Principles of Islamic Accounting

Principles of Islamic Accounting

NABIL BAYDOUN
MALIAH SULAIMAN
ROGER J. WILLETT
SHAHUL HAMEED BIN MOHAMED IBRAHIM

WILEY

Published by John Wiley & Sons Singapore Pte. Ltd.

1 Fusionopolis Walk, #07-01, Solaris South Tower, Singapore 138628

Other Wiley Editorial Offices

John Wiley & Sons, 111 River Street, Hoboken, NJ 07030, USA
John Wiley & Sons, The Atrium, Southern Gate, Chichester, West Sussex, P019 8SQ, United Kingdom
John Wiley & Sons (Canada) Ltd., 5353 Dundas Street West, Suite 400, Toronto, Ontario, M9B 6HB, Canada
John Wiley & Sons Australia Ltd., 42 McDougall Street, Milton, Queensland 4064, Australia
Wiley-VCH, Boschstrasse 12, D-69469 Weinheim, Germany

Library of Congress Cataloging-in-Publication Data is Available:

ISBN 9781119023296 (Paperback)
ISBN 9781119038856 (ePDF)
ISBN 9781119038818 (ePub)

Cover Design: Wiley
Top Image: © Semisatch/istockphoto;
Bottom Image: © isak55/Shutterstock

Typeset in 10/12pt, SabonLTStd by SPi Global, Chennai, India

Printed in Singapore by C.O.S Printers Pte Ltd

10 9 8 7 6 5 4 3 2 1

To Allah, His Prophet, his family, and companions

To the loving memories of our fathers

To our mothers, two of whom had to raise 12 children each

To our wives/husband, who continue to support us in all our endeavors

To our kids, who make our lives full of fun

Contents

Preface

This book is intended to be an introductory text for students studying the principles of Islamic accounting as part of a degree in accounting, business studies, economics, finance, or pursuing a master's degree in Islamic banking and finance. It is also intended for students studying for professional qualifications in Islamic accounting, banking, and finance.

In the past, students interested in these areas of study were obliged to use textbooks that ignore the Islamic perspective on accounting. The *Principles of Islamic Accounting* text addresses this shortcoming by providing an Islamic interpretation of the basic principles of accounting through to the trial balance, the concepts underlying and the preparation of Islamic financial statements, and accounting in a variety of important contexts, such as sukuk, zakat and Islamic contracting.

Specialized Islamic accounting textbooks are needed because of the unique aspects of accounting that are shaped by the Islamic religion. To a Muslim, religious and economic affairs are considered to be intimately connected. Accounting is more than a technical activity. It is also a cultural activity, and in the culture of Islam, religion plays an important part in the formation of accounting practices.

Religious sources in Islam influence business in specific ways. For example, the Quran specifically requires followers to keep proper records of their indebtedness and the payment of zakat. The latter is an obligatory payment of part of the wealth and income of Muslims to those more in need and can be considered analogous to a form of religious taxation. The Quran also prohibits riba (of which interest on a loan is a specific instance), waste and avarice, and all activities under the heading of *unfair trading*.

The book starts with a discussion of the Islamic business environment in which accounting takes place, explains how Islamic ethical principles apply to the practice of accounting, and describes the institutions and organisations involved in the production and use of Islamic financial reports.

Accounting concepts and principles provide the foundation of an Islamic accounting system. While Islamic accounting shares many of the principles that make the building blocks of conventional accounting, these principles also have to comply with the Islamic Sharia. Chapter 2 explains the main accounting concepts and their compliance with the

Islamic Sharia. It describes the importance of market values in Islamic accounting and explains transactions analysis and the recording, posting, and preparation of a trial balance. Chapter 3 deals with the adjustments that are made to produce an Islamic picture of the results of the accounting entity for the accounting period and its wealth at the accounting end date. Chapter 4 details the process of completing the accounting cycle using the accounting worksheet and the process of closing the accounts, correcting accounting errors, and preparing Islamic financial statements.

Bonds are an important part of the finance industry. However, the Sharia prohibition on receiving and paying interest on debts means that the issuing of bonds is not permitted in Islamic financial markets. Thus, for such markets, special Islamic bonds (sukuk) are issued in place of the bonds seen in non-Islamic financial markets. Sukuk are Sharia compliant because no interest is involved and they seek to avoid uncertainty (gharar). Sukuk provide an alternative to conventional fixed-income securities and are often used to finance developmental and capital expenditures by large corporations. The sukuk is now used as an instrument to manage liquidity in Islamic financial markets. The growth of the sukuk market globally has been rapid, as it provides an avenue for the short- and medium-term placement of funds to investors who want to follow the teachings of Islam. Accounting for sukuk is discussed in Chapter 5.

Chapter 6 deals with accounting for zakat, one of the five pillars of Islam. Every practicing Muslim whose wealth exceeds a certain nisab (minimum amount) is expected to pay zakat, the proceeds of which are distributed to those in need. Zakat leads to moral purification and growth, counteracting greed and balancing the search for profit in commerce.

Accounting is mainly concerned with businesses, and in every civilized society these are operated under a set of laws we loosely term *commercial law*. These laws prescribe the terms and conditions of various types of business contract and affect accounting practices. They also cover situations where there are no specific contracts between parties but legal responsibilities nevertheless exist, e.g. in the case of the tort law of negligence. Hence, accounting practices vary with the legal system in place. Chapter 7, therefore, deals with Islamic commercial law and how it affects Islamic accounting.

In Chapter 8, the application of Islamic financial contracts to accounting is addressed. In particular, this chapter explains murabaha contract rules in the context of AAOIFI and of IFRS standards to accounting for murabaha.

Finally, Chapter 9 provides an account of corporate social responsibility (CSR) reporting from an Islamic perspective. Justice (*adalah*) and benevolence (*ihsan*) in Islam are the basic ethos of individuals as well as corporations. While CSR is frequently interpreted from a cost-benefit perspective in the non-Islamic world, in Islam its interpretation is based on the Quran and is of central importance to the *ummah* (community of believers).

Each chapter contains a set of review questions and numerical exercises designed to help the student achieve the learning objectives set out at the beginning of each chapter. In future editions, we intend to add chapters on Islamic insurance and accounting for banks.

Finally, the authors would like to thank Mr. Jeremy Chia for his patience and accuracy in the preparation of the original manuscript.

About the Authors

Professor Nabil Baydoun (United Arab Emirates) Professor Baydoun is the Vice Chancellor for Academic Affairs at HBMSU in Dubai, the United Arab Emirates. He held senior academic positions and staffed key board committees at various institutions in Australia, Honk Kong, New Zealand, and the UAE.

Professor Baydoun has a record of accomplishment of launching innovative projects and building effective teams in large and complex organisations.

Professor Baydoun's teaching interests extend across several areas in accounting and finance. He is supportive of enhanced scholarship and research. His research interests are in international accounting and the impact of culture and religion on accounting and finance.

Dr. Shahul Hameed bin Mohamed Ibrahim (Malaysia) Dr. Shahul is an Associate Professor at Universiti Kuala Lumpur Business School. He was formerly attached to the International Centre for Education in Islamic Finance (INCEIF) and prior to that, to the Department of Accounting of the International Islamic University Malaysia. He is a Chartered Accountant (Malaysia), a Fellow of the Association of Chartered Certified Accountants (UK), and a Chartered Islamic Finance Professional (CIFP). Shahul has published a number of journal articles and conference papers and has delivered talks in Malaysia, Indonesia, the Philippines, and India. He is also the author of the first textbook on Accounting and Auditing for Islamic financial institutions.

Professor Maliah Sulaiman (Malaysia) Professor Sulaiman, the former Dean of the Kulliyyah of Economics and Management Sciences, International Islamic University Malaysia (IIUM), is a Fellow of the Association of Chartered Certified Accountants (FCCA) (UK) and holds a PhD from the University of Otago, New Zealand. She previously served as Visiting Academic at the College of Business and Management, University of Sharjah in the United Arab Emirates as well as at the School of Accounting, Curtin University of Technology in Australia. She is a board member of the Malaysian Accounting Standards Board (MASB) as well as an executive council member of the Malaysian Institute of Accountants (MIA). At the international level, she is an expert panel member of ISO 14051 and ISO 14052 on Material Flow Cost Accounting (MFCA). She has published widely and has presented papers at various conferences in Europe, Asia, and Australia.

Professor Roger J. Willett (New Zealand) Professor Willett has a BA in Economics from the University of East Anglia and a PhD from Aberdeen, in the UK. He worked in the UK as a Chartered Accountant with Coopers & Lybrand, prior to his first academic appointment. Prior to being Professor at the Victoria University of Wellington, he previously held positions in the University of Aberdeen and the University of Wales in the UK and the Australian National University and has held professorial appointments at the University of Otago, New Zealand, Queensland University of Technology, the University of Tasmania in Australia, and the University of Wollongong in Dubai. His teaching interests extend across all aspects of the discipline of accountancy. His research interests are economic modelling and theory, accounting measurement, the statistical analysis of accounting numbers, and international accounting.

About the Companion website

This book is accompanied by a companion website:

The website includes:

- Answers for all the questions given in the book.

CHAPTER 1

The Islamic Accounting Environment

Learning Objectives

After studying this chapter, you should be able to:

1. Explain the governing principles of commerce and business in Islam.
2. Describe the history of Islamic accounting.
3. Explain the relationship between ethics and Islamic accounting.
4. Explain the Islamic principles affecting financial reporting.
5. Describe Islamic accounting and list its specialised fields.
6. Describe the types of business organisations in an Islamic economy.

Islam is one of the three 'divinely inspired' religions, the other two being Christianity and Judaism. It is monotheist, with a sacred book, the Qur'an, which calls for belief in God's revelation and the teachings of the Prophet Mohammed (pbuh)[1]. With regard to business and commerce, this implies a certain type of ethical responsibility and accountability, which this first chapter will discuss. To a Muslim, religious and economic affairs are considered to be intimately connected. Accounting is more than a technical activity. It is a socio-technical activity, and in Islam religion plays an important part in moulding accounting practices.

In Islamic political economy, growth should result in social justice and equitable distribution of power and wealth in the society. The accumulation and monopolisation of wealth for its own sake without regard to its social consequences is considered undesirable, as it may result in social imbalance (Quran 59:7). An Islamic sense of accountability provides a framework

[1]pbuh stands for 'peace be upon him'. Whenever the name of Prophet Muhammad is said, it always accompanies the name.

within which society can debate matters of equity as an integral part of business affairs.

Religious sources in Islam influence business in specific ways. For example, the Quran specifically requires followers to keep proper records of their indebtedness and the payment of zakat, which is analogous to a form of religious taxation (Quran 9:60). It also prohibits riba (of which interest on a loan is a specific instance), waste and avarice, and all activities under the heading of 'unfair trading' (e.g. Quran 2:282; 2:275; 9:34, 35).

In this chapter, we discuss the Islamic environment in which accounting takes place, how Islamic ethical principles apply to the practice of accounting, and the institutions and organisations involved in producing and using Islamic financial reports.

Accounting has been called the language of business. As a process, it consists of rules of measurement and rules of disclosure and reporting. Reporting rules are more affected by cultural and religious values than are measurement rules. In this book *Islamic accounting* is treated as the language of business in an *Islamic* society, which is one that follows the principles and laws of the Sharia. In certain respects it is different from accounting practised in non-Islamic societies. Most of the differences relate to the way accounting information is reported, but some also relate to the way transactions are measured. These differences are explained in the first four chapters of this book.

ISLAMIC ACCOUNTING

Commerce is afforded an important place in Islam. How commerce should be conducted, what is lawful (*halal*) and what is prohibited (*haram*) is laid down in the Islamic Sharia. The strong interest in commerce, and its legitimacy, stem from the fact that the Prophet Mohammed (pbuh) was himself a businessman. The Prophet (pbuh) urged His followers to take up trade, farming, and other economic activities. Considerable religious weight is attached in Islam to the principles governing the conduct of businesspeople, including accounting systems and practices.

The governing principles of commerce and business in Islam, derived from the Islamic Sharia, constitute the framework that governs Muslim life. The Sharia is based on two primary sources, the Quran and the *Sunnah* and a secondary source, jurisprudence, which is a collection of the judgements of Muslim jurists.

The Quran is the most important of the three sources. It is quite specific about certain basic aspects of business life and accounting. We have already mentioned the specific prohibitions on riba and interest. More generally, it requires followers to keep proper records of their indebtedness:

> *Believers, when you contract a debt for a fixed period, put it in writing. ... Let the debtor dictate, not diminishing the sum he owes (Qur'an 2:282).*

The second, primary source of guidance is the Sunnah, which contains the teachings of the Prophet (pbuh) as reported by His followers, who sought clarification on various aspects of the Quran, sometimes by observing His behaviour. The secondary source of the Sharia, jurisprudence, consists of the judgements of Muslim jurists on issues not specifically covered by the Quran. Together, these sources make up the Islamic law.

The attitude of Islam toward economic activity is that it is legitimate and beneficial to support oneself and one's family through honest economic activity as long as specific prohibitions in the Quran, such as those described previously, are obeyed. Firms operating in an Islamic business environment are expected to seek a reasonable profit. The generation of profit, however, is not earned at the expense of, or through the exploitation of, others; the welfare of the community is held to be more important than the rights of the owners of businesses.

Accounting entities, especially corporations, may exist for many years. The actual profit that such entities will eventually make over their lifetime is known only to the Almighty. Managers, investors, and other stakeholders with an interest in such accounting entities, however, require information on a regular basis, typically at least once a year. For example, zakat is paid at the end of every year. As a result, companies report the outcome of their operations, profits or losses, and show their financial position, assets and liabilities, at the end of yearly accounting periods based on estimates that will only be known with certainty at a later date, sometimes many years hence.

To this end, firms prepare financial statements for a number of different purposes at the end of every accounting period. One of these purposes, as just noted, is to enable zakat to be calculated and paid. Some have argued that the assessment of zakat is a primary function of Islamic accounting. This is just one example of how the Sharia influences specific accounting practices in Islam. More generally, the Sharia guides the standards used by accountants in their reporting, defines what is *true and fair,* and ultimately what the principles of good corporate governance and sustainability are.

Accounting is the process of recording the economic events taking place within organisations, classifying recorded information and communicating extracts of these to interested parties in the forms of financial reports. We have already noted that accounting is often referred to as the language of business. Understanding this language is necessary to appreciate if Islamic principles are being followed by preparers of the financial reports. Experience has shown that three different types of financial report are necessary, and usually sufficient if prepared properly, to enable this judgement to be made, based on the financial position and results of operations of accounting entities: a balance sheet, as a statement of financial position; income statements of different types (e.g. a profit and loss account; a value-added statement); and a cash flow statement as a report on periodic performance.

Islamic accounting facilitates the socioeconomic objectives, which underpin the existence of business organisations in Islam. With this in mind, we define Islamic accounting to be the process of recording, classifying, and communicating information about the extent to which Islamic organisations achieve their financial and socioeconomic objectives within the general precepts of the Sharia.

A BRIEF HISTORY OF ISLAMIC ACCOUNTING

The application of the label 'Islamic' to accounting has various interpretations. *Islamic accounting* can mean, for instance, accounting in countries where Islam is the religion for the majority of the population. Under this interpretation, Islamic accounting would cover accounting in the Middle East, North Africa, much of Sub-Saharan Africa, parts of the Indian subcontinent, a large part of South-East Asia, and parts of the former Soviet Union and the Balkans. Historically, Islamic accounting would also include parts of Spain between the eighth century CE (184H) and fifteenth century CE (905H).

Islamic accounting has a long history. The existence of accounting records to track revenues and expenses dates back to the early Islamic State. It is likely that the bookkeeping principles that underpin modern accounting systems originated in the Muslim world, and that the subsequent development of accounting mechanisms elsewhere was influenced by them. For instance, it has been suggested that Pacioli's *Summa* reflected earlier accounting developments:

> *The merchants of Italy and other European countries obtained their first education in the use of sophisticated business methods from their counterparts on the opposite side of the Mediterranean, most of whom were Muslims, although a few were Jews or Christians. (Lieber, 1968, p. 230).*

Some research refers to Islamic accounting documents dating back to the end of the eleventh century CE (493H) and the beginning of the twelfth century CE (596H). Found in a Cairo synagogue, they have been interpreted as early versions of what are referred to today as journals containing lists of 'debits' and 'credits'. Other studies, using sources from the fourteenth century CE (802H) and early fifteenth century CE (905H), describe governmental accounting systems and practices used during the Islamic State and their reliance on the journal (*jaridah*) as the main record of transactions. Examples have been discovered of accounting classification systems, including agriculture, construction, and finance sectors, and the role of the 'reviewer' (auditor) in the system. Many similarities in the terminology and practices used in early Islamic accounting and those used in medieval Italian accounting have been identified. The role and character of the bookkeeper or accountant – *al-kateb* – in Islam required being well-versed in the Islamic Sharia, in addition to being technically competent and a respectable and trustworthy individual.

Part of the need for government accounting in the Islamic State was to address the collection and distribution of zakat. The spread of Islam was also an important factor, which explains the use of the *Bahi-Khata* accounting systems in India before British colonisation. Accounting in India during this period reflected the influence of the previous Muslim Mughal invaders. Scholars have also described government accounting practices, the Risale-i Felekiyye, around 1300 CE (699H) in the area that is now Iran.

Although common objectives may have led to similar recording and processing practices of accounting evolving in the West and in Islam, the detailed application of accounting procedures is influenced by cultural and religious considerations. This requires taking a *normative-deductive approach* to understanding why the rules of Islamic accounting are as they are. Any measurement and reporting system is by its nature 'normative' in the sense that it is designed by people to accomplish some purpose or purposes. In Islam, a major purpose is to adhere to and promote certain ethical principles, consistent with the Sharia. Some of the more important of these are discussed next.

ETHICAL CONSIDERATIONS IN ISLAMIC ACCOUNTING

Islam is distinctive among religions in the extent to which its precepts address directly and in detail the ethical conduct of business. Islam is unusual also in the strength of its directives concerning the desirability of community-oriented, as opposed to individualistic behaviour. It advocates the welfare of the group over the individual and the merits of long-term investments in social capital over short-term returns to the individual. This feature of Islam anticipates the emergence in Western social philosophy of a stream of thinking that is critical of open market approaches to economic management that emphasise the bottom line at the expense of other, often more qualitative, aspects of life.

Islamic religious precepts are not hostile to capitalism per se, but rather to certain consequences of its unfettered application, without the constraints imposed by a sense of what is right and wrong, just and unjust, fair and unfair, kind and unkind. Inequalities in wealth are not seen as bad in themselves, but too much inequality is seen as socially destructive. Unsustainable exploitation of natural resources and irreversible damage to the environment are also unacceptable. Although not anti-capitalist, therefore, Islam promotes those things that are often seen to be deficient in capitalism, and this adds another dimension of interest to the study of Islamic accounting. Our discussion of the Islamic precepts of business is both a description of them and, implicitly, an analysis of their compatibility with the latest Western thinking concerning such notions as sustainable human development and 'ruthless' growth. There is a moral imperative in the Sharia regarding the undertaking of any economic activity that makes ethics central to Islamic accounting. This differs from the Western attitude toward business ethics, which adopts the rationalist position of a would-be honest individual in a potentially corrupt world.

The Sharia provides a common source from which guidelines on what are considered to be ethical business practices in Islamic accounting can be derived. An important aspect of ethical business practices in Islam is the attitude of mind behind the activities, the intentions of the parties involved. An action cannot merely be 'seen' to be good; it must also be accompanied with good intentions.

Islamic ethics rests on its conception of man in relation to self, God, and society. Among the religiously based values and the specific terms describing them that underlie accounting and economic activities in an Islamic environment, the following are some of those referred to throughout this text: *adl* (justice), *amanah* (honesty), *istislah* (community interest), *infaq* (spending to meet social obligation), *iqtisad* (moderation in personal spending), and *sabr* (patience). These values shape the behaviour of the individual Muslim and constitute what is *halal* in Islam. The opposite of halal is *haram* (prohibited). What is haram is shaped by negative values such as *hirs* (greed), *iktinaz* (hoarding of wealth), *zulm* (tyranny), and *israf* (extravagance).

ISLAMIC PRINCIPLES AFFECTING FINANCIAL REPORTING

From a conceptual point of view, two approaches are available for the development of a theory about the proper form that Islamic accounting should take: The first is to derive the objectives from the principles of the Islamic Sharia and then consider these objectives in relation to conventional accounting practices. The second is to start with the objectives of conventional accounting and test these against the principles of the Islamic Sharia; those that pass the Sharia principle test will then be accepted. This book takes the former approach. The accounting standards promulgated by AAOIFI take the latter approach. However, as will become apparent, they ultimately lead to the same general form of Islamic accounting.

The unique characteristics of an Islamic society shape much of the conduct of organisations within that society. Organisations are established with the objective of serving both the owners and society at large. All operations should be in accordance with the Islamic Sharia. Unfair trading is prohibited. Transparency between the parties to a transaction is expected. Accountability goes beyond accountability to owners and even society to accountability to God for what is entrusted to each of us as individuals. For Islamic organisations, the Islamic Sharia is the reference point from which all accounting practices are derived and tested.

Several haram issues have been referred to in relation to Islamic accounting. We now discuss these in more detail.

- *Interest (riba)*: One of the strongest Islamic rules is that the charging or receipt of interest is strictly forbidden. Wealth should not be used to generate interest. The grounds given for this include reference to the undesirability of the concentration of wealth in the hands of a minority and associated concerns about the possible negative effects of disparities between rich and poor. The Quran (2:275) condemns the practice of riba:

  > *Those that live in riba shall rise up before God like men whom Satan has demented by his touch; for they claim that riba is like trading. But God has permitted trading and forbidden riba.*

  Interest is forbidden because of its potential for the transfer of risk from a stronger to a weaker party to a transaction. It is considered unfair because possibly more powerful lenders are guaranteed a fixed income while borrowers' returns are uncertain. The prohibition of interest is also partly due to its violation of the principle of social justice that underlies economic activity in Islam. There should be no reward without effort. Riba, in its various forms, is thus believed to lead to a concentration of wealth in the hands of a few rich and economically powerful people, and its prohibition has become the central factor in distinguishing Islamic banking from conventional banking.

The operation of Islamic banks relies on the profit- and loss-sharing concept, which effectively transforms them into equity-based firms. More generally, the implication of the prohibition of riba is that the profit-and loss-sharing concept becomes central to forms of business organisations. Islamic justice implies the sharing of risk and the fair division of gains and losses. Gains and losses are borne equally by the parties involved in business deals. The prohibition of interest aims to encourage money owners to actively contribute to economic activities, promoting the accumulation of wealth through hard work. The Islamic profit- and loss-sharing concept implies a partnership where the provider of capital and the entrepreneur both share the risk and reward of their venture in a format agreed to at the start of their partnership. Wealth should not, of itself, produce a guaranteed income. In an Islamic economy, therefore, the alternatives to interest-bearing instruments are the profit-sharing instruments that incorporate mudaraba (profit-sharing and loss-bearing contracts) and musharaka (equity participation and profit- and loss-sharing contracts) principles.

- *Profit and the accumulation of wealth:* The accumulation of wealth is acceptable in Islam as long as it is put to uses that result in acceptable forms of economic development. Islam considers the search for lawful earnings, in fact, to be a 'bounden duty' (Quran 3:174).

  Proper economic development in Islam is growth characterized by equity and justice. It is a community-oriented growth. The secular, Western sense of economic development, in contrast, looks at improving the well-being of the society at large as something that is achieved by the invisible hand of free markets. Distributional considerations are secondary. From an Islamic point of view, successful economic development is perceived as achieving a fair distribution of wealth as well as increased production. In this fundamental respect, the Western approach to economic development is at variance with Islamic teachings.

  For this reason, monopolization of wealth is not acceptable in Islam because it results in social imbalance (Quran 59:7). 'Excessive' profit is viewed as exploitation. This is unlike the general view in the West, which holds that high profit levels and return on investment indicate efficiency in the use of resources and are a mark of individual success. The intent in Islam is toward moderation and the sharing of wealth with the less fortunate. Individuals are responsible for the well-being of the community. Therefore, wealth should provide benefits that result in the betterment of the community at large. The Quran states (9:34, 35):

> *Proclaim a woeful punishment to those that hoard up gold and silver and do not spend it in God's cause.*

Zakat and the Islamic law of inheritance are designed to promote actions consistent with this end.

With respect to the principles that profits and losses and risk are to be shared 'justly' and that 'excessive' profit is viewed as exploitation, precise guidance as to the meaning of 'justice' and 'excess' in these contexts is not available, mirroring the problem of defining concepts such as being 'reasonable' in Western tort law. Defining such concepts is left to the judgement of the individual, their conscience, and their personal relationship with God. Justice in the provision of wages and in the price charged for goods and services are Sharia requirements, where just wages require consideration of such factors as what is required for the wage earner to support their dependents. Fair prices, similarly, reflect the cost of products and a reasonable profit to reward the entrepreneurs for their efforts.

The concept of *tawhid*, indicating the Islamic idea of oneness with God, is central to the issue of wealth distribution in an Islamic society. It is interpreted to mean the equality of all people in society. The faithful strive to create a society based on *tawhid* or brotherhood, and to promote unity and social and economic equality.

- *Social accountability*: The great advantage that a religious code, actually followed, has over a secular one is that it governs thought, intention, and motivation as well as action. The respect for God's laws encourages the believer to exercise ethical judgement and behavior from within, rather than simply following a set of rules laid down in a code of professional conduct. As already noted, the Muslim is taught to believe Islam is built on the pillars of justice (adl) and goodness (ihsan). The Sharia laws and behaviour that Islam strives to realize are directed toward this end.
- *Stewardship and accountability*: The Islamic Sharia provides the meaning and the way of achieving accountability in a society. As with other religions, the Sharia says that people are individually accountable for their actions during their lives on the Day of Judgement. The rights of private ownership are subordinated to God (Quran 6:165; 57:7). In Islam all resources are made available to individuals in the form of a trust. Individuals are entrusted as vice-regents with what they have been given by God in the form of goods, property,

talents, etc. The Quran states, 'I will create a steward on earth'. The extent to which individuals may use what has been entrusted to them is specified in the Sharia. All possessions are held in a stewardship capacity, and the reward for individuals in the life hereafter is driven by their compliance with Islamic Sharia.

The Islamic principle of *khilafa* requires individuals to be personally responsible for what is done with the resources entrusted to them, directly or through their organisations. This principle, together with the principle of *shura,* which requires consultation with those affected by organisations, makes it a duty for managers to take a personal interest in the management of their organisations. Muslim managers are therefore expected to have a hands-on, day-to-day approach to management. The interests of those affected by the operation of the organisation and its decisions are also safeguarded by the Islamic principle of *adalah* (justice) as well as shura.

Accountability in this context therefore means accountability to the society, or the public at large. In a business enterprise, both management and the providers of capital are seen as being accountable for their actions or inactions, within and outside their organisation. This means that the providers of finance, while benefiting from the use of their capital, keep its use within the rules laid down in the Sharia. In pursuing economic goals, individuals are encouraged, through the principle of *tazkiyah*, to work for the betterment of the community at large (*ummah*). Accounting to the community is promoted by the concept of social accountability in Islam.

- *Full disclosure*: The tenet of social accountability in Islam motivates businesspeople to act ethically in their day-to-day activities, and the requirement to consult implies a principle of full disclosure. This is a strict form of transparency, which parallels the rule of utmost good faith required in Western insurance contracts. In these circumstances, the business conduct of followers must be seen to be based on true, just, and fair principles. For instance, information disclosed about companies' activities and their impact on society should be accurate, complete, reliable, and free of bias and reflect equitable treatment of the parties involved. The concept of full disclosure works against window-dressing and creative accounting, and emphasises substance over legal form.

The ethical imperatives outlined here impinge on a correct Islamic accounting and are reflected in the impact of religion on Islamic financial statements. In later chapters, we illustrate these principles by including current value balance sheets and value-added social performance measures in Islamic financial statements.

Current values are more relevant for zakat than are actual costs. Moreover, when estimated accurately, market values contain more information than actual costs about risk and have the incidental advantage that they are consistent with international financial reporting standards and the pronouncement of the main Islamic standard setters.

Performance statements including information about value-added better reflect the social impact of business organisations and avoid the emphasis that the profit and loss account alone places on short-term profit maximization. The income statement is retained because it contains essential information for investors but is balanced by a measure of value-added to emphasise the social benefit of economic activity. These and other more extensive measurements and disclosures regarding the social costs and benefits of business organisations are the subject of later chapters, where we discuss the specific rules that govern how accountants measure, process, and communicate financial information.

In the remainder of this chapter, we describe the different types of users of financial reports; the various types of reports prepared by accountants to serve the purposes of the different users; the professional bodies of accountants that impose technical and professional standards on their members; and the main types of economic entities for which Islamic financial reports are prepared.

THE USERS OF ISLAMIC ACCOUNTING INFORMATION

There are various stakeholders with interests in Islamic accounting who seek information to assist them in making decisions. When organisations are small, the number of stakeholders is also small and the amount of information demanded is therefore relatively small. As organisations increase in size, the number of stakeholders increases and the demand for information likewise increases. The principles of social accountability and full disclosure require such organisations to provide more extensive reports. Corporate accounting laws in different jurisdictions require different, additional specific disclosures.

The following is a list of the main users of Islamic corporate reports and the types of information they usually seek:

- *Individuals* use accounting information in their daily business to manage their accounts, evaluate job prospects, and make investment decisions.
- *Managers of organisations* use accounting information in their planning, control, and resource allocation functions within their business organisations.

- *Investors* use accounting information to assist them in their investment decision making about the allocation of resources to various investment opportunities and in the regular evaluation of their investment.
- *Non–interest-based creditors* or *benevolent loan creditors* use accounting information to assist in assessing the ability of their clients to pay back their loans when due.
- *Government regulatory agencies* use accounting information to assess compliance with regulations and the social impact of organisations, as well as their public accountability.
- *Zakat authorities* use accounting information to assess the accuracy of the computation of zakat by individual Muslims and Islamic businesses.
- *Other users* include employees, who use accounting information in their wage demands; consumer groups; and the general public.

The needs of these users not only differ but also may conflict, making it difficult for an organisation to serve all the needs of all the users at the same time. Important or dominant user groups may determine the type and size of the information provided. Non-Islamic accounting prioritizes investors and creditors over other users of accounting information. For example, the US FASB statement of financial accounting concepts states that the objective of financial statements is to provide information to 'investors, creditors, and others'. In Islam, in contrast, the ultimate accountability is to Allah for both individual and organisation actions. Taklif, which is 'responsibility according to capacity', implies that larger organisations have greater accountability to society, and also indicates that the 'society in general' user group is of greater importance than shareholders and creditors.

FINANCIAL ACCOUNTING AND MANAGEMENT ACCOUNTING

User groups can be classified into two types: those within the organisation and those external to the organisation. Two different types of reporting, usually referred to as management accounting and financial accounting, address their respective needs:

- *Management accounting* involves the production of various types of specific reports for internal management purposes to assist managers in their planning and control activities.
- *Financial accounting* produces general-purpose standardised financial reports for users, including shareholders, creditors, outside investors, the government, and the public at large.

ISLAMIC ACCOUNTING SERVICES

Islamic accounting services include the following.

Sharia Auditing

Sharia auditing is an important service within Islamic accounting and a key pillar of the governance framework of the Sharia. Sharia auditing is an independent service that provides assurance to Muslim stakeholders. The Sharia auditor examines the extent to which organisations and their products and services conform to the requirements of Sharia. According to the *Auditing Standard for Islamic Financial Institutions No. 1*, the objective of auditing financial statement is to express an opinion as to whether the financial statements are prepared in accordance with the ruling of Sharia principles and published Islamic accounting standards as well as the relevant country-specific accounting standards and practices.

Zakat Accounting

Zakat accounting is concerned with the computation and collection of zakat. Zakat is one of the five pillars of Islam; the other four pillars are the testimony of faith, prayer, fasting during the month of Ramadan, and the pilgrimage to Mecca once in a lifetime for those who are able. Zakat is paid by all Muslims meeting the conditions for zakat liability. In Saudi Arabia, the collection of zakat is driven by national regulations under the provisions of Royal Decrees, Ministerial Resolutions and Department of Zakat and Income Tax (DZIT) circulars. Zakat is payable by Saudi nationals and nationals of other GCC countries working in the country and by companies that are wholly owned by Saudi and GCC nationals or their equity interest in companies. The payment of zakat in most Muslim countries is left to the individual Muslims. The zakat rate is fixed at 2.5% on the higher of adjusted taxable profits or the zakat base. Islamic States may impose additional taxes beyond zakat to cover essential expenditures, but should keep tax burden equitably distributed.

OTHER SPECIALIST AREAS OF ACCOUNTING

Many functions performed by accounting are common with non-Islamic organisations. These include the following.

- *Cost accounting* is a part of management accounting concerned with the analysis of costs.

- *Budgeting* is a part of management accounting associated with planning and with setting goals and forecasts.
- *Accounting information systems* are intimately related to the accounting function in organisations. Flow charts, graphs, and manuals describe the main systems, usually computerised, and the responsibilities associated with these.
- *Internal auditing* is concerned with the evaluation of whether the assets of the company are being safeguarded and used according to the organisational policies and processes.

THE ISLAMIC ACCOUNTING PROFESSION

Establishing a professional regulatory system for the Islamic accounting is a recent phenomenon. Islamic professional organisations include the Accounting and Auditing Organization for Islamic Financial Institutions (AAOIFI), the Islamic Financial Services Board (IFSB) located in Malaysia and the Islamic International Rating Agency (IIRA) established in Bahrain. A brief description of each of these organisations is given as follows.

AAOIFI is a not-for-profit organisation established with the aim of developing standards covering the accounting, auditing, governance, ethics, and Sharia aspects for Islamic financial institutions and the finance industry. It is a self-regulated, private body originally established in accordance with an agreement between Islamic financial institutions in 1990 CE (1410H) in Algiers and registered in 1991 CE (1411H) in Bahrain.

The AAOIFI structure is quite simple, consisting of a General Assembly, board of trustees, a standards board, and a Sharia Board. AAOIFI has more than 200 institutional members from over 40 countries. As of 2014, AAOIFI has issued 88 standards, 48 of which are Sharia standards, 26 accounting standards, 5 auditing standards, 7 governance standards, and 2 codes of ethics. AAOIFI standards have been adopted in several countries in the Arab world, including Bahrain, Jordan, Lebanon, Qatar, Sudan, and Syria. Relevant authorities in other countries, including Australia, Malaysia, Indonesia, Pakistan, United Arab Emirates, Saudi Arabia, and South Africa, have issued guidelines based on AAOIFI's standards.

The Islamic Financial Services Board (IFSB, located in Malaysia), was established in 2002 as a standard-setting body for the Islamic financial services industry. As of 2014, IFSB had 184 members operating. The IFSB standard-setting process is lengthy and includes issuing exposure drafts and possible invitations to public hearings. Twenty-two standards, guiding principles, and technical notes have been issued by the IFSB for the Islamic financial services industry.

The Islamic International Rating Agency (IIRA) was established in 2005 to address the needs of capital markets in the Islamic world for a rating that reflects capital instruments and Islamic financial products available in these markets. The Central Bank of Bahrain and Islamic Development Bank recognise IIRA as an approved rating agency for Islamic capital markets.

While Islamic finance has grown rapidly, education and training of Islamic finance specialists have not kept pace. As a result there are shortages of expertise throughout the industry. This is in addition to the lack of a comprehensive curriculum and specialized textbooks for the relevant disciplines.

AAOIFI offers the Certified Islamic Professional Accountant (CIPA) program, which focuses on technical accounting and professional skills for Islamic financial institutions. The program covers financial accounting; accounting rules; accounting for Islamic financial transactions; the preparation of financial statements; accounting standards, governance standards, and Sharia standards.

Another program offered by AAOIFI is the Certified Sharia Adviser and Auditor (CSAA) program. This program focuses on Sharia compliance and review processes for Islamic financial instruments. The program covers the roles of Sharia compliance and review processes in financial institutions; the Sharia Supervisory Board (SSB); AAOIFI's Sharia standards; AAOIFI's governance standards, as well as matters such as Islamic banking and finance supervision; operational structures; and Islamic jurisprudence (*fiqh*).

The Chartered Institute of Management Accountants (CIMA) offers the following four certificates in Islamic Finance: Islamic commercial law, banking and takaful, and Islamic capital markets. These were established to address the needs of professionals in these areas.

The Association of Chartered Islamic Finance Professionals (ACIFP) was established in Malaysia to promote the practice of Islamic finance and provide opportunity for continuing professional development in this area. ACFIP offers the Chartered Islamic Finance Professional (CIFP) programme as one of its certificates covering Islamic finance.

TYPES OF ISLAMIC BUSINESS ORGANISATIONS

Organisations in an Islamic economy can take one of four forms, which are parallel to non-Islamic organisations: proprietorships, partnerships, for-profit companies, and not-for-profit organisations. The accounting procedures used to report ownership interests depend on the type of business organisation. All activities involving unlawful products or services such as gambling, alcohol, pork, and riba are not permitted in any Islamic organisation.

- *Proprietorships* are individually owned businesses, with a sole trader called the proprietor, who often runs the organisation as the manager. From an accounting viewpoint, the proprietorship is a distinct accounting entity, separate from its owner. The accounts of the proprietorship do not include the personal accounts of the owner. However, the owner is responsible for settling the debts of the business if there is a shortfall of business assets.
- *Sharika (partnership)* is an organisation owned by two or more persons. The literal meaning of sharika is 'sharing'. The profit- and loss-sharing concept in Islam regulates the distribution of profits or losses between the partners. As with non-Islamic organisations, the contribution of each partner may take the form of capital, assets, skills, and more. Partners can be involved in the management of the partnership or remain sleeping partners. From an accounting perspective, the partnership is treated as a separate entity from that of each of the partners. However, as is the case with sole proprietorships, the partners are responsible for settling any debts outstanding if there is a shortfall of business assets. In musharaka, the profits are shared according to the agreed profit-sharing ratio but losses are shared according to capital contributed by the partners. Sharika can take several forms under Islamic law:
  - *Sharika al-inan* (limited partnership). Under this type, the contribution of the partners takes the form of capital, property, and labour. Partners agree to a predetermined profit- and loss-sharing ratio.
  - *Musharaka*. In this case, two or more people combine their resources to invest in a venture. The management role of each partner is stipulated.
  - *Mudaraba* is a type of partnership where one or more of the partners provides the capital. That partner is referred to as *rabb al-mal* or 'master of the property' and does not participate in the management. Another partner provides skills or work and is referred to as the *mudarib*. The mudaraba can be of a limited or general form. Limited mudaraba restricts the mudarib's activities to what is authorised by providers of capital, the *rabb al-mal*. General mudaraba allows for all sorts of uses and mixing of partnership forms, where the mudarib is authorised to combine resources made available to him by partners with his own resources, outsourcing the mudaraba, or investing in a partnership with others.

- A *company* is a business owned by a group of people called shareholders. The company is a separate legal entity from that of its owners, the shareholders. The financial responsibility of the individual shareholders is limited to the shareholder's paid-up shares in the company. It is usually easier for shareholders than for the owners of other forms of organisation to sell their interests on the market. While it is lawful to hold ordinary shares, Western-style preference shares are not permitted. The basis for this prohibition is the inequality between different owners the preference creates. Preference shares guarantee a minimum return and priority payment in case of bankruptcy.

In the next chapter, we describe the basic measurement and recording techniques used by accountants to implement the Islamic principles described in this chapter.

VOCABULARY

accounting
accounting entities
accounting periods
accounting records
assets
auditor
avarice
balance sheet
bookkeeping
capitalism
cash flow statement
colonisation
commerce
corporate governance
corporations
credits
debits
economic activity
government accounting
indebtedness

inequalities
interest (riba)
Islamic accounting
Islamic financial reports
Islamic religious precepts
Islamic Sharia
jaridah (journal)
jurisprudence
justice
liabilities
measurement rules
Piccioli's Summa
profits
profits or losses
public welfare (istislah)
reasonable profit
religious values
reporting rules
socioeconomic
Sunnah (Al-Hadith)
sustainability
sustainable human development
The Quran
unfair trading
unjust
value-added statement
waste
wealth
Western accounting
zakat

MULTIPLE-CHOICE QUESTIONS

1. Which of the following sources is not a primary source governing principles of commerce and business in Islam?

   a. The Quran
   b. Teachings of the Prophet Mohammed (pbuh)
   c. Jurisprudence
   d. Tradition
2. Which type of business organisation(s) can be owned in an Islamic business environment?
   a. Sole proprietorship
   b. Corporation
   c. Partnership
   d. All of the above
3. Which of the following is not a separate legal entity?
   a. Proprietorship
   b. Sole proprietorship
   c. Corporation
   d. Partnership
4. Which financial statement reports the status of the business data at a specific date?
   a. Balance sheet
   b. Value-added statement
   c. Income statement
   d. Statement of cash flows
5. Which of the following are considered internal users of accounting information?
   a. Creditors
   b. Investors
   c. Managers
   d. Zakat authorities
6. What does the acronym AAOIFI represent?
   a. Accounting Aspects of Islamic Financial Institutions
   b. Accounting Association of Islamic Financial Institutions
   c. Association Accounting International Financial Institutions
   d. The Accounting and Auditing Organization for Islamic Financial Institutions
7. Which of the following have not been issued by AAOIFI?
   a. Sharia standards
   b. Accounting standards
   c. Auditing standards
   d. Halal standards
8. Which of the following values is haram?
   a. Adl (justice)
   b. Amanah (honesty)
   c. Israf (extravagance)
   d. Infaq (spending to meet social obligation)

9. Which of the following values is considered haram?
   a. Zulm (tyranny)
   b. Hirs (greed)
   c. Iktinaz (hoarding of wealth)
   d. All of the above
10. Which of the following statements is FALSE according to the Islamic Sharia?
    a. Charging or receipt of interest is strictly forbidden under the Islamic Sharia.
    b. Under Islam, the rights of private ownership are ultimately subordinated to God.
    c. People are not individually accountable for their actions during their lives on the Day of Judgement.
    d. The principle of khilafa requires individuals to be personally responsible for what is done with the resources entrusted to them.

DISCUSSION QUESTIONS

1. What type of information does each of the following user groups usually seek?
   a. Individuals
   b. Managers of organisations
   c. Investors
   d. Non–interest-based creditors or benevolent loan creditors
   e. Government regulatory agencies
   f. Zakat authorities
2. Distinguish between financial accounting and managerial accounting.
3. Briefly define Sharia auditing.
4. What is Sharika al-inan?
5. What is the basis for the prohibition of preference shares in Islam?
6. What are the main reasons behind interest prohibition in Islam?
7. How does the Sharia specify the meaning and the way of achieving accountability in Islam?
8. Briefly discuss the following statement: 'The concept of full disclosure is at variance with window-dressing, and creative accounting'.
9. What is the objective of auditing Islamic financial statements according to AAOFI Auditing Standard for Islamic Financial Institutions No. 1?
10. Briefly discuss the main Islamic principles affecting accounting and financial reporting.

CHAPTER 2

Recording Transactions and Market Values in Islam

Learning Objectives

After studying this chapter you should be able to:

1. Explain the main accounting concepts and their compliance with the Islamic Sharia.
2. Describe the importance of market values to the Islamic accounting system.
3. Explain transactions analysis using the accounting equation.
4. Record, post, and analyse transactions using an accounting system.
5. Prepare a trial balance.
6. Prepare a chart of accounts.
7. Prepare a simple set of Islamic financial statements.
8. Use accounting information to make decisions in an Islamic business environment.

Accounting concepts and principles provide the foundation of an Islamic accounting system. Islamic accounting shares many of the accounting principles that make the building blocks of conventional accounting. However, in Islamic accounting, these principles also have to comply with the Islamic Sharia.

ACCOUNTING CONCEPTS AND THE ISLAMIC SHARIA

The Accounting Entity Concept

The *accounting entity* concept requires the preparers of accounts to treat the organisation as a separate entity from that of the owners and principals. Boundaries are established between the organisation, and its owners, so that only the impact of economic events related to the organisation is reflected in the organisation's accounts.

Fatina Jabir, a young Emirati girl, started her own Abaya design and fashion business, Dar Al Fatina, in Al Ain in the UAE, with AED 1,000 of her own money. Fatina had to decide how to organise her fashion business in an Islamic society. The Abaya design and fashion house Dar Al Fatina business is a proprietorship—a single-owner business—with Fatina as the owner. As her business grows, she may consider opening businesses in other countries. If she wants to expand, she could choose to go into partnership or incorporate—that is, to form a company. What role does accounting play in this situation? In addition, Fatina wants to know how well the business performed. Within a short space of time Dar Al Fatina made a profit of AED 900 after all expenses were paid. Profit and expenses are accounting terms.

The personal accounts of Fatina Jabir, the owner of Dar Al Fatina, are not reflected in the accounts of her business Dar Al Fatina. Of a AED 3,000 balance on her bank account at the end of the year, only AED 2,500 came from Dar Al Fatina's operations. The other AED 500 was a gift from her parents. Fatina follows the entity concept, so she will account for the money generated by Dar Al Fatina – the accounting entity – separately from the money she received from her family, a different economic unit. This separation makes it possible to view the financial position of Dar Al Fatina as an accounting entity, clearly. Suppose Fatina disregards the entity concept and treats the full AED 3,000 as a product of Dar Al Fatina's operations. She, and anyone using her financial statements, will be misled into believing that the business has produced more cash than it has.

Dar Al Fatina is a small, owner-managed proprietorship. The financial statements most of us see are those of publicly listed companies. These financial statements are nearly always 'consolidated' statements formed by adding together all the accounts of the holding company (chief entity) and of its many subsidiary companies (controlled entities) on an item-by-item basis. Although controlled entities are usually legally defined entities, they are also economically controlled by the chief entity. Consolidated accounts are prepared to serve the needs of the chief entity's shareholders and creditors.

The accounting entity concept was known during the early Islamic State; mosques, bayt al mal (treasury) and awqaf (endowment), and other institutions were considered separate and independent financial and legal entities (AAOIFI, 1999a). The entity concept was accepted by AAOIFI in its *Financial Accounting Standard No. 1* (FAS1) issued in January 1996. This implies that limited liability is accepted. The Second Seminar on Stock Market held in Bahrain on January 25, 1991, and the seventh session of the Islamic Fiqh

Academy held in Saudi Arabia in May 1992 both accepted the concept of limited liability for Islamic financial institutions.

The Time Period Concept

According to the *time period* concept, the life of the business is divided into periods called accounting periods. For each of these periods, sets of Islamic financial statements are prepared for the transactions related to these specific periods. Generally, one calendar year is used for each period. Accounts for shorter periods than one year are sometimes prepared, called interim periods.

If Dar Al Fatina earned another AED 1,500 by the end of December, we would need to know how long it took the company to earn this money if we wanted to find out whether the profitability of Dar Al Fatina had increased or decreased. If it was known that another venture had earned AED 2,000 and we wanted to compare its profitability with Dar Al Fatina, we would also need to know how long it had taken to earn that money.

The budget for Bayt Al-Mal (treasury), the institution that handled the finance of the Islamic State, was prepared on an annual basis. The time period concept facilitates the payment of zakat, the assessment of which is computed annually. That is, Muslims are required to compute their zakatable wealth every year, as per Prophet Mohammad's Hadith, 'No zakat is payable on property till a year passes on it'.

The Cost Principle

According to the *cost* principle, accounting transactions for the economic events taking place within the organisation are reflected in Islamic financial statements at their actual cost. Assets acquired for Dar Al Fatina are recorded at their actual cost, for example. Expenses incurred by Dar Al Fatina are recorded at the cost incurred in purchasing goods and services from suppliers. Revenues are recorded at the price of goods and services sold to customers. If Dar Al Fatima paid a bargain price of AED 2,000 for the items that would have cost the business AED 3,000 from other suppliers in the market, the cost principle requires recording the items at the actual cost of AED 2,000, not AED 3,000. The records of Dar Al Fatina will reflect the historical cost value of the company's assets for as long as they are used in the business.

The main characteristics of the cost principle are its objectivity and reliability, in that different accountants would agree on the accuracy and objectivity of what is recorded in the accounting records in the majority of cases where invoices document the cost, given the same information about the transactions involved. This ensures that Islamic financial statements are not based on just the subjective opinions of individuals.

While the cost principle enhances reliability, its relevance and the extent to which it reflects a correct Islamic moral position are questionable. This criticism has resulted in calls for the assets in Islamic financial statements to be shown in the balance sheet at their market values. However, estimating market values may take place at the expense of both objectivity and reliability. Therefore, it is often necessary to exercise a trade-off between reliability and relevance to the Islamic purpose.

AAOIFI adopted the cost concept in its conceptual framework, on the basis that it is the method that produces the most reliable information. However, given that zakat is one of the five pillars of Islam, accounting should play an important role in enabling Muslims to pay zakat. Historical cost can be misleading both as indicative of values and in the computation of zakat. Misleading values and information are at odds with the values of justice, fairness, and truthfulness in Islam. Accounting information should help in computing the zakat payment, thus requiring the use of market values. The difference between historical cost and market values is subject to zakat, but is not distributable to owners.

The Matching Principle

Economic events taking place within organisations result in expense and revenue items being recognised and recorded in the accounts. According to the *matching* principle, expense items are matched against revenue items that they generate. AAOIFI adopted the matching concept to ensure that the responsibility of the cost is assigned to the recipient of benefit. The matching concept helps to compute the actual wealth subject to zakat. Historically, *osher*, an Ottoman tax on agriculture products, was determined after deducting the cost of fertilisers and other expenses related to the production of agriculture products. Determining the profit to be distributed from mudaraba contracts also necessitates application of the matching concept. However, several authors have criticized the matching concept on the ground of the required judgement needed to assess the cost allocated to current and future periods. Arguments have been made for an asset liability approach as more acceptable in an Islamic environment, as opposed to the revenue expense approach promoted by the matching principle.

The Profit Recognition Principle

Profit is the outcome of the operations of a business over a period of time. It is computed as the difference between the revenue and expenses incurred to generate this revenue. One issue in computing the profit is whether a cash-based method or accrual-based method should be used. Should profit be recognised when cash is paid and received or when sales orders or purchases of inputs take place, irrespective of whether cash is received or paid? The latter method is usually referred to as the *accruals* method of accounting.

In its sixteenth meeting on November 11, 2000, the Sharia Advisory Council (SAC) of the Securities Commission Malaysia (SC), which is responsible for providing advice on matters pertaining to Islamic Capital Markets, agreed on the appropriateness of accrual accounting for recognising revenue. The Islamic Sharia permits both cash and accrual methods in recognising revenues. According to SAC, the accrual method is preferable. The accrual method is consistent with the Sharia, which requires credit transactions to be properly recorded. SAC refers to the following verse of the Quran in support of their resolution:

> *O believers! When you contract a debt from one another for a fixed period, put it (its amount and period of repayment) in writing. And let a scribe write it down between you justly (truthfully)... [Surah al-Baqarah, verse 282]*

Let us assume Dar Al Fatina completed a delivery to a client on August 30, but payment did not take place until the end of September. Should the profit from this transaction be recognised by Dar Al Fatina as an outcome for the August period? Alternatively, should it be recognised in the September period? According to the accrual version of the profit recognition principle, profit should be recognised in August, when transactions take place, irrespective of the timing and movement of cash.

The application of the accrual basis in an Islamic business environment results in the computation of the wealth subject to zakat that conforms to Islamic principles. AAOIFI adopted the accrual concept referring to the saying of Umar, the second Muslim caliph, to a trader, 'Evaluate it [your merchandise] and then pay its due zakat' (AAOIFI, 1999a, p. 308).

The Conservatism Principle

According to the *conservatism* principle, accountants are required to avoid anticipating profit but should ensure losses and expenses are anticipated and accounted for. This principle counters the general optimism of managers in overestimating and anticipating uncertain future revenues. It also ensures that the Islamic reality of the organisation is better reflected and that stakeholders such as creditors are better protected.

The application of the conservatism principles requires the reporting of the lowest value of assets and revenues, which may result in an understatement of assets that are subject to zakat. Conservatism thus may contradict zakat computation principles. On the other hand, companies have to avoid an overoptimistic valuation of assets and revenues, which may lead to distribution of unearned profits. Therefore, conservatism is important in measuring profits to be distributed amongst partners, although it may be adjusted in order to calculate zakat. AAOIFI was silent on the Conservatism Concept in its *Financial Accounting Standard No. 1* (FAS1).

The Going Concern Principle

The *going concern* principle reflects an assumption that the business for which Islamic financial statements are prepared will continue to operate into the future. Application of this principle justifies accountants making estimates and attributing amounts to more than one accounting period.

Islam recognises continuity as the basis of human life. The requirement to pay zakat on an annual basis emphasises the continuity of business activity. AAOIFI (1999a) adopted the going concern concept in its Statement of Financial Accounting No. 2 on the basis that mudaraba contracts associated with a specific period of time continue operating until one of the parties to the contract decides to terminate the contract. Going concern is also supported by the fact that the separation of wealth between money and goods where goods are divided into goods available for sales and those which are not and that are likely to be available for longer period.

Social Accountability and Full Disclosure

The tenet of social accountability in Islam motivates businesspeople to act for the benefit of the *ummah* in their day-to-day activities. This necessitates consultation and consensus and implies a principle of full disclosure, which is a strict form of transparency, paralleling the rule of utmost good faith required in Western insurance contracts. The concept of full disclosure ensures that any and all information of substance or interest to users, to which they are morally entitled under the Sharia, is provided to assist them in decision making. In these circumstances, the business conduct of followers must be seen to be based on true, just, and fair principles. For instance, information disclosed about companies' activities and their impact on society at large should be accurate, complete, reliable, and free of bias and reflect equitable treatment of the parties involved.

MARKET VALUE

Central to Islamic accounting is the use of current values instead of historic costs for the correct computation of zakat. Current values, when measured accurately, contain more information than actual costs about risk and have the incidental advantage that they are consistent with international financial reporting standards and the pronouncement of the main Islamic standard setters. The amount and timing of profit distribution as well as the type of capital to be maintained are important drivers of the choice of the valuation method adopted.

The principle of *tandeed* in Islam requires companies not to distribute any profit resulting from business transactions until the invested capital is recovered. While some scholars believe that the initial capital invested should be maintained prior to any distribution of profit, others argue that this principle requires the real capital or economic value to be maintained as opposed to nominal capital. This favours the use of current values. However, pragmatic difficulties associated with the implementation of market values may necessitate the use of historic cost as estimates of market values in many cases. Some writers have argued for two balance sheets in Islamic financial reports, one prepared on historical cost figures and another using market values.

These ethical imperatives impinging on a correct accounting are reflected in the impact of religion on Islamic financial statements. The considerations above indicate that companies in an Islamic business environment should disclose all necessary information about their operations to the Islamic community, even if such information is not in the interest of these companies themselves. Completeness, truthfulness, and accuracy must characterise such disclosure. This is clearly reflected in the Quran: 'And cover not Truth with falsehood, nor conceal the Truth when you know (what it is)' (al-Baqarah 2:42). Full disclosure is not intended to mean to disclose everything, but disclosure is driven by accountability to God and the society.

TRANSACTIONS AND THE ACCOUNTING EQUATION

The basis of all financial statements, whether or not they contain information about market values, lies ultimately in the classification and recording of transaction costs. The outcome of the accounting process in any Islamic organisation includes the following Islamic financial statements or reports: The balance sheet showing the financial position of the organisation, the income statement showing the results of its operations in the form of income, and cash flow statement. These statements are based on the accounting equation, which reflects resources used in the business and claims against these resources. This equation forms the basis for the derivation of the final accounts.

Assets, Liabilities, and Equity

The elements of the accounting equation are assets, liabilities, and equities. *Assets* represent the resources owned and controlled, providing the business with hope for economic benefits in the future. Examples include cash, accounts receivables, inventory, furniture, land, and buildings. *Liabilities* are claims on the assets, representing obligations the business expects to pay in the future. *Equity* is the residual interest of the owners in the business. In the accounting equation equity equals the difference between the value of assets and the value of liabilities and is often referred to as the "owners' equity" or "capital." The initial capital that Fatina invested in Dar Al Fatina is an example. What the business owns and controls, providing it with future economic benefits, equals the obligations the business expects to pay others, plus the owners' equity.

Assets Assets are economic resources entrusted to organisations by God according to the Quran. Organisations benefit from these assets, and they should be reflected in Islamic financial statements in accordance with the Islamic Sharia. AAOIFI defines assets as those acquired by the company for the purpose of keeping, using, or disposing of the asset. In conventional accounting, the criteria includes the ability of the assets to generate future economic benefit regardless of legal control by the company.

Examples of assets include:

- *Cash:* This term refers to liquid money generally placed in the bank account of the organisation to meet cash requirements resulting from business transactions. Cash at bank includes liquid cash, bank account balances, certificates of deposit, and cheques.
- *Accounts receivable:* An instance of this asset is goods sold on credit, implying a future obligation on the buyer to pay another business for the goods sometime in the future. All such credit sales transactions are reflected in the accounts receivables.
- *Bills receivable:* Sales of goods can also take the form of bills of exchange. In these, the buyer signs a written pledge to pay for the goods bought at a future date. In a court setting, bills receivable have stronger weight than accounts receivables.
- *Inventories:* This refers to the stock of goods that remain unsold at the close of an accounting period.

- *Prepaid expenses:* These are payments for services that have not yet been consumed by the company.
- *Land:* This refers to the cost or the value of the land owned by the business. In the cases where land is intended for sale, it is kept as a separate account and may be referred to as 'investment'.
- *Building:* This refers to the cost or value of the building owned by the company. As is the case with the land account, if the buildings are intended for sale, they are placed in a separate account referred to as 'investment'.
- *Equipment, furniture, and fixtures:* These accounts relate to assets owned by the company in the forms of machinery, equipment, furniture, and fixtures. A separate account is normally kept for each category.

The assets just listed are only classified as assets in Islamic financial statements if they are owned by the business. The concept of ownership in Islam has some special features that are not always commensurate with its more familiar Western accounting counterpart.

> *Whatever is in the heavens and whatever is in the earth belongs to Allah [al-Baqarah 2:284].*

According to the Sharia, individuals are only trustees for what they own. God is the ultimate owner of all wealth (Quran 6:165; 57:7). The Quran (2:284) states '. . . and to Allah belongeth the dominion of the heavens and earth'. Although individuals have the right to own resources that are made available by God, this right is not absolute. This tenet has a direct impact on the objective of accounting from an Islamic point of view.

Accountability is seen as being personal accountability to God. Accountability from the traditional western accounting perspective is interpreted by being accountable to the private stakeholder. In an Islamic accounting system, accountability to God may be interpreted as being accountable to the society at large. This shifts the emphasis in financial statements away from the traditional form of the income statement to alternative formats that include value-added concepts, giving less emphasis to the private interests of owners and more to the interest of society in general.

Liabilities A liability represents an obligation the company will have to pay at a future date. Liabilities accounts include:

- *Accounts payable:* These refer to credit purchases, the payment for which will occur later. Accounts payable are the opposite of accounts receivables discussed above. Accounts payable are sometimes referred to as trade creditors; other payables include salaries payable, zakat payable, etc.

- *Bills payable:* These represent the purchase of goods made under a bill of exchange. A business signs a written pledge to pay for goods purchased on credit at a specified future date. In a court setting, bills payable have a stronger weight than accounts payable.
- *Accrued liabilities:* These are obligations for services that have been consumed but not yet paid for by the company.

Owners' Equity The residual interest for the owners in a business is referred to as the *owners' equity*. Starting a business requires initial capital to get the business started. Withdrawals from the business by the owners may occur. Revenues generated by the business can but may not be distributed, thus increasing owners' equity accordingly. Expenses incurred represent a decrease in owners' equity. Capital, withdrawals, revenues, and expenses are all owners' equity accounts. To summarise:

- *Capital:* The initial investment made by the owners and any additional investment made after the business starts operations.
- *Revenues:* The value generated mostly through cash and credit sales of goods or provision of services. Revenues lead to an increase in owners' equity.
- *Expenses:* The payment or increased indebtedness for goods and services during the course of doing business. Expenses have the opposite effect to revenues and represent a reduction to owners' equity.
- *Drawings:* "Withdrawals," representing the cash or other assets withdrawn from the business for personal use or consumption. Drawings are not expenses against profits, but are "distributions" of profit. However, they also result in a decrease in owners' equity.

The accounting equation is usually stated in one of the following two equivalent forms:

Resources		Claims to resources
Assets	=	Liabilities + Owners' equity
Assets – Liabilities	=	Owners' Equity

The first of these forms, where the assets appear on the left side of the equation and liabilities and equity are on the right side of the equation, reflects the traditional view of assets as having opposite signs on their values compared to liabilities, as reflected in the practice of double-entry bookkeeping. You will learn about double-entry bookkeeping later in this chapter.

The second equation shows the residual amount of a company's assets after the liabilities are subtracted as the *net assets* and is equal in amount to the owners' equity. In this form it is clear that owners have a residual claim over the net assets of their business. Increasing owners' equity is an important objective for business and is usually achieved through increasing business assets as a result of increasing revenues through sales. As we will see later, these equations can be rearranged to focus greater attention on equity as social savings, as well as measuring the more narrowly focused owners' equity.

TRANSACTIONS ANALYSIS USING THE ACCOUNTING EQUATION

Islamic accounting shows the interaction between an Islamic organisation and its economic environment through a process of recording transactions. To be recorded, transactions must reflect an economic event that has financial consequences for the organisation and be reliably measured.

For example, Ahmed decided to open an accounting practice and become the sole owner of the business. How will the first few following transactions be reflected in the books of this practice?

- *Transaction 1: Investment by owner.* Ahmed invests $100,000 of his money to start a new business. He deposits the $100,000 in a bank account entitled Islamic Finance Training (IFT). The effect of this transaction on the accounting equation of the business entity is shown in Table 2.1.

TABLE 2.1 Investment by Owner

Transaction	Assets Cash	=	Liabilities	+	Owners' Equity Ahmed Capital
1	100000				100000

This transaction increased the assets of the business by increasing its cash, and increased owners' equity by increasing the capital account by the same amount. In the accounting equation, the amount on the left side must equal the amount on the right side.

- *Transaction 2: Purchase of office building.* IFT purchases an office building, paying cash of $75,000. The effect of this transaction on the accounting equation is shown in Table 2.2.

  The $75,000 reduces the cash account by the same amount. The accountant creates a new account 'office building', which increases

TABLE 2.2 Purchase of Office Building

Transaction	Assets Cash	+ Office Building	= Liabilities	+ Owners' Equity Ahmed Capital
1	100000			100000
2	−75000	75000		
Balance	25000	75000		100000

by $75,000. This transaction leads to an increase in one asset account and a decrease in another asset account, and the equality in the accounting equation is maintained. After the transaction is completed, the balance in the cash account is $25,000; the office building account has a balance of $75,000. There are no liabilities, and the owners' equity is $100,000.

- *Transaction 3: Purchase of equipment.* IFT purchases equipment, paying cash of $5,000. The effect of this transaction on the accounting equation is shown in Table 2.3.

TABLE 2.3 Purchase of Equipment

Transaction	Assets Cash	+ Office Building	+ Equipment	= Liabilities	+ Owners' Equity Ahmed Capital
1	100000				100000
2	−75000	75000			
3	−5000		5000		
Balance	20000	75000	5000		100000

The $5,000 reduces the cash account on the asset side. The accountant creates a new account, 'Equipment', which increases by the same amount, $5,000. The transaction leads to an increase in one asset account and a decrease in another asset account, retaining the equality in the accounting equation. After the transaction is completed, the balance in the cash account is $20,000, the office building account has $75,000, and the equipment account has $5,000. There are no liabilities, and owners' equity is $100,000.

- *Transaction 4: Purchase of office supplies.* IFT buys office supplies, agreeing to pay $1,000 within 30 days. The assets of the business increase as a result by $1,000. IFT owes its supplier the same amount. The liabilities increase by the same amount. Equality in the equation is preserved.

The accountant creates an account 'Office Supplies', and a liability account, 'Account Payable', to record this transaction (Table 2.4).

TABLE 2.4 Purchase of Office Supplies

	Assets				= Liabilities +	Owners' Equity	
Trans-action	Cash	Building	Equipment	Supplies	= Accounts Payable	Capital	Retained Earnings
1	100000					100000	
2	−75000	75000					
3	−5000		5000				
4				1000	1000		
Balance	20000	75000	5000	1000	1000	100000	

- *Transaction 5: Training services provided.* IFT provided Islamic finance training services to its clients, earns $10,000, and collects this amount in cash. The effect on the accounting equation is an increase in the asset Cash at Bank and an increase in Ahmed's Capital account, as shown in Table 2.5.

TABLE 2.5 Training Services Provided

	Assets				= Liabilities +	Owners' Equity	
Trans-action	Cash	Building	Equipment	Supplies	= Accounts Payable	Capital	Retained Earnings
1	100000					100000	
2	−75000	75000					
3	−5000		5000				
4				1000	1000		
5	10000						10000
Balance	30000	75000	5000	1000	1000	100000	10000

- *Transaction 6: Consultancy services provided on account.* IFT provided Islamic consultancy services for another client amounting to $4,000, and the client promised to pay within one month. This promise represents an asset for the business and will be recorded as an 'account receivable' to be collected in the future. This occurs irrespective of whether Ahmed receives the cash. The business earned revenue and the accountant reflects this in the accounting records (Table 2.6).

TABLE 2.6 Consultancy Services Provided on Account

	Assets					= Liabilities +	Owners' Equity	
Trans-action	Cash	Building	Equip-ment	Supplies	Accounts Receiv-able	= Accounts Payable	Capital	Retained Earnings
1	100000						100000	
2	−75000	75000						
3	−5000		5000					
4				1000		1000		
5	10000							10000
6					4000			4000
Balance	30000	75000	5000	1000	4000	1000	100000	14000

- *Transaction 7: Payment of expenses*. IFT pays $2,300 for advertising its services, $1,500 for Ahmed's salary, and $500 for an electricity and water invoice. Assume that IFT pays cash for all of these transactions. Table 2.7 shows the effects of these transactions on the accounting equation.

TABLE 2.7 Payment of Expenses

	Assets					= Liabilities +	Owners' Equity	
Trans-action	Cash	Building	Equip-ment	Supplies	Accounts Receiv-able	= Accounts Payable	Capital	Retained Earnings
1	100000						100000	
2	−75000	75000						
3	−5000		5000					
4				1000		1000		
5	10000							10000
6					4000			4000
7	−2300							−2300
7	−1500							−1500
7	−500							−500
Balance	25700	75000	5000	1000	4000	1000	100000	9700

Expenses, as opposed to revenues, will result in the decline of the business, as indicated by the decline in the total assets and total equity.

- *Transaction 8: Payment on credit* (on account). IFT pays the $1,000 it owes for the office supplies purchased in transaction 3. The effect of this transaction on the accounting equation is a decrease in the asset Cash at Bank and a decrease in the liability Accounts Payable, as shown in Table 2.8.

TABLE 2.8 Payment on Credit

	Assets					= Liabilities +	Owners' Equity	
Transaction	Cash	Building	Equipment	Supplies	Accounts Receivable	= Accounts Payable	Capital	Retained Earnings
1	100000						100000	
2	−75000	75000						
3	−5000		5000					
4				1000		1000		
5	10000							10000
6					4000			4000
7	−2300							−2300
7	−1500							−1500
7	−500							−500
8	−1000					−1000		
Balance	24700	75000	5000	1000	4000	0	100000	9700

- *Transaction 9: Personal transaction.* Ahmed decides to go on holiday with his family, paying $15,000 cash from his personal account. This event has no impact on the business and will not be reflected in its accounts. In accordance with the entity concept, the business transaction must not be mixed with the personal affairs of its owner.
- *Transaction 10: Receipt of Cash on Account.* ITF collects the $4,000 owed by the client in transaction 6 for the services performed on credit. This increases the cash account on the asset side of the accounting equation and reduces the account receivable accounts on the same side to reflect that the amount has been collected. The effect on the accounting equation is shown in Table 2.9.
- *Transaction 11: Dividends.* The business pays $2,000 in cash as "dividends" to Ahmed. This transaction results in a reduction of the assets of ITF through a decline in cash of $2,000 and a reduction of the equity of Ahmed by the same amount. The effect on the accounting equation is shown in Table 2.10. Although the payment for dividends is ostensibly a reward for Ahmed's investment, it is not treated as a deduction from profit but as a distribution.

TABLE 2.9 Receipt of Cash on Account

	Assets					= Liabilities +	Owners' Equity	
Trans-action	Cash	Building	Equip-ment	Supplies	Accounts Receiv-able	= Accounts Payable	Capital	Retained Earnings
1	100000						100000	
2	−75000	75000						
3	−5000		5000					
4				1000		1000		
5	10000							10000
6					4000			4000
7	−2300							−2300
7	−1500							−1500
7	−500							−500
8	−1000					−1000		
10	4000				−4000			
Balance	28700	75000	5000	1000	0	0	100000	9700

TABLE 2.10 Dividend

	Assets					= Liabilities +	Owners' Equity	
Trans-action	Cash	Building	Equip-ment	Supplies	Accounts Receiv-able	= Accounts Payable	Capital	Retained Earnings
1	100000						100000	
2	−75000	75000						
3	−5000		5000					
4				1000		1000		
5	10000							10000
6					4000			4000
7	−2300							−2300
7	−1500							−1500
7	−500							−500
8	−1000					−1000		
10	4000				−4000			
11	−2000							−2000
Balance	26700	75000	5000	1000	0	0	100000	7700

TABLE 2.11 Withdrawing of Cash

	Assets						= Liabilities +	Owners' Equity	
Trans-action	Cash	Building	Equip-ment	Supplies	Accounts Receiv-able	=	Accounts Payable	Capital	Retained Earnings
1	100000							100000	
2	−75000	75000							
3	−5000		5000						
4				1000			1000		
5	10000								10000
6					4000				4000
7	−2300								−2300
7	−1500								−1500
7	−500								−500
8	−1000						−1000		
10	4000				−4000				
11	−2000								−2000
12	−2300								−2300
Balance	24400	75000	5000	1000	0		0	100000	5400

- *Transaction 12: Drawings.* Ahmed withdraws $2,300 cash from the business for personal use. The effect on the accounting equation is shown in Table 2.11.

  The personal withdrawals of cash decrease the Cash at Bank account on the asset side. Given that these drawings are for personal use, they are not considered as business expenses. The owners' equity deceases as a result, so that the equality continues to hold. The effect on the accounting equation is the same as with the 'dividend' in transaction 11. Calling the payment something different makes no difference to the accounting treatment, which is governed by the substance of the transaction, not its form.

SUMMARY OF BUSINESS TRANSACTIONS

Table 2.12 summarises IFT's business entity transactions for the month. It is important to note that after every transaction the following equality holds:

ASSETS = LIABILITIES + OWNERS' EQUITY

TABLE 2.12 Transactions for the Month

	Assets					= Liabilities +	Owners' Equity	
Trans-action	Cash	+ Building +	Equip-ment +	Supplies +	Accounts Receiv-able	Accounts Payable +	Capital +	Retained Earnings
1	100,000						100,000	
2	−75,000	75,000						
Balance	25,000	75,000					100,000	
3	−5,000		5,000					
Balance	20,000		5,000				100,000	
4				1,000		1,000		
Balance	20,000	75,000	5,000	1,000		1,000	100,000	
5	10,000							10,000
Balance	30,000	75,000	5,000	1,000		1,000	100,000	10,000
6					4000			4000
Balance	30,000	75,000	5,000	1,000	4000	1,000	100,000	14,000
7	−2,300							−2,300
Balance	27,700	75,000	5,000	1,000	4000	1,000	100,000	11,700
7	−1,500							−1,500
Balance	26,200	75,000	5,000	1,000	4000	1,000	100,000	10,200
7	−500							−500
Balance	25700	75,000	5,000	1,000	4000	1,000	100,000	9700
8	−1000					−1000		
Balance	24700	75,000	5,000	1,000	4000	0	100,000	9700
10	4000				−4000			
Balance	28700	75,000	5,000	1,000	0	0	100,000	9700
11	−2000							−2000
Balance	26700	75,000	5,000	1,000	0	0	100,000	7700
12	−2300							−2300
Balance	24400	75,000	5,000	1,000	0	0	100,000	5400

These transactions are summarised in financial statements toward the end of this chapter. First, however, we need to see how accountants use the accounting system to achieve the same result as in the preceding transaction analysis.

KEEPING ACCOUNTING RECORDS IN ISLAMIC BUSINESSES

It would not be practical to try to analyse every transaction in businesses using the accounting equation explicitly, as have done here. As a result, for centuries dating back to the time of the Islamic State traders, investors and businesspeople have developed accounting systems and records to achieve the same end as that which would be achieved by using the accounting equation to analyse every transaction.

The Quran specifically requires followers to keep records of their indebtedness:

> *O ye who believe! When you contract a debt for a fixed period, write it down. Let a scribe write it down in justice between you. Let no scribe refuse to write as Allah has taught him, so let him write. Let him (the debtor) who incurs the liability dictate, and he must fear Allah, his Lord, and diminish not anything of what he owes.... (S2:282)*

Muslims are required to record their indebtedness as per Ayah 282 and 283 of the second Surah of al-Baqarah. The Quran requirements replaced the tribal rules that existed before Islam, and offer guidance on many aspects of life including commercial, legal, zakat, and ethical aspects of doing business. The requirements in the Quran helped to develop accounting systems in the early Islamic State. These systems helped to manage the accounts resulting from the collection of zakat.

The following procedures were applied by governments and entrepreneurs during the period of the Islamic State:

1. The recording of transactions was done immediately upon the occurrence of the economic events having financial impact on the institution.
2. Classification of recorded transactions was done on the basis of their nature. This resulted in grouping transactions under headings similar to those used today.
3. Receipts were recorded on the right-hand side and payments on the left-hand side with full explanation given for each record and transaction.
4. Blank spaces between records were not allowed.
5. Deleting or overwriting records was not allowed. Mistakes were explained in writing.
6. Accounts were signed before being closed.
7. Posting of similar transactions to a specialised book was done by a different person to the one recording the original transactions.
8. Accounts were balanced and the difference between the totals was referred to as al-Hasel ("the result").
9. Reports were produced on a monthly or annual basis.
10. Annual reports were audited and kept in the main Dewan.

Islamic enterprises in today's computerized business environment still account for the financial implications of economic events taking place within the organisation in a similar manner. Transactions reflecting economic events are reflected in individual accounts. Initial actions are recorded in a journal to reflect the need to record transactions on a daily basis, so that no transaction with a financial effect is omitted. The grouping of the accounts is done in the ledger.

The recording procedures described in this chapter are applied to the first transactions of Dar Al Fatina, the Abaya business established by the young UAE girl, Fatina Jabir. We will look at how the investment of AED1,000 is recorded immediately after the occurrence of the event, resulting in the investment of Fatina in the business. What does Fatina get in return for her investment, and how is this recorded? Three examples of transactions of the business on material supplies, office supplies, and withdrawals by the owner Fatina are recorded to show how these are reflected in the books of Dar Al Fatina. We will show what the ledgers of the business look like, and the way the data in the journal are posted to the ledgers. The trial balance of Dar Al Fatina will be prepared to ensure that the accounting cycle from recording to trial balance is complete. The role of accounting in recording, classifying, and communicating the business transactions of Dar Al Fatina is explained. Also, the use of accounting information produced by the journal, ledgers, and the trial balance to assist Fatina in her decision making will be illustrated toward the end of the chapter.

Dar Al Fatina was created by small amount of capital of AED1,000. Operating from the small city of Al Ain in the UAE was challenging. Dar Al Fatina had to address the challenge of retaining skilled labour in Al Ain and determine whether to increase salaries to match those paid in Abu Dhabi or Dubai. The impact of such increases on the results of business operations can be better understood using accounting information. Should Fatina decide to move her small factory to Dubai or Abu Dhabi, what information does she need to evaluate the decisions to stay in Al Ain or to relocate to one of these cities? The following shows how the ledger process of recording and classifying business transactions produces information that could be useful for decision making.

Double-Entry Accounting

Ayah 282 and 283 of the second Surah of al-Baqarah specifically require Muslims to record their indebtedness. It was left to individual Muslims to work out the details of their accounting system in accordance with Sharia principles. These practices became the components of what was later referred to and further developed as the double-entry bookkeeping system. The double-entry bookkeeping system thus evolved to comply with the recording requirements specified in the Quran. As the name suggests, each transaction in the double-entry system has two entries: One to the debit side of the ledger and the other to the credit side, both with the same amount to ensure the balance of the ledger remains equal.

When Fatina Jabir invested AED1,000 in her Abaya business, two accounts were created as a result of the transaction. The Cash at Bank account increased by AED1,000 and the Capital account also increased by AED 1,000. An Asset account (Cash at Bank) and an Owners' Equity account (Capital) were both equally affected.

If Fatina purchased material to make goods for sales and paid cash for the purchase, the transaction affects two accounts: Cash at Bank decreases and Material Supplies increases. If the purchase was done on credit, the accounts payable would increase instead of the cash. When Fatina pays the accounts payable for the material, then the Cash at Bank account decreases and the Accounts Payable account deceases, each by the same amount.

The T-Account

Ledger accounts are therefore affected by the recording of business transactions, either as debits or as credits. The list of debit and credit changes to a particular account is summarised in what is referred to as T-accounts. To the left side of the 'T' we list the debit amounts from the transaction affecting this particular account. To the right side of the 'T' we list all the credit amounts from transactions affecting this particular account. The T-account is divided into left side and right side, using a vertical line. The title of the account is written above the horizontal line. "Dr" and "Cr" represent the abbreviations for "debit" and "credit," respectively.

Increases and Decreases in the Accounts

The rules of debit and credit lead to the same outcome as the rules applying the accounting equation did for the transactions considered earlier in the chapter. The ledger system of bookkeeping has evolved over a long period of time to allow the consistent processing of very large numbers of transactions. As noted, the accounting equation method illustrated earlier in the chapter would be too cumbersome to be applied in practice.

Increases in assets are debits and are recorded on the left side of the T-account, and decreases are credits and are recorded on the right side of the T-account. For liabilities and owners' equity accounts, increases are credits and are recorded on the right side and decreases are debits and are recorded on the left side. These are the rules of debit and credit, and reflect the equation:

ASSETS = LIABILITIES + OWNERS' EQUITY

The effect on the ledger accounts of Fatina's business resulting from the first few transactions are illustrated next. To start the business, Fatina invested AED1,000. The Abaya business entity thus received AED1,000 cash from Fatina in exchange for an increase in equity for the owner in the business. The accounts that are affected are the business's Assets and Capital accounts: both would increase by AED1,000, as the T-accounts in Table 2.13 show.

The equality in the accounting equation is maintained and the total debit amounts always equal the total credit amounts. The amount remaining in an account is called its balance. The balance of the cash account after the first transaction of the initial investment is AED1,000 and is a debit balance. The capital account balance after the same transaction is an AED1,000 credit balance.

If Fatina purchased material to make goods for sales and paid AED100 cash for the purchase, Cash at Bank will decrease by AED100 (credit) and Material Supplies will increase by the same amount (debit). After this transaction, Cash at Bank has an AED900 debit balance (a 1,000 debit amount minus a 100 credit amount). Material Supplies then has a debit balance of AED100, and Capital has an AED1000 credit balance.

The third transaction is an AED150 purchase of office supplies on credit. This results in an increase in Accounts Payable by AED150 and a corresponding increase in Office Supplies by AED150.

When Fatina pays Accounts Payable for the material, then the Cash at Bank account decreases and Accounts Payable also deceases by the same amount.

Accounts are created as needed. When opening an account, a ledger account, represented here as a T-account, is created to start recording the transactions. For transaction 1, a Cash at Bank account and Fatina Jabir's Capital account are opened. For transaction 2, the Material Supplies account

TABLE 2.13 Ledger Accounts

Cash

Date	Item	Journal Ref	Debit	Date	Item	Journal Ref	Credit
March 3, 20X6		J.1	1,000				

Fatina Jabir Capital

Date	Item	Journal Ref	Debit	Date	Item	Journal Ref	Credit
				March 3, 20X6		J.1	1,000

is opened, and for transaction 3, Office Supplies and Accounts Payable ledger accounts are opened.

Recording Transactions in the Journal

In today's business environment, transactions are recorded as soon as possible after their occurrence, in accordance with Islamic precepts. This is done initially in the journal. Accountants follow a step-by-step approach in recording business transactions in the journal. First, the source documents supporting each transaction are identified. Second, the accounts affected by the transaction are identified, named, and grouped according to the nature of accounts: Assets, liabilities, equity, revenues, and expenses. Third, they determine the increase or decrease in the account, which account to debit, and which to credit. Finally, they journalise the transaction, entering it in the journal with a short explanation given for each entry. With advances in technology and the development of computerised accounting systems, the preceding steps are mostly completed using automated accounting systems.

Journalising the first few transactions in Fatina Jabir Dar Al Fatina is done in the following manner:

Step 1: Dar Al Fatina received AED1,000 from the owner Fatina Jabir as an initial investment in the business; the source document is Fatina's bank deposit slip.

Step 2: Cash at Bank and Owner's Capital accounts are affected by the transaction. Cash at Bank is an asset account. Owner's Capital is an owners' equity account.

Step 3: Cash at Bank is increased (debited) by 1,000 and the Owner's Capital, the owners' equity account, is increased (credited) by the same amount 1,000.

Step 4: The journal entry is shown in Table 2.14.

TABLE 2.14 Journal Entry

Date	Accounts and Explanation	Debit	Credit
March 3rd	Cash at Bank	1,000	
	Fatina Jabir, Capital		1,000
	Initial investment by owner		

Posting Entries from the Journal to the Ledger

Amounts recorded in the journal are posted to their respective accounts in the ledger. This is done maintaining the rules of debit and credit. With the use of computerised accounting systems, posting to the ledger is not done manually very often. It is automatically implemented by the system.

The initial investment transaction of Fatina Jabir in the Dar Al Fatina business is posted from the journal to the ledger, as shown in Tables 2.15 and 2.16.

Flow of Accounting Data from Transaction to Ledger

Entrepreneurs like Fatina Jabir establish their business to conduct transactions and achieve their business objectives. Events taking place in the business with financial consequences are recorded by accountants in the manner previously described. As soon as an event that has financial consequences occurs, accountants follow the aforementioned four steps to record the business transactions reflecting the event in the journal entry. Transactions are then posted to the ledger. The flow of accounting data from business transactions all the way through the accounting system to the ledger can be summarised as follows:

Event → Transaction → Source Document → Recording → Posting

TABLE 2.15 Journalising the Transaction

Date	Accounts and Explanation	Post Ref	Debit	Credit
March 3, 20X6	Cash	101	1,000	
	Fatina Jabir Capital	301		1,000
	Received AED1,000 cash investment from owner			

TABLE 2.16 Posting Transaction to the Ledger

Cash

Date	Item	Journal Ref	Debit	Date	Item	Journal Ref	Credit
March 3, 20X6		J.1	1,000				

Fatina Jabir Capital

Date	Item	Journal Ref	Debit	Date	Item	Journal Ref	Credit
				March 3, 20X6		J.1	1,000

The flow of accounting data for the first few business transactions of Dar Al Fatina is summarized as follows.

Transaction Analysis, Journalising, and Posting to the Accounts

1. Investment by owner:

Transaction

Dar Al Fatina received AED1,000 cash that Fatina Jabir invested to start her Abaya business.

Analysis

Dar Al Fatina increased its asset cash; the business also increased its owners' equity.

Debit-Credit Analysis

To record this increase in cash, debit Cash at Bank, and to record the increase in capital, credit Fatina Jabir's Capital account.

Journal Entry J.1

Dr Cash at Bank	1,000	
Cr Fatina Jabir, Capital		1,000

Received initial investment from owner.

Accounting Equation

ASSETS	= LIABILITIES	+ OWNERS' EQUITY
Cash	= Liabilities	+ Fatina Jabir Capital
1000	= 0	+ 1000

This transaction increased one asset account: Cash and increased one owner's equity account: Capital (Table 2.17)

2. Cash Purchases

Transaction

Fatina paid AED100 cash for material supplies to start making Abayas.

Analysis

The purchase decreased the business's cash and increased the entity's asset Material Supplies.

TABLE 2.17 Ledger Accounts

Cash

Date	Item	Journal Ref	Debit	Date	Item	Journal Ref	Credit
March 3, 20X6		J.1	1,000				

Fatina Jabir Capital

Date	Item	Journal Ref	Debit	Date	Item	Journal Ref	Credit
				March 3, 20X6		J.1	1,000

Debit–Credit Analysis

To record the decrease in cash, credit Cash at Bank, and to record the increase in the entity's asset material supplies, debit Material Supplies.

Journal Entry J.2

Dr Material Supplies	100	
Cr Cash at Bank		100

Paid cash for material supplies.

Accounting Equation

ASSETS		= LIABILITIES	+ OWNERS' EQUITY
Cash	+ Material Supplies	= Liabilities	+ Fatina Jabir Capital
−100	+ 100	= 0	+ 0

This transaction increased one asset, material supplies, and decreased another asset, cash. The net effect on the business's total assets was zero, and there was no effect on liabilities or owners' equity. We mostly use the term *net* in accounting to mean an amount after a subtraction (Table 2.18).

3. Purchase of office supplies on credit

Transaction

A purchase of AED150 office supplies on credit.

Analysis

Office supplies increased and accounts payable increased.

TABLE 2.18 Ledger Accounts

Cash

Date	Item	Journal Ref	Debit	Date	Item	Journal Ref	Credit
March 3, 20X6		J.1	1,000	March 10, 20X6		J.2	100

Material Supplies

Date	Item	Journal Ref	Debit	Date	Item	Journal Ref	Credit
March 10, 20X6		J.2	100				

Debit–Credit Analysis

We debit Office Supplies to record an increase in an asset, and credit Accounts Payable to reflect an increase in liabilities at the same time.

Journal Entry J.3

Dr Office Supplies	150	
Cr Accounts Payable		150

Purchased office supplies on credit.

Accounting Equation

ASSETS			= LIABILITIES	+ OWNERS' EQUITY
Cash	+ Material Supplies	+ Office Supplies	= Accounts Payable	+ Fatina Jabir Capital
0	0	150	150	0

This transaction increased one asset, Office Supplies, and increased a liabilities account, Accounts Payable (Table 2.19).

TABLE 2.19 Ledger Accounts

Office Supplies

Date	Item	Journal Ref	Debit	Date	Item	Journal Ref	Credit
March 15, 20X6		J.3	150				

Accounts Payable

Date	Item	Journal Ref	Debit	Date	Item	Journal Ref	Credit
				March 15, 20X6		J.3	150

4. Payments of accounts payable:

Transaction

Fatina paid AED100 of the account payable created in the preceding transaction.

Analysis

The payment of accounts payable decreased the asset Cash and decreased the liability Accounts Payable. It has no effect on Equity.

Debit–Credit Analysis

Credit Cash at Bank and debit Accounts Payable.

Journal Entry J.4

Dr Accounts Payable	100	
Cr Cash at Bank		100

Paid cash for accounts payable.

Accounting Equation

ASSETS			= LIABILITIES	+ OWNERS' EQUITY
Cash	+ Material Supplies	+ Office Supplies	= Accounts Payable	+ Fatina Jabir Capital
−100	0	0	−100	0

This transaction decreased one asset, Cash and decreased a liabilities account, Accounts Payable (Table 2.20).

TABLE 2.20 Ledger Accounts

Cash

Date	Item	Journal Ref	Debit	Date	Item	Journal Ref	Credit
March 3, 20X6		J.1	1000	March 10, 20X6		J.1	100
				March 20, 20X6		J.4	100

Accounts Payable

Date	Item	Journal Ref	Debit	Date	Item	Journal Ref	Credit
March 20, 20X6		J.4	100	March 15, 20X6		J.3	150

5. Cash withdrawals for personal expenses.

Transaction

Fatina Jabir withdrew AED200 cash for personal living expenses.

Analysis

The withdrawal decreased Dar Al Fatina cash; the transaction also decreased the owners' equity of the entity, although it is not an expense, because it is a distribution of equity.

Debit–Credit Analysis

Credit Cash at Bank to reflect the reduction of the Cash at Bank. Decreases in owners' equity resulting from owners' drawings are debited to a separate owners' equity account entitled Drawings. Therefore, Debit Fatina Jabir, Drawings.

Journal Entry J.5

Dr Fatina Jabir, Drawings	200	
Cr Cash at Bank		200

Drawing of cash by owner.

Accounting Equation

ASSETS			= LIABILITIES +	OWNERS' EQUITY
Cash	+ Material Supplies	+ Office Supplies	= Accounts Payable	+ Fatina Jabir Capital
−200	0	0	0	−200

This transaction decreased one asset, Cash and increased an equity account, Drawings (Table 2.21).

TABLE 2.21 Ledger Account

Cash

Date	Item	Journal Ref	Debit	Date	Item	Journal Ref	Credit
March 3, 20X6		J.1	1,000	March 10, 20X6		J.2	100
				March 20, 20X6		J.4	100
				March 25, 20X6		J.5	200

Fatina Jabir Withdrawals

Date	Item	Journal Ref	Debit	Date	Item	Journal Ref	Credit
March 25, 20X6		J.5	200				

Balancing the Accounts

After all business transactions are posted to the ledger, related accounts are grouped according to their type – that is, as assets, liabilities, owners' equities, revenues, or expenses. The balance for each account is computed by adding the total of the debit side and adding the total of the credit side; the account balance is the difference between the totals of the debit and credit sides.

Applying this to the cash account of Dar Al Fatina shows that the total debit side is AED1,000 and the total credit side is 100 + 100 + 200, or AED400. The cash account balance is 1,000 – 400 = 600. Given that the total debit side is greater than the total credit side, the balance is a debit balance.

The balance of the accounts payable is the difference between the total credit side, which is AED150, and the total debit side, which is AED100, to give a balance of AED50. Since the total on the credit side is larger than the total on the debit side, the accounts payable balance is a credit of AED50.

The Trial Balance

The trial balance is a total of all debit and credit balances shown in the ledger accounts at an accounting date. It is used as a check on the accuracy of the accounting system. If the total of all credits and debits is unequal, there is something wrong with the recording of the transactions, described earlier. The trial balance summarises important aggregates of the database from which the final accounts are prepared. It is also a classification process. The debit balances are listed in the left column of the trial balance, and credit balances are listed in the center column. The trial balance is automatically produced at the click of a mouse in computerised systems. In manual

TABLE 2.22 Dar Al Fatina Trial Balance

	Balance	
Account Titles	Debit	Credit
Cash at Bank	600	
Office Supplies	150	
Material Supplies	100	
Accounts Payable		50
Capital		1,000
Withdrawals	200	
Total	1,050	1,050

systems, recording steps sometimes contain errors and it is not unusual for the trial balance not to balance. It may then take some time to find the errors. Computerised systems save much time in these situations.

The following steps are required to prepare the trial balance:

1. List all the accounts and their balances as debits or credits in the respective debit or credit column.
2. Total the debit and credit amounts in each of the columns.
3. Ensure equality is maintained between the total of the debit and credit columns.

The trial balance of Dar Al Fatina after the first few transactions is as shown in Table 2.22.

Correcting Trial Balance Errors

Although the use of accounting software eliminates most errors, certain errors remain possible. For example, if we enter the wrong amounts on both the debit and credit sides of an entry, the trial balance will balance despite the error, and it will not be automatically identified and corrected. Other types of errors can still take place due to wrong entry and are also not necessarily detectable by the system.

Accountants need to perform certain activities in order to detect errors and correct the accounts. They may need to look for a missing account in the trial balance. If the accountant in Dar Al Fatina omitted Fatina Jabir's, drawings of AED200 from the trial balance, the total amount of the debits would be AED850. The accountant needs to be able to trace each account from the ledger to the trial balance to correct the error.

In the case where the total credit balance in the trial balance is different from the total debit balance, the accountant will need to search the journal for the difference. For example, if the total credits on the Dar Al Fatina trial balance equal AED1,250 and total debits are AED1,050, the accountant might have recorded the transaction in the journal incorrectly or incorrectly posted the transaction to the ledger. The accountant of Dar Al Fatina will need to search the journal for the erroneous transaction, which in this case could be an Accounts Payable payment of AED100 wrongly posted as a credit instead of debit, creating the difference of AED 200.

In the case where a debit balance is treated by mistake as credit balance or the other way around, the accountants will need to divide the difference between the total debit balances and total credit balances by 2. If the accountant at Dar Al Fatina posted the AED150 credit in Accounts Payable as debit, the total debits in the trial balance will be AED300 (double the amount) more than the total credit balance. If we divide the difference by 2 we will find the AED150 amount. The accountant can then search the journal for the AED150 transaction and correct the error.

The trial balance may show an error between the total credit and debit balances that is evenly divisible by 9. Errors of this nature are called slide errors. They can occur from, for example, recording AED31 as AED310 or through transposition errors such as recording AED 31 as AED13. If the accountant at Dar Al Fatina recorded the drawings of Fatina Jabir as AED2,000 instead of AED200, the trial balance will show a difference of AED1,800 (2,000 – 200), and dividing 1,800 by 9 gives AED200. The accountant can then check the ledger balances for an amount of AED200 and will most likely find the Drawing account balance with this amount.

Formats of Journals and Ledgers

The journal and ledgers contain important information. These are useful tools that serve other purposes than sourcing the data for the trial balance. For instance, data in the journal and ledger can be used as an audit trail through which records are checked. For example, the accountant can check the journal and ledgers for information on specific payments or receipts.

Table 2.23 is an example of a typical journal. The important information is the date when the transaction occurred, the title of the account, and a short explanation of the transaction; the posting reference; the debit column to

TABLE 2.23 Journalising the Transaction (Page 1)

Date	Accounts and Explanation	Post Ref	Debit	Credit
March 3, 20X6	Cash	101	1,000	
	Fatina Jabir Capital	301		1,000
	Received AED1,000 cash investment from owner			

TABLE 2.24 Ledger Accounts

Cash

Date	Item	Journal Ref	Debit	Date	Item	Journal Ref	Credit
March 3, 20X6		J.1	1000	March 10, 20X6		J.2	100
				March 20, 20X6		J.4	100
				March 25, 20X6		J.5	200

Fatina Jabir Capital

Date	Item	Journal Ref	Debit	Date	Item	Journal Ref	Credit
				March 3, 20X6		J.1	1,000

Material Supplies

Date	Item	Journal Ref	Debit	Date	Item	Journal Ref	Credit
March 10, 20X6		J.2	100				

insert the amount of debit; and the credit column to insert the credit amount. Finally, the journal pages are numbered for ease of reference.

Table 2.24 represents an example of the ledger in a T format prepared for Dar Al Fatina Cash at Bank account, Material Supplies, and the Capital account. Important data shown in the ledger account include the date, the journal reference number, the debit column, and the credit column.

Tables 2.25 and 2.26 show the typical format of the journal and ledger accounts with all the relevant headings. The journal entries of the first few transactions of Dar Al Fatina and the posting of these entries to their respective ledger accounts are shown.

Chart of Accounts

The grouping of accounts in the ledger reflects the type of accounts. A chart of accounts is a coding system applied to all the accounts in an organisation. It is the list of all the ledger accounts and their account numbers, which are used as posting references. The chart of accounts helps to keep track of all accounts and in locating individual accounts.

TABLE 2.25 Journalising the Transactions

Date	Accounts and Explanation	Post Ref	Debit	Credit
March 3, 20X6	Cash	101	1,000	
	Fatina Jabir Capital	301		1,000
	Received AED1,000 cash investment from owner			
March 10, 20X6	Material Supplies	161	100	
	Cash	101		100
	Paid AED 100 cash for material supplies			
March 15, 20X6	Office Supplies	151	150	
	Accounts Payable	201		150
	Purchased AED150 office supplies on credit			

The system of numbering accounts generally follows a standard format where the numbers given to individual accounts tend to be two or more digits; organisations with many accounts use lengthy account numbers. We usually number the asset accounts beginning with 1, liabilities beginning with 2, owners' equity accounts with 3, revenue accounts with 4, and expenses accounts with 5. The position of an individual account within a particular category is reflected in the second, third, and higher digits in an account number. For example, Cash at Bank at Dara Al Fatina has the account number 101, indicating that this is the first account in the assets category. Accounts Receivable could take number 111, the second asset account. Accounts Payable could take the number 201, the first liability account. Using this numbering system, the chart of accounts for Dar Al Fatina is shown in Table 2.27.

The gaps in these account numbers give the accountant at Dar Al Fatina the possibility to include more categories.

Owners' Equity Accounts: Revenues and Expenses

In addition to the owner's capital and withdrawals listed under owners' equity, the categories of Revenues and Expenses are the main components of the income statement affecting the owners' equity account. Fatina Jabir will always work to increase the revenues generated by Dar Al Fatina because any increase in revenue represents an increase in owner's capital. However, by the same token, she will work to reduce her expenses, as a reduction in expenses has the same effect on income as an increase in revenue.

TABLE 2.26 Ledger

Cash

Date	Item	Journal Ref	Debit	Date	Item	Journal Ref	Credit
March 3, 20X6		J.1	1,000	March 10, 20X6		J.2	100
				March 20, 20X6		J.4	100
				March 25, 20X6		J.5	200

Fatina Jabir Capital

Date	Item	Journal Ref	Debit	Date	Item	Journal Ref	Credit
				March 3, 20X6		J.1	1,000

Material Supplies

Date	Item	Journal Ref	Debit	Date	Item	Journal Ref	Credit
March 10, 20X6		J.2	100				

Office Supplies

Date	Item	Journal Ref	Debit	Date	Item	Journal Ref	Credit
March15, 20X6		J.3	150				

Accounts Payable

Date	Item	Journal Ref	Debit	Date	Item	Journal Ref	Credit
March 20, 20X6		J.4	100	March 15, 20X6		J.3	150

Fatina Jabir Withdrawals

Date	Item	Journal Ref	Debit	Date	Item	Journal Ref	Credit
March 25, 20X6		J.5	200				

TABLE 2.27 Chart of Accounts

	Balance Sheet Accounts
Code	Assets Accounts
101	Cash at Bank
111	Accounts Receivable
151	Office Supplies
161	Material Supplies
	Liabilities Accounts
201	Accounts Payable
241	Note Payables
	Owners' Equity Accounts
301	Capital
311	Withdrawals
	Income Statement Accounts
	Revenue Accounts
401	Revenue
	Expenses Accounts
501	Salaries
502	Rent
503	Marketing

The accounting equation thus incorporates revenues and expenses accounts within owners' equity, in addition to capital and withdrawals.

$$\text{Assets} = \text{Liabilities} + \overbrace{\text{Capital} - \text{Withdrawals} + \text{Revenues} - \text{Expenses}}^{\text{Owners' Equity}}$$

The rules of debit and credit governing the types of account falling under each category of the above equation are shown in Table 2.28.

The Financial Statements

Accountants record economic events taking place within a business that have financial consequences. Records are summarized and financial statements prepared for an accounting period. The financial statements summarise the impact of the financial transactions that have occurred up to the end of the

TABLE 2.28 Types of Account

Asset Accounts							
Date	Item	Journal Ref	Debit	Date	Item	Journal Ref	Credit
			Debit for increases				Credit for decreases
Liability Accounts							
Date	Item	Journal Ref	Debit	Date	Item	Journal Ref	Credit
			Debit for decreases				Credit for increases
Capital							
Date	Item	Journal Ref	Debit	Date	Item	Journal Ref	Credit
			Debit for decreases				Credit for increases
Withdrawals							
Date	Item	Journal Ref	Debit	Date	Item	Journal Ref	Credit
			Debit for increases				Credit for decreases
Revenues							
Date	Item	Journal Ref	Debit	Date	Item	Journal Ref	Credit
			Debit for decreases				Credit for increases
Expenses							
Date	Item	Journal Ref	Debit	Date	Item	Journal Ref	Credit
			Debit for increases				Credit for decreases

accounting period and in the most recent accounting period on the business. The financial statements summarise the outcome of economic events in a highly aggregated format. The primary financial statements in a conventional accounting system are the (1) income, (2) changes in owners' equity, (3) balance sheet, and (4) cash flows.

Islamic financial statements share the same broad classification. An Islamic financial accounting system should facilitate the production of a statement of financial position to reflect the status of the financial position at a particular point in time. It should also facilitate the production of an income statement to identify the results of operation over a period of time. The system should also facilitate the production of a cash flow statement to report the flow of cash in and out of the firm. A value-added statement is an important additional piece of information, especially in an Islamic context, as it identifies the value the entity brings to the community at large through its economic activities. The latter is a more significant objective of business organisations in Islam than in non-Islamic organisations.

Financial Accounting Standard No. 1 (FAS1), issued in January 1996 by AAIOFI on the General Presentation and Disclosure in the Financial Statements of Islamic Banks, requires the preparation of an income statement, balance sheet, cash flow statement, and a statement of changes in owners' equity, or a statement of retained earnings. In addition it requires additional statements of changes in restricted investments, sources and uses of zakat and charity funds (if the bank assumes the responsibility for the collection and distribution of zakat), and sources and uses of qard funds. Detailed notes to these financial statements are also mandated.

The standard lists specify Sharia disclosure requirements for Islamic banks and financial institutions. These include important aspects reflecting the nature of their business and information on the role of the Sharia's advisory board in supervising the bank's activities and the bank's responsibility towards zakat. FAS1 requires the disclosure of major accounting policies, the asset revaluation methods to be used, liabilities, and restricted investments at their cash equivalent value, earnings, or expenditures or assets not measured or calculated in accordance with Sharia requirements, and how such assets will be disposed of. FAS1 also requires the disclosure of information on restricted and unrestricted investments, the distribution of unrestricted investment accounts by type, methods of allocating profits or losses on investments between investment account holders, and returns on each type of investment accounts.

Balance Sheet The balance sheet represents the financial position of the entity at a particular point in time, and is thus often described as a snapshot of the entity at that point in time. The balance sheet contains a summary of the entity's assets, liabilities, and owners' equity.

Profit and Loss Statement The profit and loss statement presents the results of an entity's operations over a period of time. This statement lists the revenues and expenses of an entity for a specific period, such as a month or a year. The difference between the revenue and expenses indicates the net profit or loss for the period and is usually considered the most significant figure in the profit and loss statement (the "bottom line").

The income statement needs to be prepared every year for the purposes of zakat.

The profit figure in an Islamic business should not distract those involved in business from their religious duties. A profitable business may contribute positively to its owner's wealth, but primarily it should contribute to the benefit of the wider community. Ultimately the important question is: What does the bottom line contribute to the community?

Statement of Changes in Owners' Equity The changes in the entity's owners' equity over a period of time is presented in the statement of owners' equity. Investments by the owner and from net profit earned during the period increases owners' equity. Drawings and losses decreases owners' equity.

Statement of Cash Flows The statement of cash flows represents the movement in cash inflows and outflows of the company during a period of time. The outcome of the cash flow statement is the net increase or decrease in the cash account shown in the balance sheet during an accounting period and the cash balance at the end of the period. Some consider the cash flow statement to be a check on the substance of the profit and loss statement.

Statement of Sources and Uses of Funds in the Zakat and Charity Funds This statement shows the source and application of zakat funds by a business entity over a period of time. Zakat is calculated on the basis of the appreciation of net asset values over an accounting period, excluding assets acquired for consumption or used in production.

Statement of Sources and Uses of the Qard Fund This statement represents the amount of money loaned free of interest, referred to in Arabic as qard (benevolent loan). It is part of the social responsibility of companies and individuals towards others in the community. Funds that are unused should be loaned free of interest for a specific period of time. In Islam, as explained in Chapter 1, fixed-interest-based credit is illegal. Government soft loans and grants to organisations are examples of qard loans. In such cases, the providers of loans will use accounting information to assess whether their loans are used in accordance with the agreements underlying them, as well as to assess the ability of the relevant organisation to pay back their loan on time.

USING ACCOUNTING INFORMATION FOR DECISION MAKING

In Islamic societies, religion constitutes a significant part of people's lives and the meaning they attach to them. Religion is all-embracing in its impact on business and decision making. Islam is not just a religious institution.

It is inseparable from all of the affairs of believers. Religion and business decisions go hand in hand. Religion can provide insight into the behaviour of individuals in a society, so that understanding religion is an important component of understanding the way business decisions are made in religious societies. Religious tenets provide much of the foundation for business decisions as well as for the moral codes that guide individual and group behaviour.

While Islam is not alone among religions in the references it makes to business-related matters, it is distinctive in the extent to which its percepts address directly and in detail the conduct of business.

Islam is unusual in the strength of its directives concerning the desirability of community-oriented, as opposed to individualistic, behaviour. It is unequivocal in its advocacy of the welfare of the group over the individual and the merits of long-term investments in social capital over short-term returns to the individual.

The Islamic principle of *khilafa* requires individuals to be personally responsible for what is done with the resources entrusted to them. This principle, together with the principle of *shura,* which requires them to consult with those affected by their organisations, places a duty upon individual believers to take a personal interest in the management of their organisations. The interests of those affected by the operation of the organisation and its decisions are also safeguarded by the Islamic principles of *adalah* (justice).

Running a fashion house such as Dar Al Fatina in Al Ain comes with challenges that the owner, Fatina Jabir, needs to address. For instance, customer impressions of a fashion house based in Al Ain will probably be lower than those for similar businesses in Dubai or Abu Dhabi.

In an interview on the nature of this challenge, Fatina Jabir said, 'They are not expecting that you will make a high-value product', adding that ladies will pay double in Dubai for the same product in Al Ain, under the notion that it is of higher quality. For this reason, it's also been challenging to build customer loyalty.

Another challenge is finding and keeping skilled manpower in Al Ain. Dubai and Abu Dhabi are more attractive because salaries are higher. Should Fatina Jabir consider establishing a factory in Dubai or Abu Dhabi to address the problem of skilled staff retention, or can she afford higher salaries while staying in Al Ain? Will sale prices in Al Ain support salary increases? What are the responsibilities of Fatina to the communities of Dubai, Abu Dhabi, and Al-Ain, aside from the making of profits? To what extent can accounting information assist Fatina Jabir in dealing with some of these questions?

Entrepreneurs like Fatina Jabir often make decisions without taking the time to follow all the steps in an accounting system. Data related to specific issues are generally collected and used to make decisions relating to the aforementioned challenges. The decision of whether to move to Dubai or stay in Al Ain will in part depend on the financial impact of such a move. Information that is contained in financial statements should assist the decision maker in making well-informed decisions.

VOCABULARY

AAOIFI
accounting equation
accounts payable
accounts receivable
accruals
accrued liabilities
al-Hasel
assets
balance sheet
balancing the accounts
bills payable
bills receivable
bookkeeping system
business transactions
capital
cash
chart of accounts
conservatism principle
correcting trial balance errors
cost principle
debit–credit analysis
double-entry accounting
drawings
entity concept
equipment, furniture, and fixtures
expenses
fairness

financial statements
formats of journals and ledgers
full disclosure
going concern principle
increases and decreases in the accounts
inventories
Islam
justice
keeping records
ledger accounts
liabilities
market value
matching principle
normal balance of an account
owners' equity
posting entries from the journal to the ledger
prepaid expenses
preparers of accounts
profit and loss statement
profit recognition principle
recording transactions in the journal
revenues
statement of cash flows
statement of owners' equity
statement of sources and uses of funds in the qard fund
statement of sources and uses of funds in the zakat and charity funds
T-account
tandeed principle
time period concept
transaction
transactions analysis
trial balance
truthfulness

MULTIPLE-CHOICE QUESTIONS

1. Which of the following statements about the entity concept is not correct?
   a. The entity concept requires the preparers of accounts to treat the organisation as a separate entity from that of the owners.
   b. The entity concept was known during the early Islamic State.
   c. Accountants should record owner personal expenses to comply with the entity concept.
   d. An economic entity can be any organisation or unit in an economy.
2. Which of the following statements about market values is not correct?
   a. Central to Islamic accounting is the use of current values for the correct computation of zakat.
   b. Current values, when measured accurately, contain more information than actual costs.
   c. Capital maintenance is an important driver of the choice of the valuation method adopted.
   d. The maintenance of nominal capital favours the use of current values.
3. Which of the following statements is not true?
   a. Historical cost can be misleading in the computation of zakat.
   b. AAOIFI adopted the cost concept in its conceptual framework.
   c. While the cost principle ensures reliability, its relevance is sometimes questioned.
   d. The cost principle ensures that the accounts are based on the opinions of individuals in charge of the accounts.
4. Which of the following is not a step in the accounting process?
   a. Identification
   b. Auditing
   c. Recording
   d. Communication
5. On the last day of the period, Ahmed Islamic Finance Training buys a computer for $2,000 on credit. In what manner does this transaction affect the accounting equation?
   a. Office Equipment increases and Cash decreases.
   b. Office Equipment increases and Accounts Payable decreases.
   c. Office Equipment increases and Accounts Payable increases.
   d. Assets increases and Liabilities and Owners' Equity increases.
6. Which of the following statements is correct?
   a. Debits decrease liabilities and increase assets.
   b. Debits increase both assets and liabilities.
   c. Debits decrease both assets and liabilities.
   d. Debits decrease assets and increase liabilities.

7. Which of the following statements about ledgers is correct?
   a. A ledger is a collection of the asset accounts in a company.
   b. A ledger is a book to record daily transactions.
   c. A ledger is a collection of all the accounts maintained by a company.
   d. A ledger is a book that reports the outcome of the business operation.
8. If the accounts of Aafaq Islamic Finance show a cash balance of $75,000, equipment $100,000, office building $500,000, and accounts payable $150,000, what is the company owners' equity?
   a. $425,000
   b. $25,000
   c. $450,000
   d. $525,000
9. On June 10, 20X6, Dar Al Fatina purchased material supplies on account for $35,000. Which of the journal entries for this transaction in the table below is correct.

A

Date	Accounts and Explanation	Debit	Credit
June 10, 20X6	Cash	35,000	
	Material Supplies		35,000
	Purchased supplies on account		

B

Date	Accounts and Explanation	Debit	Credit
June 10, 20X6	Material Supplies	35,000	
	Sales		35,000
	Purchased supplies on account		

C

Date	Accounts and Explanation	Debit	Credit
June 10, 20X6	Material Supplies	35,000	
	Accounts Payable		35,000
	Purchased supplies on account		

D

Date	Accounts and Explanation	Debit	Credit
June 10, 20X6	Material Supplies	35,000	
	Accounts Receivables		35,000
	Purchased supplies on account		

10. The Material Supplies account at Dar Al Fatina shows the following transactions: Material supplies purchased for cash AED1,000, additional supplies purchased for cash AED500, material supplies purchased on account AED3,500. Dar Al Fatina paid AED1,000 of the accounts payable. What is the Material Supplies account balance?
    a. AED4,000
    b. AED1,500
    c. AED6,000
    d. AED5,000

DISCUSSION QUESTIONS

1. Briefly describe the steps in the accounting process.
2. Discuss the Islamic view of the profit recognition principles.
3. How was the osher (Ottoman tax on agriculture products) determined? To which accounting principle does this relate?
4. Discuss the concept of full disclosure in Islamic accounting.
5. What are the main differences between conventional accounting and Islamic accounting with regard to the definition of assets?
6. The requirements in the Quran helped to develop an accounting system for the early Islamic State. Explain the main procedures that were developed and applied by government authorities and individual entrepreneurs during the Islamic State to record, classify, and post transactions in the books.
7. Islamic financial statements share the same broad classifications as conventional financial statements. However, a value-added statement is an important outcome of the Islamic financial accounting system. Explain why the similarity exists, and indicate the reasons for the emphasis on the VAS.
8. 'Historical cost can be misleading both as indicative of values and in the computation of zakat'. Discuss.
9. Explain the principle of tandeed in Islam.

EXERCISES

1. Post the following journal entries from the books of Aafaq Islamic Finance to their respective T-accounts and compute the October 31 balances.

General Journal

Date	Account Titles and Explanation		Debit	Credit
Oct. 20X6				
3	Material Supplies		3,500	
		Accounts Payable		3,500
7	Material Supplies		4,000	
		Cash		4,000
9	Accounts Receivable		1,500	
		Revenue		1,500
12	Cash		6,000	
		Revenue		6,000
16	Rent Expense		2,000	
		Cash		2,000
22	Cash		1,000	
		Accounts Receivable		1,000

General Ledger

Cash		Accounts Receivable	

Revenue		Rent Expense	

Accounts Payable		Material Supplies	

2. The ledger accounts of Dar Al Fatina show the following account balances as of March 31, 20X6. Prepare a trial balance for the company as of the same date.

Accounts Payable	4,500	Rent Expense	1,500
Accounts Receivable	6,000	Service Revenue	9,000
Cash	3,000	Supplies	600
Owner Capital	6,600	Salaries	3,000
Dividends	3,000	Office Equipment	3,000

3. During the month of June, the following transactions took place at the Islamic Finance Training Company. Prepare the journal entry for each of these transactions.
   a. Received 75,000 from owner.
   b. Purchased office equipment for $5,000 for cash.
   c. Purchased material supplies for $7,000 on account.
   d. The rent for the month of $4,000 was paid in cash.
   e. Conducted tow training program for a client and received $18,500 in cash.
   f. Salaries for the month were $9,000 and were all paid.
   g. Conducted one training program for $10,000 for a client who will pay next month.
   h. Paid dividends to stockholders of $4,000.
   i. Received $4,000 cash for training services previously performed on account.
4. The general journal book of Al Markkas shows the following entries for the month of November 20X6 transactions. You are required to post these entries to their respective accounts in the general ledger and prepare a trial balance as of November 30, 20X6.

General Journal

Date	Account Titles and Explanation	Debit	Credit
Nov 20X6			
1	Cash	75,000	
	Owner Capital		75,000
Investment by owner in the company			
3	Material Supplies	5,000	
	Cash		5,000
Material Supplies cash purchase			
5	Company Car	20,000	
	Cash		20,000

General Journal			
Date	**Account Titles and Explanation**	**Debit**	**Credit**
Company car purchased by cash			
8	Office Equipment	3,000	
	Cash		3,000
Office equipment cash purchases			
10	Material Supplies	7000	
	Accounts Payable		7000
Material supplies purchased on account			
12	Rent Expense	2,000	
	Cash		2,000
Paid September rent			
14	Accounts Receivable	3,000	
	Revenue		3,000
Invoiced customers for sales			
16	Cash	3,500	
	Revenue		3,500
Cash sales			
	Accounts Receivable	1,000	
	Revenue		1,000
Invoiced customer for sales			
20	Utility Expense	200	
	Cash		200
Paid month utilities expenses for cash			
30	Dividends	750	
	Cash		750
Cash dividend paid			
30	Salaries	1,500	
	Cash		1,500
Monthly salaries paid by cash			

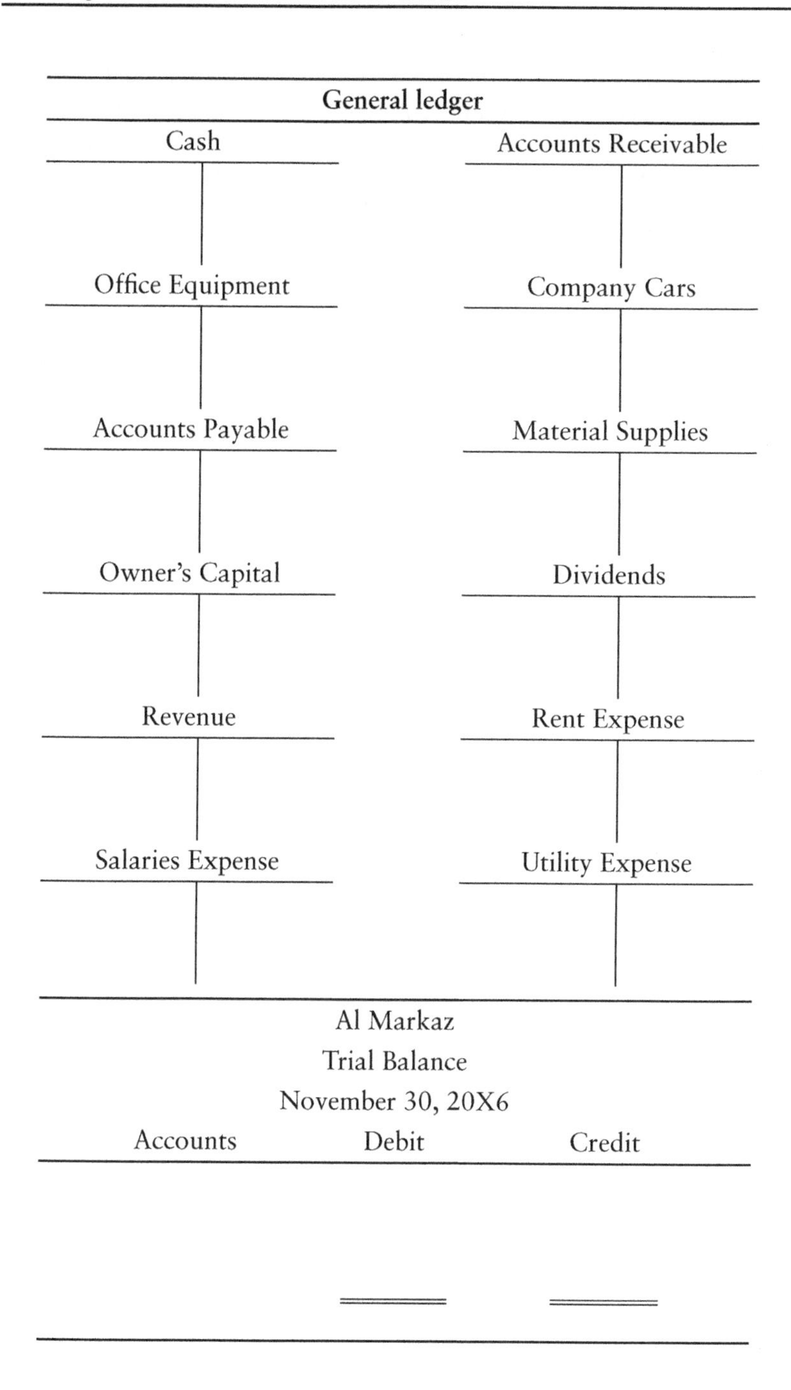
General ledger
Cash
Accounts Receivable
Office Equipment
Company Cars
Accounts Payable
Material Supplies
Owner's Capital
Dividends
Revenue
Rent Expense
Salaries Expense
Utility Expense
Al Markaz
Trial Balance
November 30, 20X6
Accounts
Debit
Credit

5. During a routine check on the accounts of Dar Al Fatina, the following errors were identified. You are required to state which of these errors causes an unequal total in the trial balance and which of these errors causes the trial balance to be misstated but not unequal.
   a. Accounts payable payments of AED900 were recorded as debit Accounts Payable AED90 and credit Cash AED900.
   b. Office equipment purchases of AED650 for cash were recorded as debit Office Equipment AED65 and credit Cash AED65.
   c. Payment of accounts receivable for AED1,500 were recorded as debit Cash AED1,500 and debit Accounts Payable AED1,500.
   d. Cash payment to accounts payable of AED750. The record was debit Accounts Payable AED750 and credit Accounts Receivable AED750.

Errors	Error causes an unequal total in the trial balance	Error causes the trial balance to be misstated but not unequal
1		
2		
3		
4		

CHAPTER 3

Adjusting Islamic Accounting Records at the Close of the Accounting Period

Learning Objectives

After studying this chapter, you should be able to:

1. Explain the accrual accounting system and its suitability to an Islamic business environment.
2. Make the necessary end-of-period adjustments to the accounts.
3. Journalise and post closing entries.
4. Prepare an extended trial balance, taking into account the necessary adjustments to the accounts.
5. Prepare the profit and loss account and balance sheet from the extended trial balance.

Chapter 2 dealt with recording transactions as the transactions take place in time. This chapter will deal with all the adjustments that must be made to produce a true Islamic picture of the results of the accounting entity for the accounting period and its wealth at the accounting date.

Trade and commerce are encouraged in Islam. Many verses in the Quran promote honest trade and business activities. People are encouraged to work toward respectful living for their families and support others less fortunate through charitable donations. This can be done through business and trading activities that result in reasonable profits. The generation of profits is, however, not done at the expense of, or through the exploitation of, others, and the welfare of the community is promoted over the rights of the owners of the business.

Companies prepare their financial reports or statements at the end of the accounting period to serve different purposes, including zakat calculation and payment. Zakat is paid at the end of every year. For this and other reasons, Islamic financial statements are produced annually. How do these businesses compute the results of their operations?

As already noted, FAS1 requires the production of a profit and loss account, which shows the revenue generated by a business during an accounting period minus all the expenses paid to generate these revenues. The result of that difference is the profit or loss figure. This is a significant metric for an Islamic business but is not the only important indicator of success in an Islamic environment, since a profitable business contributes positively not only to the owners' wealth but also to the betterment of the community and the wider economy.

The benefits of the economic activities of a business to society generally are seen in the calculation of value-added. This rearranges the information in an income statement so that the difference between sales and 'intermediate' purchases of goods and services, i.e. the value added to society by firm activities, is shown as being distributed to employees and lenders, as well as owners, or retained in the business, rather than showing wages and the other distributions as expenses. As this is merely a reclassification of certain items in the profit and loss account, the information needed to produce a measure of value-added is essentially the same as that needed to prepare the income statement. The process of completing the accounting cycle therefore supports the calculation of both income and value-added. We discuss the measurement of value added in Chapter 4.

The process of completing the accounting cycle starts with the trial balance, which shows all the account balances as a list of debits and credits. In addition to balancing the accounts in the trial balance, firms bring their accounts up to date, a process known as adjusting the books. The computation of the profit or loss and value-added therefore involves the trial balance, adjusting entries, and finally the preparation and presentation of the financial statements. The previous chapter dealt with the trial balance. This chapter deals mainly with the adjusting process and the next chapter deals with the presentation of the financial statements.

The system accountants use to prepare the financial statements is the accrual system of accounting, which stands in contrast to the cash basis of accounting. The accrual basis allows for recognising revenues when they occur irrespective of whether cash is received. This system also allows recognising the expenses when they take place irrespective of the whether they are paid.

The accrual system of accounts is the one mostly used around the world and is based on certain accounting concepts and principles including periodicity, realization, going concern, entity, and others described in previous chapters.

ACCRUAL ACCOUNTING

You will recall that the Quran requires records of indebtedness to be kept by followers. Surat Al-Baqra verse 2:282 states, 'Believers, when you contract a debt for a fixed period, put it in writing. Let a scribe write it down fairly... and let the debtors dictate, not diminishing the sum he owes...' In an Islamic business, accountants are, therefore, required to record the Sharia compliant economic events, which have financial implications. Effectively, we interpret this as requiring accountants to follow accrual principles.

These records must be identified with a particular date, in order to prepare the final accounts related to the period in which the transaction took place. For instance, the accounts prepared for a particular year are used to assess the zakat due for that particular year.

As indicated earlier, the accrual system of accounting is used to prepare the financial statements of business entities. The system allows for recognising revenue when it occurs irrespective of whether cash is received. This system also allows recognising the expenses when they take place, irrespective of whether they are paid.

According to the Malaysian Financial Reporting Standard i-12004, 'Presentation of Financial Statements of Islamic Financial Institutions', with the exception of the cash flow statement, the financial statements must be prepared on the basis of the accrual accounting system. Any departure from this rule must be approved by the Sharia Advisory Council of Bank Negara Malaysia.

FAS1 includes a recommendation to use the accrual basis of accounting as the primary treatment with cash basis provided as an alternative. In the case where cash basis is used, this must be explained in the notes to the account together with a reconciliation to reflect the financial position using the accrual system.

Accrual accounting provides a comprehensive picture of the results of the operations and financial position of businesses. If a business earned revenue prior to the end of the accounting period without collecting cash, using the cash-basis of accounting method, the financial statements would not report the revenue or the related account receivable, because no collection has occurred. This omits important information about the financial position of the business. A similar argument holds for the recording of expenses. According to AAOIFI's SFA2, 'Revenues should be recognised when realized'. Realization of revenues is subject to the legal right that the entity is to receive the expected revenue and the receipt of revenue is known with a reasonable degree of certainty.

ADJUSTING THE ACCOUNTS AT THE ACCOUNTING PERIOD END

The Islamic Sharia requires financial statements to be prepared at the end of each accounting period. The financial statements are prepared from the accounting balances of the various accounts available on the books and summarised in the trial balance. Prior to the preparation of the financial statements, the trial balance will need to be adjusted for items affecting more than one accounting period.

The adjustment process, which takes place prior to the preparation of end of accounting period financial statements, allocates revenues and expenses transactions to the period in which they occur. The assets and liability accounts will also be adjusted to reflect their accrual basis balance at the balance sheet date.

Prepaid and Accrued Expenses

Prepaid and accrued expenses are adjusted in the books to ensure they are accounted for in the correct period in which they occur, according to accrual principles. To reiterate the most important point: The accruals concept requires the recognition of expenses when incurred rather than when paid and income recognised when earned, not received.

Prepaid Expenses These arise when expenses are paid in advance. A business may have to pay for certain services in advance—that is, prior to when the service is delivered. Such practice gives rise to an asset account named *prepaid expenses*. Prepaid expenses represent payments made for expenses that are not yet incurred. Examples of prepaid expenses include rent paid in advance, where the landlord requires payment at the beginning of the month or the year. Other examples include prepaid insurance, which is typically paid in advance for the period insured.

According to the Application Guidance of the Malaysian FRS 132 Financial Instruments: Disclosure and Presentation (AG11): 'Assets (such as prepaid expenses) for which the future economic benefit is the receipt of goods or services, rather than the right to receive cash or another financial asset, are not "financial" assets. Similarly, items such as deferred revenue and most warranty obligations are not "financial" liabilities because the outflow of economic benefits associated with them is the delivery of goods and services rather than a contractual obligation to pay cash or another financial asset'. These transactions therefore result in the creation of what are considered 'non-financial' assets and liabilities rather than 'financial' assets and liabilities.

Rent payments in the United Arab Emirates, for example, are usually settled using one, two, or three cheques. Business tenants sometimes negotiate different arrangements. When rent is paid in advance, giving rise to prepaid rent, a business is buying the benefits to use the asset for a period of time in the future. This creates an asset, usually referred to as prepaid rent, in the balance sheet of the business.

Example: Dar Alhikma pays advance rent to its landowner of $15,000 on December 31, 2017, in respect of bookshop rent for the following year. Dar Alhikma will recognise the payment as an asset of $15,000 in the 2017 financial statements. This will be reflected in the 2017 books of Dar Alhikma as follows:

Debit	Prepaid rent	$15,000	
Credit	Cash		$15,000

In 2018, the period for which the prepaid expenses were intended, the prepaid expenses will then be recognised as an expense related to this year. The 2018 books will reflect this as follows:

Debit	Rent expense (income statement)	$15,000	
Credit	Prepaid Rent		$15,000

Example: Tecom signed a contract with Tamimi law firm to provide legal services for a three-month period from March 1, 2018, to May 31, 2018, and paid $15,000 cash in advance for this service. This transaction will be reflected in Tecom books in the following manner:

March 1, 2018

Debit	Prepaid legal services	$15,000	
Credit	Cash		$15,000

The prepaid legal service represents an asset account.

March 31, 2018

Debit	Legal expense	$5,000	
Credit	Prepaid legal services		$5,000

April 30, 2018

Debit	Legal expense	$5,000	
Credit	Prepaid legal services		$5,000

May 31, 2018

Debit	Legal expense	$5,000	
Credit	Prepaid legal services		$5,000

Depreciation of Fixed Assets Fixed or noncurrent assets are assets entrusted to the business to assist in its operations and are not intended for sales. The word *entrusted* is used because according to the Islamic Sharia, the ultimate ownership of assets remains with God. The Quran in Al Baqarah, 2:284 specifically mentions that whatever is in heavens and whatever on earth belong to Allah. This rule applies to assets held in a business.

In an Islamic business, fixed or noncurrent assets, therefore, refer to assets that are entrusted to the business to perform its operations and are not intended for sale. Examples include machines and equipment, building, land, and furniture. According to the Malaysian FRS116, the costs of property, plant, and equipment are recorded as assets if future economic benefits could be associated with the use of these assets, and their cost can be measured reliably. All fixed assets, with the exception of land, tend to decline in value over time. Companies create a depreciation account to capture the decline in the value of fixed assets. FRS 116 defines depreciation as 'the systematic allocation of the depreciable amount of an asset over its useful life'. FRS116 requires that depreciation is recorded in the income statement unless it is included in the carrying amount of another asset, in which case the carrying amount of the other asset will include the depreciation charges

Depreciation Method Depreciation can be computed using various methods, including the straight-line method, the declining-balance method, and the units of production method. According to the straight-line depreciation method, the cost of an asset is equally distributed over the useful life of the asset. According to the declining-balance method, a decreasing charge over the useful life of the asset is allocated based on the written-down value at the close of the previous period. The use of the units of production method results in a charge based on the expected output of the asset, where this can be reliably measured. The selection amongst these methods is a reflection of the use of the asset by the company. The most commonly used depreciation methods are the straight-line and declining-balance methods.

Example: Dugas has acquired a new machine during the year at a cost of $20,000. The machine has an expected useful life of five years, after which time it will be sold for $5,000.

If Dugas decides to use straight-line depreciation, it will allocate the cost of the machine less salvage value equally through the life of the machine – that is, the annual depreciation charge will be

$$\text{Annual depreciation} = (\$20{,}000 - \$5{,}000)/5 = \$3{,}000$$

This charge will be used every year for the five-year life of the machine.

If Dugas chose to use the declining-balance method and apply a 25% rate, the resulting depreciation charge would be as follows:

$$\text{Annual Depreciation charge} = 25\% \times \text{Carrying value}$$

$$\text{Year 1 Depreciation charge} = 25\% \times \$20{,}000 = \$5000$$

$$\text{Year 2 Depreciation charge} = 25\% \times (\$20{,}000 - \$5{,}000) = \$3{,}750$$

$$\text{Year 3 Depreciation charge} = 25\% \times (\$15{,}000 - \$3{,}750) = \$2{,}812$$

$$\text{Year 4 Depreciation charge} = 25\% \times (\$11{,}250 - \$2{,}812) = \$2{,}109$$

$$\text{Year 5 Depreciation charge} = 25\% \times (\$8{,}438 - \$2{,}109) = \$1{,}582$$

This shows that different depreciation methods lead to different charges applied in the income statement, thus leading to different profit figures.

FRS 116 requires the depreciation method to be reviewed each financial year-end to ensure that companies reflect any significant changes in the expected pattern of future economic benefits associated with the use of fixed assets.

Accumulated Depreciation

Accumulated depreciation represents depreciation to date. That is the total depreciated amount since the asset was first bought. It is the sum of the depreciation amounts to date. The accumulated depreciation is a contra-asset account. That is, it will have the relevant fixed asset as its companion. While the balance of the fixed assets is always a debit balance, its accumulated depreciation will always have a credit balance.

Using the preceding Dugas example, the journal entry in the books of Year 2 will be:

Straight line

DR Depreciation expense	3,000	
CR Accumulated depreciation provision		3,000

Reducing balance

DR Depreciation expense	3,750	
CR Accumulated depreciation provision		3,750

Carrying Amount

Fixed assets are shown in the balance sheet on the asset side at their carrying amount. This is their original cost or valuation minus accumulated depreciation and any accumulated impairment losses. The carrying amount is also referred to as the asset net book value. The assets side of the balance sheet shows fixed assets as per the following example. The respective carrying values appearing in Year 2 balance sheet under each method would be as follows:

Straight line

Cost	20,000
Accumulated depreciation provision	6,000*
Carrying amount (or net book value)	14,000
*Depreciation year 1 + Depreciation year 2	

Reducing balance

Cost	20,000
Accumulated depreciation provision	8,750*
Carrying amount (or net book value)	11,250
*Depreciation year 1 + Depreciation year 2	

Accrued Expenses These arise when expenses are incurred but not yet paid. Accrued expenses are the counterpart of prepayments. They are expenses for services already delivered but not yet paid for. Examples of accrued expenses include salaries payable or accrued salaries, which represents the salaries due for work performed by employees not yet paid for.

Adjusting entries are prepared at the end of the accounting period to account for accrued expenses. The accountant will record each expense and its corresponding liability prior to the preparation of the financial statements.

Example: The December 31, 2018, financial statements of Dar Alhikma showed a water and electricity account balance of $200 accrued. The 2019 books would show a credit balance of this amount on January 1, 2019. The total payment for water and electricity invoices for the first 11 months up to November 30, 2019, was $4,600.

The books of Dar Alhikma would show the following charges for the water and electricity account to reflect the preceding transactions.

The adjusting entry for accrued water and electricity account on December 31, 2018, would be:

Dr	Electricity expense	$200	
Cr	Accruals		$200

This adjustment is to ensure that the water and electricity costs incurred up to December 31, 2018, are recognised as an outstanding amount that remains at the end of the year. The 2019 books would show this amount at the beginning of the following year to offset against the payment made during the year of $4,600, which included the amount that was accrued in 2018.

The payment of $4,600 does not include the water and electricity already consumed for December 2019. The amount for this month must therefore be accrued. On the basis of the payment of $4,600 for the 11 months of the year and the outstanding amount from last year, one can assume that the amount due for December would be $400, i.e. ($4,600 – $200)/11, and the following entry would therefore be made in the accounting records on December 31, 2019.

Dr	Electricity expense	$400	
Cr	Accruals		$400

Accrued Revenues Accrued revenues refer to the revenue earned by the companies for which the cash has not yet been received. The cash will be collected later.

Example: On March 3, 2019, Dar Alhikma sold books to the university bookshop for $7,000 and received the payment on March 15, 2019. This transaction will be reflected in the books as follows:

March 3, 2019

	Debit	Credit
Accounts receivable	7,000	
Sales		7,000

March 15, 2019

	Debit	Credit
Cash	7,000	
Accounts receivable		7,000

Unearned Revenues Unearned revenues refer to the advance payment for work not yet performed. These are amounts collected from customers for services not yet delivered. Given that the work is not yet performed, any advance payment represents an obligation and must appear in the liability side under unearned revenues or deferred revenues. Revenue becomes earned only when the work is performed or the service or product is delivered.

Example: On April 1, 2019, Tecom leased office space to Infosys and signed a one-year contract. Tecom received $8,000 from Infosys as rent for April and May 2019 in advance.

April 1, 2019	April 30 and May 31, 2019
Cash is received.	Revenue is recognised at the end of April 2019 and May 2019.

Tecom should only recognise revenue when its services are provided to Infosys. This transaction would be reflected in the books of Tecom as follows:

April 1, 2019

	Debit	Credit
Cash	8,000	
Unearned rent revenue		8,000

Until the services are provided by Tecom, the unearned rent revenue account represents liability in Tecom accounts. Therefore, 'Unearned revenue' refers to amounts received prior to services for which the amount is received are provided.

April 30, 2019

	Debit	Credit
Unearned rent revenue	4,000	
Rent revenue		4,000

May 31, 2019

	Debit	Credit
Unearned rent revenue	4,000	
Rent revenue		4,000

Summary of the Adjusting Entries

The adjusting entries are four types; prepaid expenses, accrued expenses, accrued income, and unearned revenue.

Prepaid expenses: If an expense is prepaid, it means that the service being paid for has not yet been received at the time the payment was made. The Cash account has been credited and a Prepaid expense account debited to reflect that it was an asset, not an expense, at the time of payment. At the end of an accounting period some, perhaps all, of the service for which the prepayment was originally made may have been received. The adjusting entry for prepaid expenses transfers the part of the prepayment relating to the service received from the Prepaid expense account, which is credited, to the appropriate expense account, which is debited.

Accrued expenses: These are the opposite of prepayments in the sense that services have been received but not yet paid for, i.e. the service has been purchased 'on credit' or 'on account'. If a purchase invoice has been entered in the records, an expense account will have been debited and Accounts payable credited. However, if no invoice has yet been received this entry will not have been made in the ledger and it is then necessary to make an adjusting entry to debit the relevant expense account and credit an Accrued expense account. The balance on this account is shown as part of Current liabilities along with Accounts payable.

Accrued income: Accrued income is income that has been earned from a service provided but the income not yet been received. As with Accrued expenses, if no invoice has been raised at the accounting period end to reflect the service provided, it is necessary to make an adjusting entry by crediting Income account and debiting Accrued income account. The latter is a receivable, included in Current assets.

Unearned revenue: This is the opposite of Accrued income in the sense that cash has been received before it has been earned in providing a service to a customer. In this case Cash account will have been debited and an Unearned revenue account credited, the latter reflecting the fact that the Unearned revenue is a liability to repay the cash should the service not be provided as promised. At the accounting period end it is necessary to review how much of the originally unearned revenues have now been earned and to make an adjustment to credit the earned revenues to Revenues account and to debit the Unearned revenues account to reflect the consequent reduction in the liability.

Example:

The ledger accounts of Afaaq show the following balances as of December 31, 2019:

a. Prepaid insurance	$4,000
b. Equipment	$10,000
c. Service income	$1,500
d. Unearned income	$3,000

Additional Information:

a. The $4,000 prepaid insurance represents the cost of an insurance policy covering two years, effective from January 01, 2019.
b. The depreciation rate on the equipment is 20%. The estimated residual value is zero.
c. Services provided but not billed at December 31, 2019, are valued at $500.
d. Half of the unearned income has been earned during the year.

Requirements: Prepare the adjusting entries for the year to December 31, 2019.

Solution:

Adjusting Entries

Date	Account Title and Explanation	Ref.	Debit	Credit
Dec. 31, 2019	Dr. Insurance expense		2,000	
	Cr. Prepaid			2,000
	Insurance expense expired for the year.			
Dec. 31, 2019	Dr. Depreciation expense		2,000	
	Cr. Accumulated dep. – Equip.			2,000
	Yearly depreciation charged.			
Dec. 31, 2019	Dr. Accounts receivable		500	
	Cr. Service income			500
	Income accrued for services realized.			
Dec. 31, 2019	Dr. Unearned income		1,500	
	Cr. Service income			1,500
	Unearned income realized.			

The Extended or Adjusted Trial Balance

The balances of all accounts in the ledger are listed in the trial balance. Adjustments are required to produce the adjusted trial balance from which the financial statements will be prepared. We complete this process for the Al Madani Group below. The company trial balance as of December 31, 2019, is shown in Table 3.1.

Assume the insurance expense for the month of December was $600, rent expense for the same month was $1,200, supplies used during the month amounted to $1,500, and the depreciation allowance for December was $2,250. Fixed assets consist of property, plant, and equipment purchased on December 31, 2018. Also, assume $6,300 of the sales received in advance

TABLE 3.1 Al Madani Group Trial Balance as on December 31, 2019

Account Title	Trial Balance	
	Dr.	Cr.
Cash	31,950	
Accounts receivable	19,200	
Supplies on hand	4,200	
Prepaid insurance	7,200	
Prepaid rent	56,550	
Account payable		9,390
Fixed assets	63,450	
Sales received in advance		13,500
Capital		150,000
Dividends	9,000	
Sales		32,100
Advertising expenses	150	
Gas and oil expenses	2,040	
Salaries expenses	10,800	
Utilities expenses	450	
Total	**204,990**	**204,990**

account has been earned by December 31, unbilled sales were $3,000, and salaries not yet paid at year-end were $540.

Recording the Adjusting Entries

The worksheet provides information that assists in identifying the accounts that need adjustment. Data used to record adjusting entries in the journal and post these entries to the ledgers. The adjusting entries from the preceding Al Madani group worksheet will be as follows:

Dec. 31	Dr. Insurance expenses	600	
	Cr. Prepaid insurance		600
Dec. 31	Dr. Rent expenses	1200	
	Cr. Prepaid rent		1200
Dec. 31	Dr. Supplies expense	1500	
	Cr. Supplies		1500
Dec. 31	Dr. Depreciation	2250	
	Cr. Accumulated depreciation		2250
Dec. 31	Dr. Sales received in advance	6300	
	Cr. Sales		6300
Dec. 31	Dr. Unbilled sales	3000	
	Cr. Sales		3000
Dec. 31	Dr. Salaries expense	540	
	Cr. Accrued salaries		540

Posting the preceding entries to the ledgers is as follows:

Supplies Expense	
1,500	

Supplies on hand	
4,200	1,500

Insurance Expense	
600	

Prepaid Insurance	
7,200	600

Rent Expense	
1,200	

Prepaid Rent	
56,550	1,200

Depreciation	
2,250	

Accumulated Depreciation	
	2,250

Sales Received in Advance	
6,300	13,500

Sales	
	32,100
	6,300
	3,000
Balance	41,400

Unbilled Sales	
3,000	

Salaries Expenses	
10,800	
540	

Accrued Salaries	
	540

The Financial Statements

The adjusted trial balance shown in Table 3.2 can be used to prepare the financial statement for the Al Madani Group. The accounts listed in the

TABLE 3.2 Al Madani Group Adjusted Trial Balance as on December 31

Account Title	Trial Balance		Adjustments		Adjusted Trial Balance	
	Dr.	Cr.	Dr.	Cr.	Dr.	Cr.
Cash	31,950				31,950	
Account receivable	19,200				19,200	
Supplies on hand	4,200			1,500	2,700	
Prepaid insurance	7,200			600	6,600	
Prepaid rent	56,550			1,200	55,350	
Account payable		9,390				9,390
Fixed assets	63,450				63,450	
Accumulated depreciation				2,250		2,250
Sales received in advance		13,500	6,300			7,200
Capital		150,000				150,000
Dividends	9,000				9,000	
Sales		32,100		9,300		41,400
Advertising expenses	150				150	
Gas and oil expenses	2,040				2,040	
Salaries expenses	10,800		540		11,340	
Utilities expenses	450				450	
Insurance expense			600		600	
Rent expense			1,200		1,200	
Supplies expense			1,500		1,500	
Depreciation			2,250		2,250	
Interest revenue						
Salaries payable				540		540
Unbilled Sales			3,000		3,000	
Total	204,990	204,990	15,390	15,390	210,780	210,780

adjusted trial balance are allocated to their relevant financial statements. The income statement lists all the revenues generated by the company and the expenses paid to generate these revenues. The assets, liabilities, and owners' equity accounts are taken to prepare the balance sheet. The income statement for Al Madani Group is shown in Table 3.3.

TABLE 3.3 Al Madani Group Income Statement for the Year Ending December 31, 20X4

Revenue		
Sales		41,400
Expenses		
Advertising expenses	150	
Gas and oil expenses	2,040	
Salaries expenses	11,340	
Utilities expenses	450	
Insurance expense	600	
Rent expense	1,200	
Supplies expense	1,500	
Depreciation	2,250	
Total Expenses		19,530
Net Profit		21,870

The statement of changes in owners' equity, which represents the movement in the owners' equity of Al Madani, is shown in Table 3.4.

The balance sheet of Al Madani as of December 31, 20X4, should be as shown in Table 3.5.

TABLE 3.4 Al Madani Group Statement of changes in Owners' Equity for the Year Ended December, 31, 20X4

Capital at the beginning of period	150,000
Add: Net Profit	21,870
	171,870
Less: Dividend	9,000
Capital as at end of period	162,870

TABLE 3.5 Al Madani Group Balance Sheet as of December, 31, 20X4

Assets		Liabilities	
Cash	31,950	Account payable	9,390
Account receivable	19,200	Salaries payable	540
Unbilled sales	3,000	Sales received in advance	7,200
Supplies on hand	2,700	**Total Liabilities**	**17,130**
Prepaid insurance	6,600	**Owners' Equity**	162,870
Prepaid rent	55,350		
Fixed assets	63,450		
Less: Accumulated depreciation	2,250		
Fixed assets net	61,200		
Total Assets	180,000	**Total Liabilities and Owners' Equity**	180,000

VOCABULARY

accrual system of accounting
accrued expenses
accrued revenues
accumulated depreciation
adjusting entries
adjusting the accounts
balance sheet
capital reserve
carrying amount
cash basis of accounting
changes in restricted investment statement
charity fund
current value of asset
declining balance method
depreciation
financial statements of Islamic banks
fixed or noncurrent assets
income statement

Madarinah contracts
prepaid (deferrals)
retained earnings statement
statement of cash flows
statement of changes in owners' equity
statement of sources and uses of funds in the zakat
straight-line method,
the adjusted trial balance
the replacement value of the asset
the units of production method
unearned revenues
ward fund

MULTIPLE-CHOICE QUESTIONS

1. Which accounting principle requires expenses to be matched against the revenues which they help to generate?
   a. Historical cost principle
   b. Accounting entity principle
   c. Expense recognition principle
   d. Matching principle
2. Before adjustment, what type of account will result in assets being overstated and the expenses understated?
   a. Unearned revenues
   b. Accrued revenues
   c. Prepaid expenses
   d. Accrued expenses
3. Which of the following statement about accrual accounting is not correct?
   a. Expenses are recorded only when cash is paid and cash from revenues received.
   b. Expenses are recorded when incurred irrespective of whether cash is paid.
   c. Revenues are recorded when earned irrespective of whether cash is received.
   d. Recording of the economic events affecting the financial statements of the company is done in the period during which these events occur.

4. The adjusting entry for prepaid expenses should
   a. debit the expenses account and credit the asset account.
   b. debit the expenses account and credit the liability account.
   c. debit the asset account and credit the income account.
   d. debit the liability account and credit the income account.
5. The adjusting entry for unearned revenue should
   a. debit the expenses account and credit the asset account.
   b. debit the expenses account and credit the liability account.
   c. debit the asset account and credit the income account.
   d. debit the liability account and credit the income account.
6. The adjusting entry for accrued revenue should
   a. debit the expenses account and credit the asset account.
   b. debit the expenses account and credit the liability account.
   c. debit the asset account and credit the income account.
   d. debit the liability account and credit the income account.
7. The adjusting entry for accrued expenses should
   a. debit the expenses account and credit the asset account.
   b. debit the expenses account and credit the liability account.
   c. debit the asset account and credit the income account.
   d. debit the liability account and credit the income account.
8. Asset book value can be defined as
   a. historical cost
   b. market value
   c. replacement value
   d. cost less accumulated depreciation

DISCUSSION QUESTIONS

1. Discuss the main reasons for adjusting entries, and list the main types of adjusting entries.
2. Explain the main difference between depreciation expense and accumulated depreciation. How are they related?
3. List the main factors affecting the computation of depreciation charges.
4. Explain the main difference between the accrual basis of accounting and cash basis of accounting systems.
5. Why would an accrual system help in the accurate computation of zakat?

EXERCISES

1. Diamond Advertising was established on June 1, 2019. The company's trial balance as of June 30, 2019, shows the following account balances:

Advertising revenue	$18,000
Unearned revenue	$42,000
Office equipment	$20,000
Prepaid insurance	$4,800

The following additional information was provided:

- Advertising services not yet billed at the end of June were $10,000.
- Prepaid six months advertising packages of $1,800 each were paid on June 1 and services for the month of June were carried out.
- Depreciation of office equipment was done at the rate of $400 per month.
- A two-year insurance policy was effective June 1.

Requirements:

prepare the adjusting entries for the month of June, 2019.

2. The following transactions took place during the month of June at Mashreq Company. Prepare the journal entries for the month of June.

Transaction No.	Date	Transaction Detail
1.	June 5	Purchased equipment on account for $9,000.
2.	June 6	Received $5,000 for services rendered on account.
3.	June 8	Paid cash $2,000 to a supplier to settle an account.
4.	June 10	Purchased office supplies worth of $1,500 on account.
5.	June 14	Paid $1,000 advertising expenses in cash.
6.	June 17	Received $2,000 advance payment for services to be rendered in September.
7.	June 19	Paid $3,000 rent expenses in cash.
8.	June 20	Invoiced a customer $2,000 for a services rendered but not collected during June.
9.	June 25	Paid cash $500 advertising expenses for an ad that will run in July.
10.	June 30	Cash dividends of $1,500 were paid to stockholders.

3. The following transactions took place during 2018 at Diamond Company. Prepare the adjusting journal entries for the year ended December 31, 2018.

Transaction Details

1. Diamond has 10 employees who earn $2,000 per month each. At December 31, two months' salaries have been earned by the employees but not paid to them.
2. Received $10,000 cash from a customer on December 1, 2018, for services to be rendered equally for two months starting from December 1, 2018. The receipt was credited to a liability account.
3. Purchased equipment costing $72,000 on January 1, 2018. Monthly depreciation is $1,500.
4. Services provided but not billed amounts to $1,000.
5. Purchased $6,000 in supplies during the year and have $1,500 on hand at December 31. There were no supplies on hand at the beginning of the year. Supplies were debited to an asset account when purchased.
6. A three-year insurance policy was purchased for $9,000 on July 1, 2018, debiting an asset account at that time.
7. Purchased Emaar stock on January 1, 2018. Dividend of $500 has been earned but not received or recorded prior to December 31.

4. For each of the following accounts, indicate which has a normal debit balance and which has a normal credit balance.

_____	1. Retained earnings	_____	6. Common stock
_____	2. Machinery	_____	7. Unearned revenue
_____	3. Depreciation	_____	8. Accumulated depreciation
_____	4. Dividends	_____	9. Accounts payable
_____	5. Revenue	_____	10. Prepaid rent

5. Use the following information to answer the below questions pertaining to the adjusting entries of Afaaq Company and Noor Takaful.

   Afaaq Company purchased an insurance policy for $5,000 on December 1, 2018, from Noor Takaful. The premium paid on December 1 to Noor Takaful for the 12 months beginning December 1 is $1,200. This premium was recorded on December 1 by Afaaq as Dr. Prepaid Insurance account and Cr. Cash account. Noor Takaful recorded the $1,200 receipt as of December 1 with a debit to the current asset Cash and a credit to the current liability Unearned Revenues.

Both Afaaq Company and Noor Takaful prepare monthly financial statements at the end of each month.

a. Adjusting entries in both companies are recorded on which date?
b. State the number of accounts involved in the adjusting entries of Afaaq Company.
c. Which account should be debited in the books of Afaaq Company?
d. Which account should be credited in the books of Afaaq Company?
e. What is the amount of the debit and the credit in the books of Afaaq Company?
f. If Afaaq fails to make the necessary adjusting entry on December 31, what would be the effect of this on the financial statements?
g. State the number of accounts involved in Noor Takaful's adjusting entry.
h. Which account should be debited in Noor Takaful's books?
i. Which account should be credited in Noor Takaful's books?
j. What is the amount of the debit and the credit in Noor Takaful's books?
k. If the company fails to make the adjusting entry on December 31, what would be the effect of this on Noor Takaful's financial statements?

6. Use the following information to answer the following questions pertaining to the adjusting entries of Smart Ideas.

   Smart Ideas started operation on December 1. The company purchased $3,000 of supplies. The transaction was recorded as a debit to Supplies and a credit to Accounts Payable. Smart Ideas' financial statements are prepared on a monthly basis at the end of each month. On December 31, remaining supplies were estimated at $500.

   a. State the date for the record of the December adjusting entry.
   b. State the number of accounts involved in the adjusting entry.
   c. Which account should be debited?
   d. Which account should be credited?
   e. State the debit and the credit amounts.
   f. If the adjusting entry was not made on December 31, what would be the effect on the company's financial statements?

CHAPTER 4

Islamic Financial Statements

Learning Objectives

After studying this chapter, you should be able to:

1. Prepare an accounting worksheet.
2. Complete the accounting cycle using an accounting worksheet.
3. Close the accounts of revenue, expense, and drawings.
4. Correct accounting errors.
5. Prepare a classified balance sheet.
6. Prepare basic Islamic finance statements.

THE ACCOUNTING CYCLE

The value chain from recording transactions in the journal, posting these records to the ledger, preparing the trial balance, and finally producing the financial statements is referred to as the accounting cycle. Once Dar Al Fatina was established in the City of Al Ain in the UAE, the accounting cycle starts with opening the books and recording the transactions taking place at the company, including the first transaction of the initial investment of AED1,000 as the capital of the owner Fatina Jabir. The accounting cycle ends with the preparation of the end-of-period financial statements. The accounting cycles for the following periods start with the balances of the accounts of the preceding period; new transactions are recorded, posted, a trial balance is prepared; and end-of-period financial statements are also prepared. This is done during every accounting period until the business is liquidated or sold.

At the end of the accounting period, the fair values of some assets and liabilities are estimated based on market conditions existing at the balance sheet date. In this chapter we show how the methods of accounting in the form of bookkeeping practices provide the basic transaction cost data for

Islamic financial statements. At the end of the chapter we explain the role that fair values play in Islamic accounting and the way social income of the Islamic community can be reported in a value-added income statement. First, though, we focus on the basis of all accounting data, in market values or any form of financial performance measurement, that is the processing of transaction costs.

The accounting cycle starts with journalising the business transactions taken place during the accounting period and ends with the preparation of the financial statements at the end of the period after adjusting and closing the accounts and journalising and posting the adjusted entries. The end-of-year account balances are taken forward to the following period as starting balances for these accounts.

The Worksheet

The trial balance, which includes the debit and credit balances of all the accounts in a business, is the principal source of data for the preparation of the end-of-period financial statements. This process of moving information from the trial balance to the financial statement can be done using a worksheet. This summarises data for the financial statements. It lists the account balances from the unadjusted trial balance, helps identify the accounts that need adjustment, and lists ending adjusted balances for all accounts. It is important to note that the worksheet is not part of the accounting system but is a document that facilitates transferring information from the unadjusted trial balance to the related financial statements. A typical worksheet includes 11 columns. These are explained as follows:

1. The first three columns of the worksheet have the title of the account and the unadjusted account balances as debits and credits.

Worksheet: Step 1

Account Title	Trial Balance	
	Debit	Credit
Cash	....	
Capital		...

2. Columns four and five cover the adjustments to the trial balance accounts

Worksheet: Steps 1 and 2

Account Title	Trial Balance		Adjustments	
	Debit	Credit	Debit	Credit
Cash	....		....	
Capital		...		...

3. Columns six and seven will have the adjusted account balances, which represent the combination of the adjusted and unadjusted figures.

Worksheet: Steps 1, 2, and 3

Account Title	Trial Balance		Adjustments		Adjusted Trial Balance	
	Debit	Credit	Debit	Credit	Debit	Credit
Cash	....		....		....	
Capital		...		...		...

4. Each of the balances in the adjusted trial balance is transferred to the income statement and balance sheet according to the type of account: assets, liabilities, owners' equity, revenues, or expenses.

Worksheet: Steps 1, 2, 3, and 4

Account Title	Trial Balance		Adjust-ments		Adjusted Trial Balance		Income state-ment		Balance Sheet	
	Debit	Credit	Debit	Credit	Debit	Credit	Debit	Credit	Debit	Credit
Cash	....		....		....		....		....	
Capital		...		...		...		...		...

The profit or loss for the period is simply the difference between the total revenues and total expenses. This figure is then entered as a balancing

TABLE 4.1 Al Madani Group Trial Balance as of December 31, 20X4

Account Title	Trial Balance	
	Dr.	Cr.
Cash	31,950	
Accounts receivable	19,200	
Supplies on hand	4,200	
Prepaid insurance	7,200	
Prepaid rent	56,550	
Accounts payable		9,390
Sales received in advance		13,500
Capital stock		150,000
Dividends	9,000	
Fixed assets	63,450	
Accumulated depreciation		
Sales		32,100
Advertising expenses	150	
Gas and oil expenses	2,040	
Salaries; expenses	10,800	
Utilities expenses	450	
Insurance expense		
Rent expense		
Supplies expense		
Depreciation		
Interest revenue		
Salaries payable		
Accounts receivable		
Net profit		
Total	204,990	204,990

amount in the income statement and balance sheet columns. The totals in the final two columns are then computed. A worksheet showing a trial balance of this extended type, as of December 31, 20X4, is displayed in Table 4.1 for the Al Madani Group

The following adjusting entries, which were shown in Chapter 3, are reproduced to allow easy reference. The insurance expense for the month of December was $600, rent expense for the same month $1,200, supplies used during the month $1,500, and depreciation for December $2,250. Also, assume $6,300 of the sales received in advance account has been earned by December 31 and that unbilled sales were $3,000, and accrued salaries were $540. This information would be entered into the worksheet in the extended trial balance form as in Table 4.2.

TABLE 4.2 Al Madani Group Worksheet as of December 31

Title of Account	Trial Balance		Adjustments		Adjusted Trial Balance		Income Statement		Balance Sheet	
	Dr.	Cr.	Dr.	Cr.	Dr.	Cr.	Dr.	Cr.	Dr.	Cr.
Cash	31,950				31,950				31,950	
Accounts receivable	19,200				19,200				19,200	
Supplies on hand	4,200			1,500	2,700				2,700	
Prepaid insurance	7,200			600	6,600				6,600	
Prepaid rent	56,550			1,200	55,350				55,350	
Accounts payable		9,390				9, 390				9,390
Sales received in advance		13,500	6,300			7,200				7,200
Capital		150,000				150,000				150,000
Dividends	9,000				9,000				9,000	
Fixed assets	63,450				63,450				63,450	
Accumulated depreciation				2, 250		2,250				2,250
Sales		32,100		9, 300		41,400		41,400		
Advertising expenses	150				150		150			
Gas and oil expenses	2,040				2, 040		2,040			
Salaries expenses	10,800		540		11,340		11,340			
Utilities expenses	450				450		450			
Insurance expense			600		600		600			
Rent expense			1,200		1,200		1,200			
Supplies expense			1,500		1,500		1,500			
Depreciation			2,250		2,250		2,250			
Interest revenue										
Salaries payable				540		540				540
Unbilled sales			3,000		3,000				3,000	
Net profit							21,870			21,870
Total	204,990	204,990	15,390	15, 390	210,780	210,780	41,400	41,400	191,250	191,250

Completing the Accounting Cycle An important purpose of the accounting worksheet is to summarise data to assist in the preparation of financial statements at the end of the accounting period.

Preparing the Financial Statements The worksheet shows the total revenue and total expenses in two different columns. The difference between the two represents the net profit or loss for the period. The income statement is essentially these two columns presented separately as a statement with a specific format. The income statement for Al Madani group is shown in Table 4.3.

Figure 4.1 shows a real-world illustration of the consolidated income statement for Bahrain Islamic Bank for the year ended December 31, 2015.

The statement of changes in owners' equity, which represents the movement in the owners' equity of Al Madani, is shown in Table 4.4.

As an illustration of this format in practice, the statement of changes in owners' equity for Bahrain Islamic Bank for the year ended December 31, 2015, is shown in Figure 4.2.

TABLE 4.3 Al Madani Group Income Statement Year Ended December 31, 20X4

Revenue		
Sales		41,400
Expenses		
Advertising expense	150	
Gas and oil expense	2,040	
Salaries expense	11,340	
Utilities expense	450	
Insurance expense	600	
Rent expense	1,200	
Supplies expense	1,500	
Depreciation	2,250	
Total Expenses		19,530
Net Profit		21,870

TABLE 4.4 Al Madani Group Owners' Changes in Equity Statement for the Year Ended December 31, 20X4

Capital at the beginning of period	150,000
Add: Net profit	21,870
	171,870
Less: Dividend	9,000
Capital as at end of period	162,870

Consolidated Statement of Income
For the year ended 31 December 2015

	Note	2015 BD'000	2014 BD'000
INCOME			
Income from financing	17	33,530	28,702
Income from investment in Sukuk		3,659	2,535
		37,189	31,237
Return on equity of investment accountholders		(21.582)	(23,379)
Group's share as Mudarib		16,395	16,092
Net return on equity of investment accountholders	13.4	(5,187)	(7,287)
Net financing income		32,002	23,950
Expense on placements from financial institutions		(546)	(252)
Fee and commission income		7,746	6,452
Income from investment securities	18	739	3,990
Income from investment in real estate	19	1,194	8,988
Share of results of associates, net	7	(711)	(1,550)
Net gain from foreign currencies		1,223	1,273
Other income		72	–
Total net income		41,719	42,851
EXPENSES			
Staff costs		10,212	11,482
Depreciation	9	1,554	1,641
Other expenses	20	9,795	8,502
Total expenses		21,561	21,625
Profit before impairment allowances		20,158	21,226
Impairment provisions on financing assets	21.1	(5,203)	(7,593)
Impairment provisions on investments	21.2	(3,750)	(4,336)
PROFIT FOR THE YEAR		11,205	9,297
BASIC AND DILUTED EARNINGS PER SHARE (fils)	23	14.02	11.76

FIGURE 4.1 Consolidated statement of income
Source: Bahrain Islamic Bank, Annual Report, 2015.

Consolidated Statement of Changes in Owners' Equity
For the year ended 31 December 2015

			Shares under employee share incentive scheme BD'000		Reserves						Equity attributable to owners of the parent BD'000	Non-controlling interest BD'000	Total owners' equity BD'000
	Share capital BD'000	Treasury shares BD'000	Shares under employee share incentive scheme BD'000	Share premium BD'000	Statutory reserve BD'000	General reserve BD'000	Real estate fair value reserve BD'000	Investments fair value reserve BD'000	Retained earnings/ (accumulated losses) BD'000	Total reserves BD'000	Equity attributable to owners of the parent BD'000	Non-controlling interest BD'000	Total owners' equity BD'000
Balance at 1 January 2015	93,967	(563)	–	–	11,809	1,000	7,361	1,101	(35,591)	(14,320)	79,084	11	79,095
Profit for the year	–	–	–	–	–	–	–	–	11,205	11,205	11,205	–	11,205
Shares issued during the year	940	–	(940)	–	–	–	–	–	–	–	–	–	–
Shares allocated during the year	–	–	61	30	–	–	–	–	–	–	91	–	91
Rights issue	17,094	–	–	2,794	–	–	–	–	–	–	19,888	–	19,888
Write off of accumulated losses	(14,560)	–	–	(30)	(11,809)	(1,000)	–	–	27,399	14,590	–	–	–
Net movement in investments fair value reserve	–	–	–	–	–	–	–	(480)	–	(480)	(480)	–	(480)
Net movement in real estate fair value reserve	–	–	–	–	–	–	(276)	–	–	(276)	(276)	–	(276)
Transfer of profit to statutory reserve	–	–	–	–	1,121	–	–	–	(1,121)	–	–	–	–
Net movement in noncontrolling interest	–	–	–	–	–	–	–	–	–	–	–	(11)	(11)
Balance at 31 December 2015	**97,441**	**(563)**	**(879)**	**2,794**	**1,121**	**–**	**7,085**	**621**	**1,892**	**10,719**	**109,512**	**–**	**109,512**
Balance at 1 January 2014	93,967	(563)	–	–	10,879	1,000	11,301	4,248	(43,958)	(16,530)	76,874	1,242	78,116
Profit for the year	–	–	–	–	–	–	–	–	9,297	9,297	9,297	–	9,297
Net movement in investments fair value reserve	–	–	–	–	–	–	–	(3,147)	–	(3,147)	(3,147)	–	(3,147)
Net movement in real estate fair value reserve	–	–	–	–	–	–	(3,940)	–	–	(3,940)	(3,940)	–	(3,940)
Transfer of profit to statutory reserve	–	–	–	–	930	–	–	–	(930)	–	–	–	–
Net movement in noncontrolling interest	–	–	–	–	–	–	–	–	–	–	–	(1,231)	(1,231)
Balance at 31 December 2014	93,967	(563)	–	–	11,809	1,000	7,361	1,101	(35,591)	(14,320)	79,084	11	79,095

FIGURE 4.2 Consolidated changes in owners' equity statement
Source: Bahrain Islamic Bank, Annual Report, 2015

The balance sheet of Al Madani as at December 31, 20X4, should be as shown in Table 4.5.

As an illustration of an actual statement of financial position, the balance sheet for the Bahrain Islamic Bank as of December 31, 2015, is shown in Figure 4.3.

Closing the Accounts

Closing the account is the process of journalising and posting closing entries as well as zeroing all revenue and expense accounts to prepare for the next period's accounts. Balance sheet accounts (assets, liabilities, and capital or equity accounts) are not closed but their balances are carried forward from one period to the next. These are *permanent* accounts. The revenue and expense accounts are *temporary* or *nominal* accounts. Owners' drawings are considered to be a distribution (*withdrawals*) of capital and the drawings account is closed at the end of the period in the same manner as expense accounts.

The income statement of Al Madani group reports the results of operation for one accounting period ending December 31, 20X4. At December 31, the accountants of Al Madani close the firm's revenues and expense accounts for the year. For example, Al Madani's balance of sales at December 31, 20X4, is $41,400. This balance relates exclusively to the accounting period ending December 31, 20X4, and must be zeroed out before Al Madani group starts accounting for the following period.

TABLE 4.5 Al Madani Group Balance Sheet as of December 31, 20X4

Assets		Liabilities	
Cash	31,950	Accounts payable	9,390
Accounts receivable	19,200	Salaries payable	540
Unbilled sales	3,000	Sales received in advance	7,200
Supplies on hand	2,700	Total liabilities	17,130
Prepaid insurance	6,600		
Prepaid rent	55,350	Owners' equity	
		Capital at the beginning of period	150,000
Fixed Assets	63,450	Add: Net profit	21,870
Less: Accumulated depreciation	2,250	Less: Dividend	9,000
		Capital as at end of period	162,870
Total assets	180,000	Total liabilities and owners' equity	180,000

Consolidated Statement of Financial Position
As at 31 December 2015

	Note	2015 BD'000	2014 BD'000
ASSETS			
Cash and balances with banks and Central Bank	3	**61,114**	52,118
Placements with financial institutions	4	**73,150**	68,567
Financing assets	5	**475,648**	408,021
Investment securities	6	**130,635**	123,561
Ijarah Muntahia Bittamleek	8	**118,061**	102,277
Ijarah rental receivables	8	**15,692**	14,065
Investment in associates	7	**28,116**	30,835
Investment in real estate	10	**43,601**	53,934
Property and equipment	9	**16,640**	17,101
Other assets	11	**13,691**	4,728
TOTAL ASSETS		**976,348**	875,207
LIABILITIES, EQUITY OF INVESTMENT ACCOUNTHOLDERS AND OWNERS' EQUITY			
Liabilities			
Placements from financial institutions		**93,516**	75,570
Customers' current accounts		**141,244**	137,423
Other liabilities	12	**16,616**	16,518
Total Liabilities		**251,376**	229,511
Equity of Investment Accountholders	13	**615,460**	566,601
Owners' Equity			
Share capital	14	**97,441**	93,967
Treasury shares	14	**(563)**	(563)
Shares under employee share incentive scheme		**(879)**	-
Share premium		**2,794**	-
Reserves		**10,719**	(14,320)
Equity attributable to owners of the parent		**109,512**	79,084
Noncontrolling interest		**-**	11
Total Owners' Equity		**109,512**	79,095
TOTAL LIABILITIES, EQUITY OF INVESTMENT ACCOUNTHOLDERS AND OWNERS' EQUITY		**976,348**	875,207

FIGURE 4.3 Consolidated statement of financial position
Source: Bahrain Islamic Bank, Annual Report, 2015

The process of closing the accounts involves transferring the revenue, expenses, and owners' drawings account balances from their respective accounts to the Capital account. This step is done by creating an intermediate holding account called Profit and Loss Summary or, Income Summary, where the total debit for the sum of all expenses and drawings and the total credit for the sum of all the revenue accounts for the period are collected. The Income Summary account is balanced and the balance is transferred to the Capital account.

Closing the accounts of Al Madani group is done as in the following journal:

Dec 31

Sales	41,400	
Income Summary		41,400

Dec 31

Income Summary	19,530	
Advertising Expense		150
Gas and Oil Expense		2,040
Salaries Expenses		11,340
Utilities Expense		450
Insurance Expense		600
Rent Expense		1,200
Supplies Expense		1,500
Depreciation		2,250

Dec 31

Income Summary	21,870	
Capital		21,870

Posting the preceding entries to the ledgers is as follows, where 'Closing' refers to the total entries in the relevant account at the year-end:

Supplies Expense			
Closing	1,500	Income Summary	1,500

Insurance Expense			
Closing	600	Income Summary	600

Rent Expense			
Closing	1,200	Income Summary	1,200

Depreciation			
Closing	2,250	Income Summary	2,250

Sales			
			32,100
			6,300
			3,000
Income Summary	41,400	Closing	41,400

Salaries Expenses			
	10,800		
	540		
Closing	11,340	Income Summary	11,340

Advertising Expenses			
Closing	150	Income Summary	150

Gas and Oil Expenses			
Closing	2,040	Income Summary	2,040

Utilities			
Closing	450	Income Summary	450

Dividends			
Closing	9,000	Capital	9,000

Income Summary			
Closing	19,530	Closing	41,400
Capital	21,870		

Capital			
Dividends	9,000	Opening Balance	150,000
		Income Summary	21,870
		Closing Balance	162,870

TABLE 4.6 Al Madani Group Post-Closing Trial Balance as of December 31, 20X4

Cash	31,950	
Accounts receivable	19,200	
Unbilled sales	3,000	
Supplies on hand	2,700	
Prepaid rent	55,350	
Prepaid insurance	6,600	
Fixed assets	63,450	
Accumulated depreciation		2,250
Accounts payable		9,390
Salaries payable		540
Sales received in advance		7,200
Capital as at end of period		162,870
Total	182,250	182,250

Post-Closing Trial Balance

The post-closing trial balance represents the end of the accounting cycle. It lists all the ledger account balances after the closing process. This is the final check on the accuracy of the adjusting process, the journalising of the adjusting entries, and their posting to their respective ledger accounts. The steps show what goes to the next period and their balances.

Given that all temporary accounts – revenues , expenses, dividends, and withdrawals – are transferred to capital as per the previous step, only balance sheet accounts, namely assets, liabilities, and capital accounts, are reflected in the post-closing trial balance. The post-closing trial balance for Al Madani group is shown in Table 4.6.

ASSETS AND LIABILITIES CLASSIFICATIONS

The two sides of the accounting equation contain lists of assets and liabilities, respectively. The assets represent the resources controlled, providing the business with future economic benefits. Examples include cash, accounts receivable, inventory, furniture, land, and buildings. Liabilities are the claims on the assets; they represent the obligations the business will have to pay in the future. Examples include creditors and long-term loans. The residual interest for the owners in the business is referred to as the owners' equity or capital. The initial capital that Fatina invested in Dar Alfatina is an example. Owners' equity is measured by subtracting liabilities from assets. What the business owns and controls, providing it with future economic benefits, must always equal the obligations the business will have to pay others plus the owners' equity. The residual amount of a company's assets after the liabilities are subtracted is the net assets and is referred to as owners' equity.

Financial Accounting Disclosure in Islamic Business Environments

Financial Accounting Standard No.1, published by AAOIFI, lists the following financial statements required by Islamic financial Institutions: A balance sheet, a statement of income, a statement of cash flow, changes in owners' equity, or a statement of retained earnings and the notes to the annual reports. The standard lists the following three additional statements that could be useful to users of Islamic financial institutions' financial reports: Changes in restricted accounts, sources and uses of zakat and charity funds, and sources and uses of qard funds statements. Specific disclosure requirements stated by the standard include:

- The role of the Sharia Supervisory Board in overseeing the bank's Islamic finance activities
- The bank's responsibility toward zakat
- Disclosure of activities prohibited by the Sharia and how the bank intends to dispose of assets generated by these activities
- Unrestricted and restricted account information
- Information on the distribution of unrestricted accounts
- Investment profits allocation methods
- Information on returns and the rate of return for each type of investment

Islamic corporate reports should comply with Islamic Sharia social accountability and full disclosure requirements. Such reports require additional information beyond what is currently provided in financial statements. Specifically, current values should be the basis of the balance sheet because zakat is computed on the basis of the current value of assets, and current value information is needed for the calculation of shares in mudaraba contracts. We return to this matter at the end of this chapter.

The Dubai Financial Service Authority (DFSA) Rulebook contains the Islamic finance rules regulating the activities of firms carrying out Islamic financial business in or from the Dubai International Financial Center (DIFC). It requires these firms to have systems and controls that allow compliance with the Islamic Sharia requirements, including establishing a Sharia Supervisory Board (SSB) specifying the role and authority of the SSB in overseeing the Islamic financial business undertaken by the firm. Firms with

Islamic window activities must, according to the DFSA Islamic finance rules, disclose whether they commingle funds resulting from Sharia-compliant transactions with funds resulting from non–Sharia-compliant transactions. In terms of financial reports, the DFSA requires firms to prepare a funds mobilised statement according to Sharia rules and an income statement showing the results of the firm's Islamic financial business.

Balance Sheet

The balance sheet represents the financial position of the entity at a particular point of time, so it is like a snapshot of the entity at that point in time. As already explained, the balance sheet lists the entity's assets, liabilities, and owners' equity. In the case of Islamic banks, AAOIFI FAS1 requires the balance sheet to include the assets, liabilities, and equity of their unrestricted investment accountholders (para. 31).

The following assets must be disclosed in the body of the balance sheet or in the notes to the financial statements (para. 37):

- Cash and cash equivalent
- Accounts receivable
- Investment in securities
- Mudaraba financing
- Musharaka financing
- Investment in other entities
- Inventories
- Real estate investment
- Assets acquired for leasing
- Other investments
- Fixed assets
- Other assets

With regard to the liability side of the balance sheet of Islamic banks, FAS1 requires the following items to be disclosed (para. 41 to 44):

- Current, savings, and other accounts
- Deposits of other banks
- Salam payables
- Istisna payables
- Profits not distributed
- Zakat and taxes payable
- Other accounts payable

Unrestricted investment accounts are disclosed as a separate item between liabilities and owners' equity. Minority interests are disclosed in the consolidated balance sheet as a separate item between unrestricted investment accounts and owners' equity.

The equity side of the balance sheet should include:

- Capital
- Reserve
- Retained earnings

FAS1 provides the following template of a consolidated statement of financial position for an Islamic Bank, shown in Figure 4.4.

Assets in Islam are entrusted by God to the business to assist in its operations. The use of assets must therefore be consistent with the teachings of the Sharia.

Assets are divided in the balance sheet into two categories: Current assets and fixed assets.

Current Assets Current assets are those assets that are mostly expected to be converted into cash within the current operating cycle. Examples of current assets include cash at bank, accounts receivable, and prepaid expenses.

Fixed or Noncurrent Assets In an Islamic business, fixed or noncurrent assets refer to assets that are entrusted to businesses by God and used to perform their operations. They are not intended to be sold. Examples include machines and equipment, building, land, and furniture. According to the Malaysian FRS116, 'The cost of an item of property, plant and equipment shall be recognised as an asset if, and only if: (a) it is probable that future economic benefits associated with the item will flow to the entity; and (b) the cost of the item can be measured reliably'. Most fixed assets, with the exception of land, tend to decline in value over time.

Liabilities are claims on the assets. They represent the obligations the business will have to pay in the future. Examples include creditors and long-term loans. Tag El-Din (2004) provides the following breakdown of liabilities in an Islamic statement of financial position of a financial institution:

1. Current accounts, saving accounts, and other accounts
2. Deposits of other banks
3. Salam payable
4. Istisna payable
5. Declared but undistributed profits
6. Zakat and taxes payable
7. Other accounts payable

Financial Accounting Standard No. (1):
General Presentation and Disclosure in the Financial Statements of
Islamic Banks and Financial Institutions

(Name of Bank or Institution)
Consolidated Statement of Financial Position
as at xxx Year xxx (last year)

	Note	xxx (year) Monetary Unit	xx (last year) Monetary Unit
Liabilities, Unrestricted Investment Accounts, Minority Interest and Owners' Equity			
Liabilities:			
Current accounts and saving accounts	21	18,550,000	15,400,000
Current accounts for banks and financial institutions		1,200,000	1,200,000
Payables	22	936,112	133,611
Proposed dividends		5,000,000	5,000,000
Other liabilities	23	5,069,750	2,192,321
Total liabilities		30,755,862	23,925,932
Equity of Unrestricted Investment Accountholders (Para. 42 of the standard)	24,34	7,838,500	6,572,000
Minority Interest (Para. 43 of the standard)		3,450,600	3,240,550
Total Liabilities, Unrestricted Investment Accounts, and Minority Interest		42,044,962	33,738,482
Owners' Equity			
Paid-up capital	25	350,000,000	350,000,000
Reserves	26	3,368,864	1,649,796
Retained earnings		3,475,453	1,599,184
Total owners' equity (Para. 44 of the standard)		356,844,317	353,248,980
Total Liabilities, Unrestricted Investment Accounts, Minority Interest and Owners' Equity (Paras. 41 to 44 of the standard)		398,889,279	386,987,462
Assets:			
Cash and Cash Equivalent	8	95,041,890	51,281,906
Sales Receivable	9	3,804,889	875,556
Investments:			
Investment securities	10	14,850,000	15,000,000
Mudaraba financing	11	10,000,000	1,500,000
Musharaka investments	12	–	5,000,000
Participations	13	102,500,000	102,500,000
Inventories	14	–	2,000,000
Investment in real estate	15	58,500,000	71,750,000
Assets for rent	16	89,000,000	94,500,000
Istisna'a	17	–	1,000,000
Other investments			
–		–	–
–		–	–
–		–	–
Total investments	18	274,850,000	293,250,000
Other Assets	19	322,000	15,510,000
Fixed Assets (net)	20	24,870,500	26,070,000
Total Assets (Paras. 30, 38 of the standard)		398,889,279	386,978,462

FIGURE 4.4 Consolidated statement of financial position for an Islamic bank
Source: AAOIFI (2015).

Liabilities are classified into short-term liabilities and long-term liabilities.

Current Liabilities Current liabilities are mostly short-term obligations that are expected to be paid within one year after the end of the accounting period. Examples include accounts payable, salary payable, and unearned revenue.

Long-Term Liabilities Long-term liabilities are mostly obligations expected to be paid more than one year after the end of the current accounting period. Examples of long-term liabilities include Islamic bonds (sukuk).

Owners' equity represents the residual value of the accounting entity. The residual is what remains after liabilities are subtracted from the value of the assets. These net assets are usually interpreted as representing the claims for the owners over the value of the business.

Classified Balance Sheet

The balance sheet presented earlier was unclassified. A classified balance sheet has the assets divided into their two classes: Current and fixed; and liabilities divided into two classes: Current and long term. This is the form of balance sheet most often used in practice. A classified version of the balance sheet of Al Madani group is shown in Table 4.7.

TABLE 4.7 Al Madani Group Balance Sheet as of December 31, 20X4

Assets		Liabilities	
Current assets		**Current liabilities**	
Cash	31,950	Current liabilities Accounts payable	9,390
Accounts receivable	19,200	Salaries payable	540
Unbilled sales	3,000	Sales received in advance	7,200
Supplies on hand	2,700	**Non-current liabilities**	0
Prepaid insurance	6,600	**Total liabilities**	17,130
Prepaid rent	55,350	**Owners' equity**	
	118,800	Capital at the beginning of period	150,000
Fixed assets	63,450	Add: Net profit	21,870
Less: Accumulated depreciation	2,250	Less: Dividend	9,000
	61,200	Capital as of end of period	162,870
Total assets	180,000	Total liabilities and owners' equity	180,000

Other Formats of the Balance Sheet

Having the assets on the left side and liabilities and owners' equity on the right side is known as the 'account format' of the balance sheet. The balance sheet can also be presented as a report format where the assets are listed first, followed by liabilities and owners' equity. Both forms are used in practice.

Income Statement

The income statement shows the results of operations over a period. It lists the revenue generated during this period and the expenses incurred in order to generate this revenue. FAS1 requires the following items to be disclosed in the income statement of an Islamic bank (para. 50):

- Revenue
- Other revenue
- Expenses
- Income (loss) from investment
- Share of unrestricted investment accountholder income (loss) from investment before bank's share as mudarib
- Islamic bank share income (loss) from investment
- Islamic bank share in unrestricted investment income as mudarib
- Islamic bank share in restricted investment income as mudarib
- Islamic bank fees for restricted investment agency
- Other expenses
- Administrative expenses
- Net income (loss) before zakat and taxes
- Zakat
- Taxes
- Net income (loss)

If the Islamic bank is paying the zakat on behalf of its owners, the zakat base should be disclosed.

FAS1 provides a template of an income statement for an Islamic Bank, as shown in Figure 4.5.

Cash Flow Statement

The cash flow statement shows the movement of cash during an accounting period, reconciling the opening and closing cash balances shown in the balance sheet. Cash flows are categorized into cash flow from operating activities, financing activities, and investing activities.

FAS1 provides an example of a statement of cash flows for an Islamic bank, as shown in Figure 4.6.

Financial Accounting Standard No. (1):
General Presentation and Disclosure in the Financial Statements of
Islamic Banks and Financial Institutions

(Name of Bank or Institution)
Income Statement
for the Year Ended xxx (year) xxx (last year)

	Note	xxx (year) Monetary Unit	xx (last year) Monetary Unit
Income			
Deferred sales	(29A)	97,500	36,389
Investments	(29B)	5,120,000	4,168,000
	28,29	5,217,500	4,204,389
Less			
Return on Unrestricted Investments			
Accounts Before the Bank's Share as a Mudarib		551,480	455,673
Bank's Share as a Mudarib		(110,296)	(91,135)
Return on Unrestricted Investments			
Accounts Before Zakat		(441,184)	(364,538)
Bank's Share in Income from Investments (as a Mudarib and as fund owner)		4,776,316	3,839,851
Bank's Income from Its Own Investments	29B	12,000,000	10,000,000
Bank's Share in Restricted Investments			
Profit as a Mudarib		158,000	140,000
Bank's Fees as an Investment Agent for Restricted Investments		528,000	400,000
Revenue from Banking Services		2,000	1,000
Other Revenue	30	3,000	2,000
Total Bank Revenue		17,467,316	14,382,851
Administrative and General Expenditures		(3,890,000)	(2,468,000)
Depreciation		(2,089,500)	(2,030,000)
Net Income (loss) Before Zakat and Tax		11,487,816	9,884,851
Provision for Zakat		(2,887,479)	(1,632,871)
Net Income Before Minority Interest		8,600,337	8,251,980
Minority Interest		(5,000)	(3,000)
Net Income		8,595,337	8,248,980
(Paras. 46 to 52 of the standard)			

FIGURE 4.5 Income statement for an Islamic bank or institution
Source: AAOIFI (2015).

Financial Accounting Standard No. (1):
General Presentation and Disclosure in the Financial Statements of
Islamic Banks and Financial Institutions

(Name of Bank or Institution)
Statement of Cash Flows
for the Year Ended xxx (year) xxx (last year)

	Note	xxx (year) Monetary Unit	xx (last year) Monetary Unit
Cash flows from financing activities			
Net increase in unrestricted investment accounts		825316	–
Net increase in current accounts		3,150,000	–
Dividend paid		4,800,000	–
Increase in credit balances and expenses		805,501	–
(Decrease) in accrued expenses		(10,050)	–
Increase in minority interest		210,050	–
Decrease in other assets		15,188,000	–
Net cash flows provided by financing activities		15,365,817	–
Increase (decrease) in cash and cash equivalent		43,759,984	–
Cash and cash equivalent at beginning of year	(37)	51,281,906	–
Cash and cash equivalent at end of year		95,041,890	–
(Paras. 53 to 57 of the standard)			
Cash flows from operation			
Net income (loss)		8,595,337	–
Adjustments to reconcile net income			–
Net cash provided by operating activities			
Depreciation		2,089,500	–
Provisions of doubtful accounts		10,000	–
Provision for Zakat		2,887,479	–
Provision for taxes		–	
Zakat paid		(200,000)	–
Taxes paid		–	
Return on unrestricted investment accounts		441,184	–
Gain on sale of fixed assets		–	
Depreciation of leased assets		8,750,000	–
Provision for decline in value of investment securities		150,000	–
Bad debts		(6,000)	–
Purchase of fixed assets		(890,000)	–
Net cash flows provided by operations		21,827,500	–
Cash flows from investing activities			
Sale of rental real estate		–	–
Purchase of rental real estate		–	–
Sale of real estate		15,000,000	–
Acquisition of investment securities		–	–
Increase in Mudaraba investments		(8,500,000)	–
Sale of inventory		2,000,000	–
Sale of Istisna'a		1,000,000	–
Net increase in receivables		(2,933,333)	–
Net cash flows from (used in) investing activities		6,566,667	–

FIGURE 4.6 Statement of cash flows for an Islamic bank or institution
Source: AAOIFI (2015).

Statement of Changes in Owners' Equity

This statement shows the changes in the owners' equity over a period. It typically shows contributions to capital during the period, the income or loss for the period, and distributions to owners during the period, reconciling these to the opening and closing balances on each of these equity accounts.

FAS1 requires the following items to be disclosed in the statement of changes in owners' equity (para. 60):

- Retained earnings at the beginning of the accounting period
- Net income (loss) for the period
- Transfers to and from reserves
- Distributions to owners during the period
- Retained earnings at the end of the accounting period

FAS1 provides the following example of a statement of changes in owners' equity for an Islamic bank, as shown in Figure 4.7.

Statement of Sources and Uses of Zakat and Charity Funds

The sources and uses of the Zakat funds statement is prepared by companies authorised to collect Zakat and distribute these funds as per the Sharia requirements. This statement includes sources of Zakat and charity funds and the application of these funds during a particular period of time and the fund balance as the end of the period. Muslims pay Zakat based on a percentage of the amount their net assets have appreciated in value over time. Assets that have been purchased for consumption purposes or are used in production are exempt.

In the case where Zakat is directly borne by the owner, the company should indicate this in the notes to the accounts as per AAOIFI recommendation in the case of an Islamic financial institution. The notes to the accounts of the Kuwait Finance House Malaysia Bernhard (incorporated in Malaysia) includes the following statement:

> *'Kuwait Finance House K.S.C who is the shareholder of Kuwait Finance House (Malaysia) Berhad paid Zakat on behalf of the Bank. The Bank does not pay Zakat on behalf of the shareholder or depositors.'*

Charity funds are funds donated directly by customers, or funds that arise from certain transactions, including those that a company cannot recognise as income, such as penalties on loan default payment. While Zakat is an obligation, charitable donations are discretionary. The use of charity funds can be made in the form of contributions to fund, for example, education initiatives for the needy, support for the poor, and supplementary

Financial Accounting Standard No. (1):
General Presentation and Disclosure in the Financial Statements of
Islamic Banks and Financial Institutions

(Name of Bank or Institution)
Statement of Changes in Owners' Equity
for the Year Ended xxx (year) xxx (last year)

Description	Paid-up Capital	Reserves (NOTE 25)		Retained Earnings	Total
	Monetary Unit	Legal Monetary Unit	General Monetary Unit	Monetary Unit	
Balance as at xxx (year)	350,000,000	–	–	–	350,000,000
Issue of () shares					
Net income				8,248,980	8,248,980
Distributed profits				(5,000,000)	(5,000,000)
Transfer to reserves		824,898	824,898	(1,649,796)	–
Balance as at xxx (year)	350,000,000	824,898	824,898	1,599,184	353,248,980
Net income				8,595,337	8,595,337
Distributed profits				(5,000,000)	(5,000,000)
Transfer to reserves		859,534	859,534	1,719,068	–
Balance as at xxx (year) (Paras. 58 to 60 of the standard)	350,000,000	1,684,432	1,684,432	3,475,453	356,844,317

FIGURE 4.7 Statement of changes in owners' equity for an Islamic bank or institution
Source: AAOIFI (2015).

Financial Accounting Standard No. (1):
General Presentation and Disclosure in the Financial Statements of
Islamic Banks and Financial Institutions

(Name of Bank or Institution)
Statement of Sources and Uses of Funds
in the Zakat and Charity Funds
for the Year Ended xxx (year) xxx (last year)

	Note	xxx (year) Monetary Unit	xx (last year) Monetary Unit
Sources of Zakat and charity funds			
(See notes 6 and 7)			
Zakat due from the bank (institution)		2,887,479	-
Zakat due from accountholders		893,445	-
Donations		200,500	-
Total sources		3,981,424	-
Uses of Zakat and charity funds			
Zakat for the poor and the needy		206,280	-
Zakat for the wayfarer		203,000	-
Zakat for the heavily indebted and freedom of slaves		73,945	-
Zakat for new converts to Islam		350,000	-
Zakat for the cause of Allah		330,000	-
Zakat collection and distribution to staff (administrative and general expenditures)		130,720	-
Total uses		1,293,945	-
Increase (decrease) of sources over uses		2,687,479	-
Undistributed Zakat and charity at the beginning of year		1,632,871	-
Undistributed Zakat and charity funds at end of year (Paras. 65 to 68 of the standard)		4,320,350	-

Restricted funds are to be used only for the following specific purposes:

Zakat – these funds are solely used for the relief of need and financial hardship of Muslims in Northern and Western Africa.

The funeral fund represents money donated to provide for funerals in accordance with the Islamic tradition whatever their family means.

Madrassa fund represents donations for classes and activities to educate children and young adults in the speaking and comprehension of the Qur'an in Arabic and for others specific classes teaching about Islam.

Healthy living fund represents grants and donations supporting a project aimed at bringing appropriate health information to members of the community and to provide consultations by an experinced General Practitioner.

Summer camp is an activity programme for children and young people within the community whilst state schools are closed over the summer and is funded by grants and donations.

The English language programme is a grant-funded teaching project working with new residents from North Africa to ensure that they are able to become proficient in the English language.

The New Resident School Support Programme is a grant-funded project working with school-age children who have recently arrived in the UK. This project provides learning and emotional support to pupils in their first two years in the UK.

FIGURE 4.8 Statement of sources and uses of funds in the Zakat and charity funds for an Islamic bank or institution
Source: AAOIFI (2015).

interest-free loans. Limited liability companies and corporations are liable to Zakat as per the first Zakat conference held in Kuwait in 1984. In FAS1, AAOIFI provides a template shown in Figure 4.5 as an illustration for Islamic financial institutions to use in presenting their sources and uses of charity funds.

Figure 4.9 shows the sources and uses of Zakat and charity funds statement of the Bahrain Islamic Bank for the period ended December 31, 2015.

The distribution of the Zakat funds is stated in the Quran as follows:

> *'Alms are for the poor and the needy, and those employed to administer the (funds); for those whose hearts have been (recently) reconciled (to the truth); for those in bondage and in debt in the cause of Allah and the wayfarer. (Thus is it) ordained by Allah, and Allah is full of knowledge and wisdom (Chapter 9: verse 60)' (Para 58).*

Consolidated Statement of Sources and Uses of Zakat and Charity Fund

For the year ended 31 December2015

	2015 BD'000	2014 BD'000
Sources of Zakat and charity funds		
Undistributed Zakat and charity funds at the beginning of the year	282	225
Non-Islamic income/late payment fee	616	659
Donations	–	150
Total sources of Zakat and charity funds during the year	898	1,034
Uses of Zakat and charity funds		
Philanthropic societies	103	441
Aid to needy families	323	311
Total uses of funds during the year	426	752
Undistributed Zakat and charity funds at the end of the year	472	282

FIGURE 4.9 Consolidated statement of sources and uses of Zakat and charity funds
Source: Bahrain Islamic Bank, Annual Report, 2015.

The extracts from 2013 Annual Report of the Mosque Foundation (Figure 4.10) explain the collection and distribution of Zakat funds.

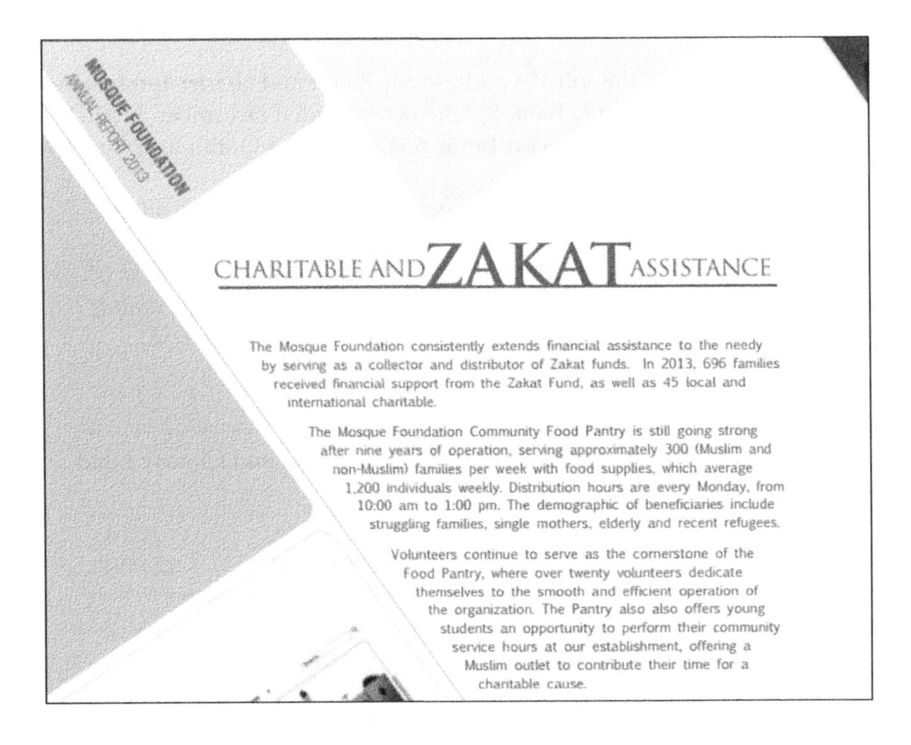
MOSQUE FOUNDATION
ANNUAL REPORT 2013

CHARITABLE AND ZAKAT ASSISTANCE

The Mosque Foundation consistently extends financial assistance to the needy by serving as a collector and distributor of Zakat funds. In 2013, 696 families received financial support from the Zakat Fund, as well as 45 local and international charitable.

The Mosque Foundation Community Food Pantry is still going strong after nine years of operation, serving approximately 300 (Muslim and non-Muslim) families per week with food supplies, which average 1,200 individuals weekly. Distribution hours are every Monday, from 10:00 am to 1:00 pm. The demographic of beneficiaries include struggling families, single mothers, elderly and recent refugees.

Volunteers continue to serve as the cornerstone of the Food Pantry, where over twenty volunteers dedicate themselves to the smooth and efficient operation of the organization. The Pantry also also offers young students an opportunity to perform their community service hours at our establishment, offering a Muslim outlet to contribute their time for a charitable cause.

THE MOSQUE FOUNDATION
SUMMARY STATEMENT OF RECEIPT AND DISBURSEMENT
FOR THE PERIOD ENDING DECEMBER 31, 2013

ACTIVITIES	RECEIPTS		DISBURSEMENTS		SURPLUS (DEFICIT)
General Services & Operations	2,203,151	58%	(1,456,212)	44%	746,940
Community Center	140,637	4%	(307,459)	9%	(166,822)
Al-Siddiq School	435,001	11%	(411,609)	12%	23,392
Zakat Fund	1,042,911	27%	(1,125,414)	34%	(82,503)
NET INCREASE (DECREASE)	3,821,699	100%	(3,300,693)	100%	521,006

FIGURE 4.10 Extracts from 2013 Annual Report of the Mosque Foundation
Source: http://mosquefoundation.org/images/annual-reports/pdf/2013_MF_Annual_Report.pdf

COLLECTION	GENERAL SERVICES & OPERATIONS	COMMUNITY CENTER	AL-SIDDIQ SCHOOL	ZAKAT FUND	TOTAL MOSQUE FOUNDATION	%
Book Service	56,104	–	–	–	56,104	1.47%
Community Services & Events	113,599	–	16	618,740	732,355	19.16%
Discount Income	499	–	–	–	499	0.01%
Eid Market	7,156	–	–	–	7,156	0.19%
Food Service	21,606	–	–	–	21,606	0.57%
Grant & Food Pentry Donation	–	–	–	27,243	27,243	0.71%
Investment and Financial Services	9,353	–	–	–	9,353	0.24%
Martial Arts	–	6,060	–	–	6,060	0.16%
Matching Donations	541	–	–	–	541	0.01%
Media and Outreach Service	54,545	–	–	–	54,545	1.43%
Membership	3,060	17,084	–	–	20,144	0.53%
Program & Other Activities	–	43,221	19,404	–	62,625	1.64%
Quranic School	–	36,536	–	–	36,536	0.96%
Registration Fee	–	–	155,075		155,075	4.06%
Rental	–	30,300	600		30,900	0.81%
Tuition Fees	–	–	227,758	–	227,758	5.96%
Vending	–	1,842	–	–	1,842	0.05%
Water Park	–	–	32,100	–	32,100	0.84%
Donations	1,936,689	5,594	47	396,927	2,339,258	61.21%
TOTAL SUPPORT AND REVENUE	2,203,151	140,637	435,001	1,042,911	3,821,699	100.00%

DISBURSEMENT	GENERAL SERVICES & OPERATIONS	COMMUNITY CENTER	AL-SIDDIQ SCHOOL	ZAKAT FUND	TOTAL MOSQUE FOUNDATION	%
Advertisement Expense	1,799	–	–	–	1,799	0.05%
Automobile Expenses	2,636	–	–	–	2,636	0.07%
Awards & Gifts	1,131	2,380	876	–	4,387	0.11%
Bank Fees & Charges	5,361	–	–	–	5,361	0.14%
Book Service Supplies	24,598	–	–	–	24,598	0.64%
Computers & Equipment	14,564	4,300	13,077	–	31,941	0.84%
Food & Refreshments	10,362	–	972	–	11,335	0.30%
Food Pantry Expense	–	–	–	54,738	54,738	1.43%
General Insurance	16,084	1,682	1,514	–	19,280	0.50%
Janitorial	–	16,800	3,650	–	20,450	0.54%
Multi-Media & Publications	92,141	1,264	1,100	–	94,504	2.47%
Outreach	14,017	–	–	–	14,017	0.37%
Paid for Education	–	–	–	18,493	18,493	0.48%
Paid for Funeral Service	–	–	–	11,350	11,350	0.30%
Paid to Needy	–	–	–	338,727	338,727	8.86%
Paid to Organisation	–	–	–	22,300	22,300	0.58%
Paid to Vendors	–	–	–	11,450	11,450	0.30%
Payroll & Adminstrative Exp	858,840	220,569	198,296	49,616	1,327,322	34.73%
Penalties and Fees	4,177	–	–	–	4,117	0.11%
Postage & Delivery	22,715	–	–	–	22,715	0.59%
Professional Services	5,660	–	–	–	5,660	0.15%
Programs, Events, and Activities	75,482	–	–	–	75,482	1.98%
Property Tax (Balance sheet Item)	87,148	–	–	–	87,148	2.28%
Rent	18,186	1,260	114,880	–	134,326	3.51%
Repairs & Maintenance	73,278	8,030	4,304	–	85,612	2.24%
Restricted and Org. Dist.	–	–	18,946	618,740	637,686	16.69%
Supplies	31,780	32,207	33,394	–	97,381	2.55%
Training and Education	8,541	1,962	18,010	–	28,513	0.75%
Travel Expense	2,330	–	–	–	2,330	0.06%
Utilities	85,439	17,005	2,589	–	105,033	2.75%
TOTAL DISBURSEMENT	1,456,212	307,459	411,609	1,125,414	3,300,693	86.37%
NET PROCEED (DEFICIT)	746,940	(166,822)	23,392	(82,503)	521,006	13.63%

FIGURE 4.10 (*Continued*)

The Birchfiled Mosque and Community Center financial statement for the year 2009 notes on the Zakat[1] includes the following:

> *Zakat: It is a part of our faith that all who are able should offer Zakat. Zakat is collected in proportion to a person's means, in accordance with the teaching of Islam, and is the giving of money for a number of specific purposes, including to help others, and to further the teachings of Islam. A Muslim need not give Zakat through the Mosque but we do provide the opportunity for those attending the Mosque to give Zakat and we arrange its distribution for approved purposes. The Zakat Committee of the Mosque collects and distributes the Zakat, none of which is used to fund the Mosque. The Mosque makes no charge for the collection and distribution of Zakat. This year Zakat was distributed to help Muslims in North and West Africa suffering poverty or in need with no means of support. The Zakat Committee travelled to Africa to meet with local Muslim leaders to establish personally who was going to receive Zakat and their needs.*
>
> *The amount of Zakat collected is supplemented by the interest earned on cash held by the Mosque on deposit which we consider to be a gift of the banking system in the UK. The trustees have decided to use this gift of interest for the relief of poverty and need in the same way as the distribution of Zakat. Once a reckoning of need had been made, the funds were sent to Muslim leaders in the locality selected with instructions for its distribution. Members of the Zakat Committee obtain a written report of how funds were distributed, or where justified, visit the locality to ensure the proper distribution of the funds.*

The notes to the accounts include the extract in Figure 4.11 on charity funds activities.

The collection and distribution of Zakat funds is undertaken differently in different countries. In Malaysia, the government is in charge of Zakat collection and distribution. In other countries, religious departments have established wholly owned companies to undertake these tasks. In Pakistan, for instance, this function is left to specific committees at the national, provincial, district, and village levels. The Dubai Financial Service Authority (DFSA) Rulebook, which contains the Islamic Finance Rules regulating the

[1]https://www.gov.uk/government/uploads/system/uploads/attachment_data/file/350997/arbmosquepb.pdf

5. Incoming resources from charitable activities

	Unrestricted funds £	Restricted funds £	Total 2009 £	Total 2008 £
Faith and worship:				
Hearse receipts	5,460	–	5,460	6,243
Nikkah Certificates	320	–	320	260
Literature sales	243	–	243	5,157
	6,023	–	6,023	11,660
Community activities:				
Birchwood Borough Council - grant	–	104,133	104,133	15,000
Wessex Muslim Council - grant	–	122,511	122,511	11,655
Other grants	2,145	–	2,145	2,978
	2,145	226,644	228,789	29,633
Total	**8,168**	**226,644**	**234,812**	**41,293**

6. Resources expended

	Unrestricted funds Direct costs £	Restricted funds Direct costs £	Support costs £	Total 2009 £	Total 2008 £
Cost of generating funds	**896**	**–**	**3,820**	**4,716**	**3,639**
Charitable activities					
Faith and worship:					
Mosque	162,325	–	30,799	193,124	194,586
Zakat	21,645	83,825	–	105,470	104,250
Funerals	–	64,204	5,080	69,284	65,974
Madrassa classes	–	12,916	4,560	17,476	15,459
	183,970	160,945	40,439	385,354	380,269
Community activities:					
Community facilities	60,106	–	14,100	74,206	81,247
English programme	–	118,540	12,540	131,080	45,199
School programme	–	91,821	8,504	100,325	32,219
Other activities	–	6,297	1,450	7,747	15,348
	60,106	216,658	36,594	313,358	174,013
Total charitable activities	**244,076**	**377,603**	**77,033**	**698,712**	**554,282**

FIGURE 4.11 Charity fund activities

Source: https://www.gov.uk/government/uploads/system/uploads/attachment_data/file/350997/arbmosquepb.pdf

15. Analysis of charitable funds

Analysis of Fund movements	Balance b/fwd £	Incoming resources £	Resources expended £	Transfers £	Fund c/fwd £
Unrestricted funds:					
Unrestricted general funds	2,648,492	425,646	(315,796)	(200,000)	2,558,342
Designated Masque extension fund	–	–	–	200,000	200,000
	2,648,492	425,646	(315,796)	–	2,758,342
Restricted funds:	**Balance b/fwd £**	**Incoming resources £**	**Resources expended £**	**Governance costs £**	**Fund c/fwd £**
Zakat	–	83,825	(83,825)	–	–
Funeral fund	7,171	76,908	(69,284)	–	14,795
Madrassa classes	4,639	20,914	(17,476)	–	8,077
Healthy Living	2,113	4,467	(2,647)	–	3,933
Summer camp	–	6,453	(5,100)	–	1,353
English language programme	27,668	122,511	(131,080)	(3,297)	15,802
New residents school support programme	25,642	104,133	(100,325)	(2,504)	26,946
	67,233	419,211	(409,737)	(5,801)	70,906
Total	2,715,725	844,857	(725,533)	(5,801)	2,829,248

FIGURE 4.11 (*Continued*)

activities firms that carry on Islamic Financial Business in or from the Dubai International Financial Center (DIFC) requires firms to disclose:

- 'the method used in the calculation of the Zakat base;
- whether Zakat has been paid by the Authorised Person;
- where Zakat has been paid by the Authorised Person, the amount which has been paid; and
- where Zakat has not been paid by the Authorised Person, sufficient information to allow a shareholder or other investor to compute the amount of his own liability to Zakat' (DFSA Rule book, Appendix I).

Statement of Sources and Uses of Qard Funds

AAOIFI requires Islamic financial institutions to prepare statement of qard funds. Funds available for lending as a non–interest-bearing loan in accordance with the Sharia are referred to as qard funds. Transactions affecting qard funds during a period of time are reflected in the qard fund statement, including the sources and uses of funds during a period and the fund balance at a given date.

Financial Accounting Standard No. (1):
General Presentation and Disclosure in the Financial Statements of Islamic Banks and Financial Institutions

(Name of Bank or Institution)
Statement of Sources and Uses of Qard Funds
for the Year Ended xxx (year) xxx (last year)

	xxx (year) Monetary Unit	xx (last year) Monetary Unit
Opening balance		
Good loans	xxx	xxx
Funds available for loans	xxx	xxx
Sources of Qard Funds		
Allocation from current accounts	xxx	xxx
Allocation from earnings prohibited by Shari'a	xxx	xxx
Source outside the bank	xxx	xxx
Total of sources during the year	xxx	xxx
Uses of Qard Funds		
Loans to students	(xxx)	(xxx)
Loans to craftsmen	(xxx)	(xxx)
Settlement of current accounts	(xxx)	(xxx)
Total uses during the year	(xxx)	(xxx)
End-of-year-balance		
Good loans	xxx	xxx
Funds available for loans	xxx	xxx
(Paras. 69 to 73 of the standard)		

FIGURE 4.12 Statement of sources and uses of qard funds for an Islamic bank or institution
Source: AAOIFI (2015).

Sources of funds include funds from current accounts at the bank, funds from the owners of the bank, and funds from non–Sharia-compliant transactions. Fund balance in the qard fund account refers to the outstanding collectible loans and the other funds not loaned or used for other purposes. AAOIFI in FAS1 provides the template shown in Figure 4.12 to guide the presentation of the statement of sources and uses of qard funds.

Figure 4.13 shows the statement of sources and uses of qard funds for Bahrain Islamic Bank for the period ended December 31, 2015.

Consolidated Statement of Sources and Uses of Good Faith Qard Fund
For the year ended 31 December 2015

	Qard Hasan receivables BD'000	Funds available for Qard Hasan BD'000	Total BD'000
Balance at 1 January 2015	80	48	128
Uses of Qard fund			
Marriage	9	(9)	–
Others (Waqf)	9	(9)	–
Total uses during the year	18	(18)	–
Repayments	(38)	38	–
Balance at 31 December 2015	60	68	128
Balance at 1 January 2014	79	49	128
Uses of Qard fund			
Marriage	22	(22)	–
Others (Waqf)	3	(3)	–
Total uses during the year	25	(25)	–
Repayments	(24)	24	–
Balance at 31 December 2014	80	48	128

	2015 BD'000	2014 BD'000
Sources of Qard fund	125	125
Contribution by the Bank	3	3
Donation	128	128

FIGURE 4.13 Consolidated statement of sources and uses of good-faith qard fund
Source: Bahrain Islamic Bank, Annual Report, 2015.

Statement of Changes in Restricted Investments

Islamic Banks must keep the use of restricted investment accounts within the conditions imposed by their holders. Restricted investment assets are not included in the assets category of the bank's financial statements.

The statement of changes in restricted investments shows the movement in these investments over a period of time and their balance at a given date. This includes restricted investments deposits and withdrawals, profits or losses on restricted accounts, and the bank's share of profits from the investments.

FAS1 requires the following to be disclosed in the statement of changes in restricted investments:

- Restricted investments at the beginning of the period
- The number of investment shares in each of the investment portfolio, and the value per share at the beginning of the period
- Deposits received or investment shares issued during the period
- Withdrawals or shares repurchased during the period
- Islamic bank's share of profit as a mudarib or fee as agent
- Allocated overhead expenses to restricted investment profit (loss) during the period
- Restricted investments at the end of the period
- Number of investment shares at the end of the period and the value per share

FAS1 provides the template shown in Figure 4.14 for the statement of changes in restricted investments.

Mosques and community centres prepare similar financial statements using terms that reflect the nature of their operations. For example, the UK Birchfield Mosque and Community Center financial statement for the year 2009 includes a statement of financial activities, which lists the incoming resources to the institution divided into unrestricted and restricted funds and the application of resources during the accounting year (Figure 4.15).

The UK Birchfield Mosque and Community Center financial statement for the year 2009 also includes a balance sheet as of the end of accounting year (Figure 4.16).

The financial statements shown in the figure are examples of those contained in Islamic reports based on current AAOIFI standards. These are designed, as far as possible, to be compatible with IFRS and US GAAP. Islamic ethical beliefs require a special interpretation of the fair value and income concepts referred to in the latter two standard setting systems. We illustrate an Islamic interpretation of these concepts with the Al Madani Group financial statements.

Market Values

The financial statements of the Al Madani Group illustrated earlier show its accountability based on the results of actual transaction costs. There is therefore a clear relationship between the debt and the changes in debt of the

(Name of Bank or Institution)
Statement of Changes in Restricted Investments
for the Year Ended xxx (year) XXX (last year)

Description	Units of Restricted Investment Portfolio[1]							
	Marketable equity Securities portfolio		Real Estate Trading Portfolio		Murabaha Portfolio		Total	
	XXX (Last year) Monetary Unit	XXX (Last year) Monetary Unit	XXX (Last year) Monetary Unit	XXX (Last year) Monetary Unit	XXX (Last year) Monetary Unit	XXX (Last year) Monetary Unit	XXX (Last year) Monetary Unit	XXX (Last year) Monetary Unit
Investments at beginning of year	6,000,000		15,000,000		10,000,000		31,000,000	
Number of investment units at beginning of year	6,000		15,000		10,000		-	
Unit value it beginning of year	1,000		1,000		1,000		-	
Deposits and issues	4,000,000		-		-		4,000,000	
Repurchased investment units and withdrawals	-		-		(2,000,000)		(2,000,000)	
Investment profits (losses)	1,800,000		750,000		880,000		3,430,000	
Administrative expenditures	(2,200)		(1,500)		(2,500)		(6,200)	
Bank's fees as an agent (1)	(360,000)		(150,000)		(176,000)		(686,000)	
Investments at end of year	11,437,800		15,598,500		8,701,500		35,737,800	
Number of investment units at end of year	1,000		15,000		8,000		-	
Unit value at end of year	1,143		1,039		1,087		-	

(Paras. 61 to 64 of the standard)

The attached notes from No. () to No. () form an integral part of the financial statements (Para. 7 of the standard)

[1] or the Bank's share in investment profits as a Mudarib if the relationship between the bank and the holders of restricted investment accounts is based on the Mudaraba contract (Note 43)

FIGURE 4.14 Statement of changes in restricted investments for an Islamic bank or institution
Source: AAOIFI Financial Accounting Standard No.1 General Presentation and Disclosure in the Financial Statements of Islamic Banks and Financial Institutions, Appendix E, Examples of the Financial Statements and Disclosures Therein, AAOIFI,

Birchfield Mosque Statement of Financial Activities for the year ended 31 March 2009					
	Note	Un-restricted Funds £	Restricted Funds £	Total Funds 2009 £	Total Funds 2008 £
Incoming resources					
Incoming resources from generated funds:					
Voluntary income:					
Friday Prayers	3	329,431	108,742	438,173	446,041
Zakat		–	83,825	83,825	91,122
		329,431	192,567	521,998	537,163
Investment income		21,645	–	21,645	13,128
Activities for generating funds	4	66,402	–	66,402	70,095
Incoming resources from charitable activities	5	8,168	226,644	234,812	41,293
Total incoming resources		**425,646**	**419,211**	**844,857**	**661,679**
Resources expended					
Costs of generating funds:	6	4,716	–	4,716	3,639
Charitable activities:	6	288,975	409,737	698,712	554,282
Governance costs:	6	22,105	5,801	27,906	25,511
Total resources expended		**315,796**	**415,538**	**731,334**	**583,432**
Net movement in funds		**109,850**	**3,673**	**113,523**	**78,247**
Reconciliation of funds					
Total funds brought forward		2,648,492	67,233	2,715,725	2,637,476
Total Funds carried forward		**2,758,342**	**70,906**	**2,829,248**	**2,715,725**

The Statement of Financial Activities includes all gains and losses in the year. All incoming resources and resources expended derive from continuing activities.

FIGURE 4.15 Statement of financial activities for the year ended March 31, 2009
Source: https://www.gov.uk/government/uploads/system/uploads/attachment_data/file/350997/arbmosquepb.pdf

Birchfield Mosque Balance Sheet as at 31 March 2009					
	Note		2009		2008
		£	£	£	£
Fixed assets:					
Tangible assets	11		2,366,800		2,363,210
Current assets:					
Debtors	12	40,482		73,473	
Cash at bank and in hand		451,337		292,542	
Total current assets		491,819		366,015	
Liabilities:					
Creditors falling due within one year	13	(29,371)		(13,500)	
Net current assets			462,448		352,515
Net assets			2,829,248		2,715,725
The funds of the charity:	15				
Unrestricted funds:					
Designated funds		200,000		–	
General funds		2,558,342		2,648,492	
Total unrestricted funds			2,758,342		2,648,492
Restricted income funds			70,906		67,233
Total charity funds			2,829,248		2,715,725

The notes at pages 10 to 15 form part of these accounts

FIGURE 4.16 Balance sheet as of March 31, 2009
Source: https://www.gov.uk/government/uploads/system/uploads/attachment_data/file/350997/arbmosquepb.pdf

Al Madani accounting entity. Its asset and equity values show the accumulated financial results of completed activities (equities) and incomplete activities (assets).

Current market values are not disclosed in the Al Madani Group financial statements shown in the classified balance sheet section. In Islam, wealth is measured using current market values. Market values are necessary for Zakat computation, for example. This makes market values especially important in Islamic accounting. When measured accurately, market values contain more information than single transaction costs about risk and the broader social value of assets and liabilities. When interpreted as 'fair' values, they are also consistent with both international financial reporting standards and AAOIFI pronouncements.

Illustrative Example of a Multicolumn Balance Sheet for Al-Madini Group

The challenge with going outside the firm's own accounting records to estimate fair values lies in the reliability and verifiability of such estimates. Fair value accounting remains, however, a reasonable method of extending the accountability of firms in the Islamic business environment to the social domain. Given the requirement of full disclosure and accountability to the Ummah in an Islamic business environment, both actual costs and fair values should be disclosed in Islamic financial statements.

The balance sheet should therefore ideally consist of a multicolumn statement showing cost and fair values. To illustrate, Table 4.8 presents a multicolumn balance sheet for Al-Madani Group.

TABLE 4.8 Al Madani Group Balance Sheet as of December 31, 20X4

Assets Current assets	Cost	Fair value	Liabilities Current liabilities	Cost	Fair value
Cash	31,950	31,950	Accounts payable	9,390	9,200
Accounts receivable	19,200	19,000	Salaries payable	540	540
Unbilled sales	3,000	2,500	Sales received in advance	7,200	7,100
Supplies on hand	2,700	2,650	**Total current liabilities**	**17,130**	**16840**
Prepaid insurance	6,600	6,600			
Prepaid rent	55,350	50,000			
Total current assets	**118,800**	**112,700**			
Fixed assets			**Long-term liabilities**	0	0
			Total liabilities	**17,130**	**16,840**
Fixed assets	63,450				
Accumulated depreciation	−2,250		**Equity**		
			Equity at end of period	**162,870**	**162,870**
Total fixed assets	**61,200**	**75,000**	**Revaluation reserve**		**7,990**
Total assets	**180,000**	**187,700**	Total liabilities and owners' equity	**180,000**	**187,700**

The differences between the original cost amounts and the estimated market values are taken to a revaluation reserve to balance the balance sheet. When items are sold, or otherwise disposed of, the differences are transferred to the income statement.

All assets and liabilities are valued at the amounts that it is expected would be agreed in a transaction between a willing buyer and seller, i.e. the principle of fair value. In Islam, as just noted, a fair value is similar to the same concept in IFRS, specifically in IFRS 13 Fair Value Measurement. The term *fair value* was used by AAOIFI in it mudaraba and musharaka standards for the measurement of capital provided in kind. AAOFI explained fair value as follows:

> *'the value representing estimate of the amount of cash or cash equivalent that would be received for an asset sold or amount of cash or cash equivalent paid for a liability extinguished or transferred in an orderly transaction between a willing buyer and a willing seller at the measurement date' (Accounting and Auditing Organization for Islamic Financial Institutions (AAOIFI, 2010).*

However, there are differences in the techniques that are used in Islamic accounting to determine fair values. Generally, discounted future values are avoided.

In the case of current assets, cash usually has the same value whether shown at cost or fair value. Receivables may have a different value if it is believed the full amount is not recoverable. Under the reporting method shown here, it is more informative to the user to display the full amount of actual receivables in the cost column without deducting 'bad debts', since the recoverable amounts are shown in the fair value column. A similar principle applies in the case of inventories. The fact that the fair value of inventories may be lower than their original cost is stated with similar effect as it is in non-Islamic accounting but without suggesting a foretelling of the future.

In the case of noncurrent assets, the 'cost' value of depreciable assets represents the original cost, less accumulated depreciation, whereas the fair value simply reflects a judgement about the current price the asset would be exchanged for in an open market transaction. Both values act as a check on the reliability and information content of the other.

The same Islamic logic carries over to the valuation of short-term and long-term liabilities. We do not discount values and we do not second-guess what the future might hold with regard to how much of a liability or accrued amount might be eventually settled, but we do take note of and measure current market values of liabilities. Since the debts that underlie cost measurement are additive, so are the expected debts represented by fair values, and we therefore add the different values in the cost and fair value columns to arrive at totals that are balanced by the Revaluation Reserve account. From an Islamic perspective, this represents the as-yet-unrealised difference in wealth accruing to the owners of the business and forms part of the equity base upon which Zakat is levied.

The Value-Added Income Statement

The presentation of market values in the way just described is suggested by the Islamic criteria of full disclosure. It is also implied by the importance of social accountability in Islam. In the market value balance sheet the social dimension of value is reflected in the fair value of total assets. This represents the current social value placed on the total assets held in trust for society by the Al Madani Group. The principle of social accountability can be accommodated in the income statement by embedding within it a line item showing the calculation value-added and showing the deductions for outflows to factors of production such as wages and salaries, rent, and dividends as 'distributions' of value-added.

The value-added calculation moves the focus on financial performance of an Islamic organisation from the bottom line, which is a single focus on the profit and loss account, to the contribution a company makes to the community it serves. The emphasis is on cooperative economic activities, as opposed to competitive activities, in accordance with the religious principles of fair and considerate trading contained in the Sharia.

The value-added elements in the income statement therefore show the value created during a particular period of time that is attributable to all stakeholders, including shareholders, directors, the providers of capital, the capital provided for maintenance, payments to employees, government, and the community in general.

As can be seen in the illustration below, value-added is integrated into the income statement by rearranging some of its elements, emphasising the idea that some deductions from revenues are in the nature of intermediate flows used up in producing outputs while others are in the nature of distributions of value-added to different stakeholders.

Table 4.9 illustrates a value-added statement as an integral part of the income statement.

In general, the distribution of value-added in the income statement would include taxes, Zakat, Qard and charitable donations, as well as the items shown in Table 4.9, salaries, depreciation, rent, dividends, and savings. In this format net profit remains an important measurement of performance from the owners' perspective but it is now readily and more easily related to the broader idea of performance from the perspective of society.

The statement of changes in owners' equity, which represents the movement in the owners' equity of Al Madani, would then appear as shown in Table 4.10.

TABLE 4.9 Al Madani Group Value-Added Income Statement for the Year Ended December 31, 20X4

Revenue	
Sales	41,400
Expenses	
Gas and oil expense	2,040
Supplies expense	1,500
Insurance expense	600
Utilities expense	450
Advertising expense	150
Total intermediate expenses	4,740
Value-added	36,660
Distribution of value-added	
Salaries	11,340
Depreciation	2,250
Rent	1,200
Total expenses	**19,530**
Net profit	**21,870**
Dividends	9,000
Retained earnings (savings)	12,870
Total distribution of value-added	**36,660**

TABLE 4.10 Al Madani Group Statement of Owners' Equity for the Year Ended December 31, 20X4

	Capital	Retained Earnings	Revaluation Reserve
Balances at beginning of accounting period	100000	150000	2700
Income for year		21870	
Increase in market value of net assets			5290
Dividends		9000	
Balances at end of accounting period	100000	162870	7990

The Statement of Changes in Owner's Equity is similar to what is reported under IFRS standards. An additional column could be included for undistributed value-added, the equivalent of savings by Al Madani, which would be the sum of the retained earnings and accumulated depreciation in this simple case. If value-added were to include changes in the market value of net assets, which we have assumed not to be the case here, the revaluation reserve would also be added to retained earnings to measure the accumulated value-added at market value.

When market values and value-added are integrated into IFRS and US GAAP style financial statements in the manner illustrated, our proposition is that they represent a way of reporting the financial position and performance of Islamic organisations that better reflects the concerns of Islamic societies. In the following chapters, you will be able to judge for yourselves if this proposition holds true in the context of reporting various aspects of Islamic financial transactions.

VOCABULARY

accounting cycle
adjusting entries
assets
cash flow statement
charity funds
classified balance sheet
closing the accounts
current assets
current liabilities
Dubai Financial Service Authority (DFSA)
Dubai International Financial Center (DIFC)
fair values
Financial Accounting Standard 1
fixed or noncurrent assets
income statement,
Islamic financial statements
Kuwait Finance House
liabilities
long-term liabilities
market values
mosques and community centres
multicolumn statement
owners' equity
post-closing trial balance

revaluation reserve
Shariah supervisory board
social income
statement of changes in owners' equity
statement of changes in restricted accounts
statement of financial position
statement of retained earnings
statement of sources and uses of qard funds
statement of sources and uses of Zakat
The Accounting and Auditing Organization for Islamic Financial Institutions (AAOIFI)
trial balance
value-added statement
worksheet
Zakat

MULTIPLE-CHOICE QUESTIONS

1. Gross profit is equal to
   a. sales minus cost of goods sold.
   b. sales minus total operating expenses.
   c. sales minus advertising expenses.
   d. sales minus depreciation expenses.
2. The net income after tax for Dutac for the year 2018 was $1,500,000. The number of shares outstanding at the end of 2018 was 600,000. Dutac issued 100,000 new shares on January 1, 2019. Net income after tax for 2019 was 25% higher than in 2018. What are earnings per share in 2019?
   a. $2.22
   b. $2.68
   c. $4.13
   d. $2.75
3. The sales for Jadco were $384,000 and cost of goods sold was $134,400. What is the company's gross profit margin (ratio of gross profit to sales)?
   a. 45%
   b. 65%
   c. 56%
   d. 35%

4. All the following are current assets except
   a. marketable securities.
   b. investments.
   c. prepaid expenses.
   d. cash.
5. Obligations that will have to be paid within the current year are classified as
   a. fixed assets.
   b. accrued expenses.
   c. current liability.
   d. long-term debt.
6. All the following are sections within the cash flow statement except
   a. cash flows from operating activities.
   b. cash flows from management activities.
   c. cash flows from investing activities.
   d. cash flows from financing activities.
7. The purchase of machinery is classified in the cash flow statement as
   a. cash flow from operating activities.
   b. cash flow from assets purchases.
   c. cash from investment activities.
   d. cash flow from financing activities.

Use the following information to answer questions 8–11:

Yasco Office Supplies
Balance Sheet
December 31, 20XX

Cash at bank	$149,500	Accounts payable	$161,000
Prepaid insurance	$ 69,000	Salaries payable	$ 23,000
Accounts receivable	$115,000	Mortgage payable	$207,000
Inventory	$161,000	**Total liabilities**	$368,000
Investment land	$172,500		
Land	$207,000		
Building	$230,000	Common stock	$276,000
Less: Accumulated depreciation	($ 46,000)	Retained earnings	$575,000
	$184,000	**Total stockholders' equity**	$851,000
Trademark	$161,000		
Total assets	$1,219,000	**Total liabilities and stockholders' equity**	$1,219,000

8. The assets classified as current assets are equal to
   a. $667,000.
   b. $494,500.
   c. $414,000.
   d. $333,500.
9. Assets classified as property, plant, and equipment are equal to
   a. $736,000.
   b. $391,000.
   c. $563,500.
   d. $437,000.
10. Assets classified as investments are equal to
    a. $0.
    b. $345,000.
    c. $172,500.
    d. $414,000.
11. The total amount of working capital is
    a. $310,500.
    b. $678,500.
    c. $172,500.
    d. $138,000.

DISCUSSION QUESTIONS

1. In the balance sheet, what is meant by assets, liabilities, and owners' equity?
2. How does a profit and loss account differ from a balance sheet?
3. How does cash-based accounting differ from accrual-based accounting?
4. Define double-entry accounting.
5. Define a ledger account.
6. What is the difference between a general journal and general ledger?
7. Define trial balance.
8. Why are different financial statements needed for Islamic business organisations?
9. What are the key criteria that should be applied when preparing financial statements for Islamic business organisations?
10. Illustrate the key characteristics underlying financial statements for an Islamic business.
11. In addition to the balance sheet, income statement, and cash flow statement, AAOIFI recommends additional statements. Briefly describe the

purpose of each of these and why is it necessary for Islamic business organisations.
12. Highlight the key items in the balance sheet of an Islamic bank.
13. What are the main advantages of disclosing value-added in financial statements from an Islamic viewpoint?
14. Discuss the main difference between value-added and profit.
15. What are some of the alternative ways of calculating value-added?

EXERCISES

1. Classify the following balance sheet items into assets, liabilities, and owners' equity:

ITEMS	ASSETS	LIABILITIES	EQUITY
Cash			
Equipment			
Accounts payable			
Land			
Accounts receivable			
Common stock			
Building			
Notes payable			
Cash			
Supplies			
Furniture			
Retained earnings			

2. Draw the general format of a balance sheet.
3. Use the following information from the financial statement of Datco to prepare the current assets section of the balance sheet:

Accounts receivable	\$11,000
Prepaid insurance	\$2,100
Cash	\$19,500
Supplies	\$2,000
Short-term investments	\$5,000

4. Use the following information from the financial statement of Dugaz to prepare a classified balance sheet for the year ended December 31, 2019.

Accounts payable	24,300
Building not currently used	85,500
Accumulated depreciation, equipment	36,000
Retained earnings	144,000
Common stock	43,200
Intangible assets	22,500
Notes payable (due in 5 years)	67,500
Accounts receivable	13,500
Cash	23,400
Short-term investments	9,000
Land	90,000
Equipment	67,500
Long-term investments	3,600

5. The following items are included in the financial statement of Ducab for the year ended December 31, 2019. Prepare an income statement for the year ended December 31, 2019.

Cost of goods sold	$2,485,000
Net sales	$4,476,500
Administrative expenses	$836,500
Interest expense	$238,000
Dividends paid	$133,000
Selling expenses	$157,500

6. The following items are included in the financial statement of Rafco for 2019:

Accounts payable	$37,500
Accounts receivable	$27,500
Accumulated depreciation—Video equipment	$70,000
Advertising expense	$52,500
Cash	$60,000
Common stock	$225,000
Depreciation expense	$30,000
Dividends	$37,500
Insurance expense	$7,500

Note payable (due 2022)	$175,000
Prepaid insurance	$15,000
Rent expense	$42,500
Retained earnings (beginning)	$30,000
Salaries expense	$85,000
Salaries payable	$7,500
Service revenue	$362,500
Supplies	$10,000
Supplies expense	$15,000
Video equipment	$525,000

Instructions

a. Compute the net profit for the year.

b. What is the retained earnings figure that would appear on the balance sheet at December 31, 2019?

c. Prepare a classified balance sheet for Rafco at December 31, 2019, assuming the note payable is a long-term debt.

7. Classfiy the following items into Revenue and Expenses

ITEMS	REVENUE	EXPENSES
Sales		
Salaries		
Rent		
Insurance		
Utilities		
Cost of goods sold		
Service revenue		
Depreciation		

CHAPTER 5

Accounting for Sukuk

Learning Objectives

After studying this chapter, you should be able to:

1. Explain the principles and nature of sukuk.
2. Demonstrate an understanding of the differences between conventional bonds and sukuk.
3. Describe how sukuk are issued and the different parties to sukuk.
4. Evaluate the different types of sukuk.
5. Deliberate on the differences between asset-backed and asset-based sukuk.
6. Provide accounting entries for sukuk under IFRS and AAOIFI.

A company can raise funds for its operations and expansion either by issuing shares or by raising debt capital. The latter consists of borrowing from banks or through the issuance of bonds. Bonds are an important part of the financial sector. However, the Sharia prohibition of charging and giving interest means that the issuing of bonds is not allowed in Islamic financial markets. Thus, for such markets, *sukuk* are issued instead. Sukuk aim to provide Sharia-compliant instruments for investment. These instruments are Sharia compliant primarily because there is no interest involved and it avoids excessive uncertainty (gharar). Given this, it is no surprise that the emerging economies of the Islamic world are turning to sukuk to manage their capital needs.

Sukuk provide an alternative to conventional fixed-income securities and are mainly used to finance large developmental and capital expenditures of big corporations. More important, sukuk are now used as an instrument to manage liquidity. The growth of the sukuk market globally has been phenomenal, as the market provides an avenue for the short- and medium-term placement of funds to astute investors who want to follow strictly the teachings of Islam.

The Accounting and Auditing Organization for Islamic Financial Institutions (AAOIFI) defines sukuk as

> *certificates of equal value representing undivided shares in ownership of tangible assets, usufruct, and services or (in the ownership of) the assets of particular projects or special investment activity.*

Put simply, sukuk are entitlement to rights in certain assets with varying degrees of asset ownership.

DIFFERENCES BETWEEN BONDS AND SUKUK

A bond is a debt certificate that requires the issuing company to pay to the bondholders a stated interest at scheduled intervals and to pay the principal amount on its maturity date. Similarly, in sukuk, given that sukuk holders also provide capital to the sukuk issuer, such investors are also entitled to some returns. However, such returns are not based on interest rates. Instead, the returns to sukuk holders are based on the returns of the underlying assets that the sukuk certificates are tied to. Thus, in sukuk, funds raised must be identifiable to specific assets or projects. It is important to note that sukuk represent trust certificates, whereas a bond is a contractual debt obligation.

Table 5.1 provides a summary of the main differences between conventional bonds and sukuk.

ISSUING SUKUK

Sukuk can be issued through a third party using a special-purpose vehicle (SPV) or directly by the company that needs the capital for its operations or expansion. Generally, sukuk will be issued through an SPV.

Sukuk Issued Through the SPV

There are three parties involved in a basic sukuk structure where the sukuk are issued through an SPV (Figure 5.1):

1. The originator: The company that needs the funds,
2. The special-purpose vehicle: The intermediary handling the issue
3. The investors: The sukuk holders

TABLE 5.1 Differences between Bonds and Sukuk

	Sukuk	Bonds
I	Three parties: 1. Originator 2. The special-purpose vehicle (SPV) 3. Sukuk holders (investors) This is the general case.	Two parties: 1. Issuer 2. Bondholders (investors)
II	Sukuk are like trust certificates. Sukuk holders have ownership stakes in specific tangible assets.	Bonds are debt obligations due from the issuer to the investors. Thus, bondholders hold investments that offer fixed or variable rates of interest.
III	Funds raised can only be used for activities that are permissible in Islam.	Funds raised can finance *any* activity.
IV	The subject matter must be based on a defined business undertaking between the *sukuk* holders and the originator.	The bondholders generally have no knowledge of what the funds are to be used for.
V	The sale of *sukuk* represents a sale of a share of the specified asset.	The sale of bonds is basically the sale of debt.

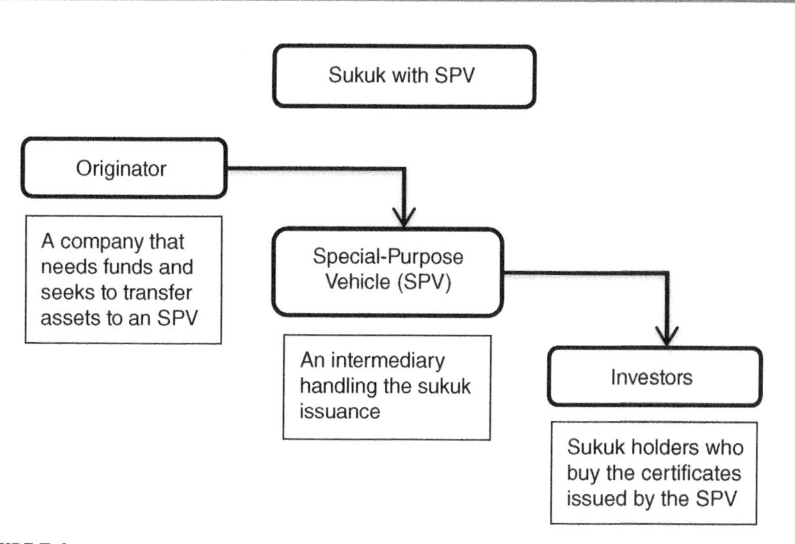

FIGURE 5.1 Sukuk with SPV

Sukuk without SPV

Some sukuk are issued without an SPV. In its simplest form, the company that requires financing issues the sukuk itself, as in Figure 5.2.

However, sukuk that are issued without an SPV normally appoint a trustee to undertake the role of the SPV. The trustee has the responsibility of managing the cash flows and the sukuk assets, such as collecting the initial investments from sukuk holders. In the case of sukuk ijara, the trustee will act on behalf of sukuk holders (who are the lessors) (Figure 5.3).

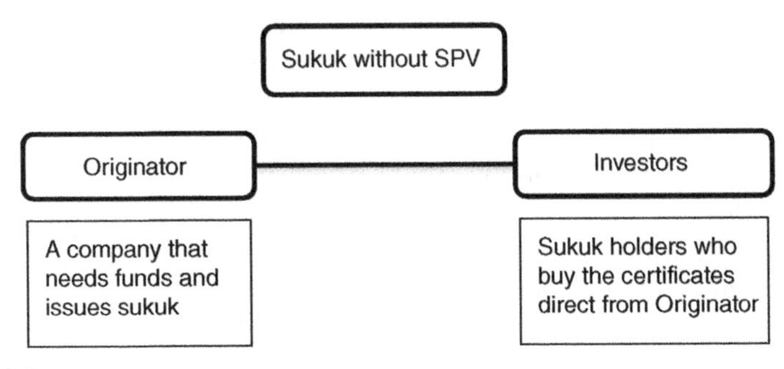

FIGURE 5.2 Sukuk without SPV

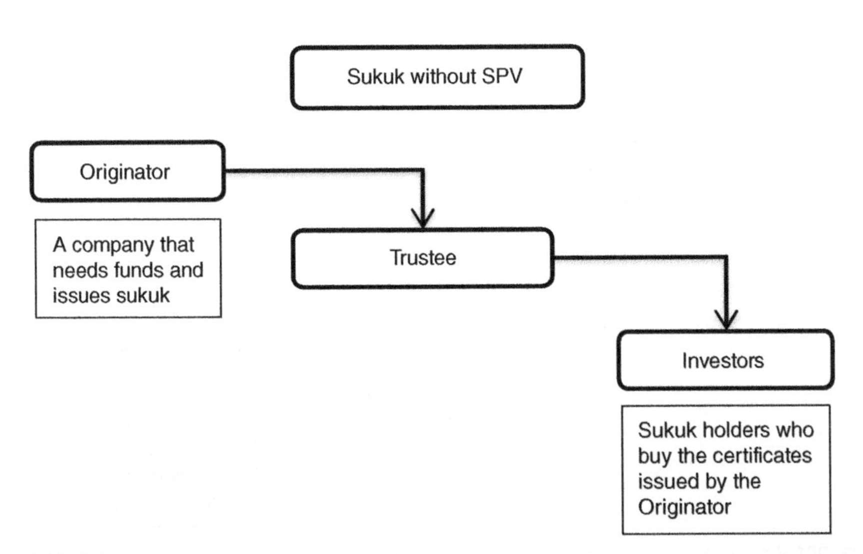

FIGURE 5.3 Sukuk without SPV (ijarah)

ASSET-BACKED OR ASSET-BASED SUKUK

Sukuk can be issued as asset backed or asset based. These have significant differences in credit risks and thus have implications for investor protection. Asset-backed sukuk are sometimes termed secured sukuk, while asset-based sukuk are sometimes called unsecured sukuk.

Asset-Backed Sukuk

For asset-backed sukuk, the sukuk holders actually own a share of a specific tangible asset of the business. Thus, the orginator's bankruptcy will not affect the sukuk holders' rights to the cash flows arising from that specific asset. Accordingly, the risks associated with the ownership of that asset will also be borne by the sukuk holders. In such a case, there would be a legitimate sales transaction, as the originator would sell that specific asset to an SPV. The SPV would hold the asset as a trustee and issue sukuk backed by the asset. It is important to note that the sukuk holders will not have recourse to the originator should there be a default in the payment of the principal or the dividends. Additionally, it will be the sukuk holders that assume any losses in case of impairment of sukuk assets. Thus, asset-backed sukuk has the characteristic of an equity as opposed to a debt.

Asset-Based Sukuk

Asset-based sukuk are structured to replicate conventional bonds. Bonds require issuers (borrowers) to guarantee both fixed (interest) income as well as the principal amount of the loan to creditors. Similarly, this debt-like structure is used to structure asset-based sukuk by incorporating income and capital guarantees. There is no sale of the underlying asset of the originator to the sukuk holders. Thus, sukuk holders do not have full recourse to the underlying assets of the business but to the originator. This implies that asset-based sukuk focuses on the creditworthiness of the originator but not on the risks of the assets.

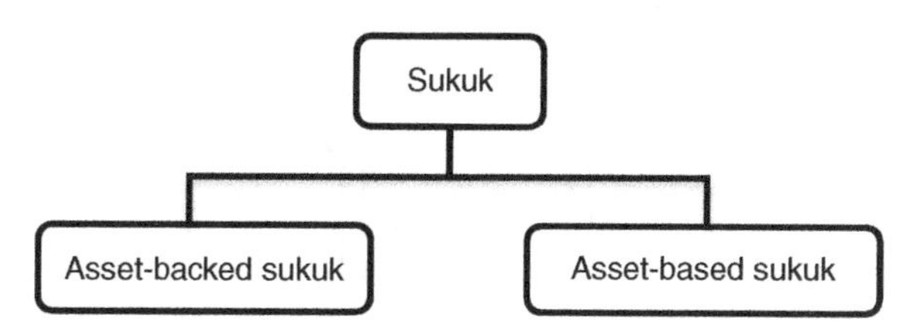

FIGURE 5.4 Asset-backed and Asset-based sukuk

TYPES OF SUKUK

Sukuk can be structured according to various contracts, including sukuk mudaraba, sukuk musharaka, sukuk murabaha, sukuk ijarah, sukuk salam, and sukuk istisna (Figure 5.5).

Sukuk Mudaraba

Mudaraba is a profit-sharing contract between a capital provider and an entrepreneur. While profits are shared according to agreed profit-sharing ratios, losses will be solely borne by the capital provider. Proceeds received from sukuk holders will be the capital raised. The owners of such sukuk are the rabbul-mal (capital provider). Thus, sukuk holders own the assets in the mudaraba. Typically, an SPV acts as the manager and is paid a management fee for the services.

Sukuk Musharaka

Musharaka is a partnership where the parties in the joint arrangement share profits and losses. All capital providers have an entitlement to participate in the management of the venture, but they are not required to do so. The partners share the profit according to the profit-sharing ratio they have agreed to, while losses are borne by the partners in accordance with their contributions of capital.

Sukuk musharaka are certificates of equal value issued with the aim of using the mobilised funds to establish a new project or the development of an existing project, on the basis of partnership contracts. Holders of these certificates (sukuk holders) become the owners of the project or the assets of the activity according to their respective shares. Musharaka certificates can function as negotiable instruments and can be bought and sold in the secondary market.

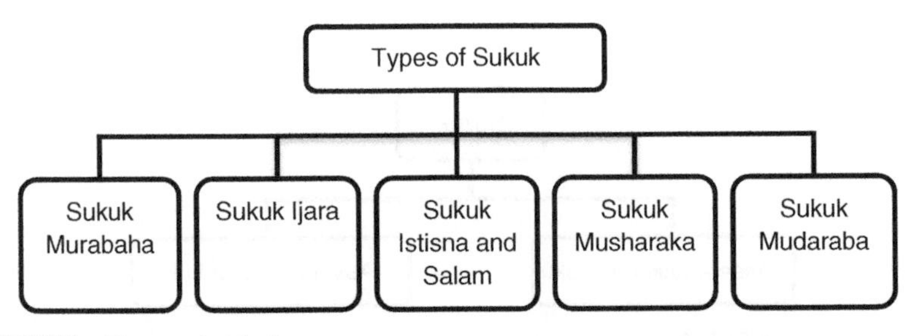

FIGURE 5.5 Types of sukuk

Sukuk Murabaha

Murabaha is when an asset is sold at cost plus a markup that has been agreed to by both the buyer and the seller. In sukuk murabaha, the originator (or the SPV) will issue the sukuk certificates and the proceeds will be used to buy assets. Thus, sukuk holders will have ownership interests in the assets bought. These assets will then be sold at cost plus markup. Buyers of these assets will pay on an instalment basis, and such payments will be paid to sukuk holders after deducting relevant expenses of the transaction.

Sukuk Ijarah

Ijarah is similar to a conventional lease. In sukuk ijarah, the assets to be leased or the right to use specific assets (the usufruct) are transferred from the originator to the SPV. Investors then purchase sukuk certificates from the SPV. This gives the investors the right of ownership in the assets or the usufruct that were transferred. The SPV would subsequently lease the underlying assets to a lessor. As the lessor makes scheduled lease payments, such payments are distributed to the sukuk holders. The payment to sukuk holders can be immediate (i.e. upon receipt of monies from lessor) or at scheduled intervals.

Sukuk Salam

Salam is a contract of sale where payment is immediate upon the conclusion of the sale contract but the goods are delivered at a future predetermined date. The seller issues sukuk certificates for cash. Such certificates represent ownership of the goods that will be delivered.

Sukuk Istisna

Istisna is a contractual agreement to manufacture goods where the purchase price can be deferred. The manufacturer of the goods would then issue sukuk certificates. Such certificates represent ownership interests in the goods that will be manufactured. At the time the goods are delivered, sukuk holders would own their respective portion of those goods. These may be sold by the SPV, and the proceeds would then be given to sukuk holders. Sukuk istisna can also be used as a financing facility for the construction of roads and buildings.

Note that in both sukuk salam and sukuk istisna, the sukuk certificates can neither be sold nor traded before their maturity date. Accordingly, these sukuk are treated as investments held to maturity by the sukuk holders.

ACCOUNTING FOR SUKUK

In order to understand the accounting for sukuk, the discussion will focus on sukuk ijarah. Additionally, let us assume that the sukuk were issued through an SPV and the originator owns an office building. As explained next, there are differences as to how sukuk are accounted for under IFRS and AAOIFI standards.

ACCOUNTING FOR SUKUK UNDER IFRS

The Originator

The originator is the party that requires funds. In the books of the originator (and assuming that IFRS is adopted), the sukuk transaction is regarded purely as a financing transaction. Thus, the originator would recognise the sukuk as a financial liability and continues to maintain the office building as its fixed asset. This is despite the fact that the originator is no longer the owner of the building since it has sold the building to the SPV (for sukuk issuance through an SPV). The emphasis of IFRS is the economic substance of the transactions. Thus, the originator cannot derecognise the asset (the office building).

The SPV

In the case of sukuk issued through an SPV, the SPV is merely a trustee. Thus, the legal title to the building is held by the SPV while the originator retains the beneficial interest. Given this, when the asset is sold, the cash flows arising from it are not shown on the SPV's statement of financial position. The SPV is accountable only for its trusteeship fee and its own operating expenses. Essentially, although owned by the SPV, the building is held in trust for the sukuk investors. Thus, the asset is neither included as an asset nor the sukuk recorded as a liability in the statement of financial position of the SPV.

The Sukuk Holder (Investor)

Under IFRS 139, sukuk will be treated as an investment categorized as follows (Figure 5.6):

- Investments: Held for trading
- Investments: Available for sale
- Investments: Held to maturity

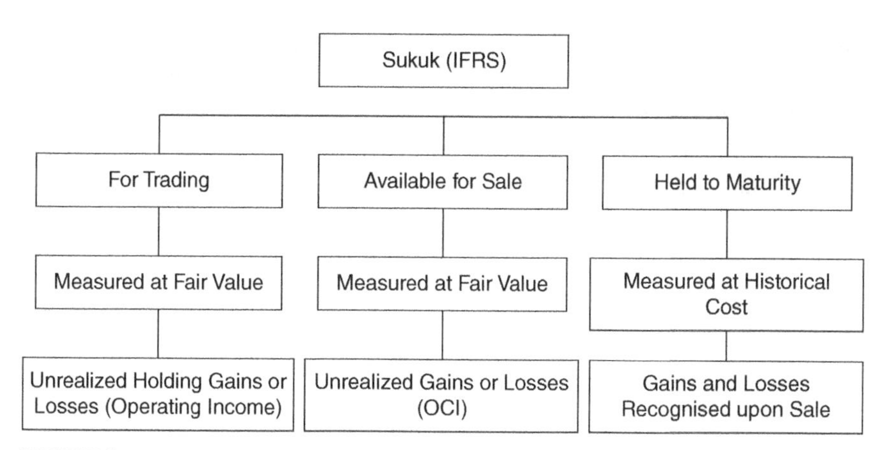

FIGURE 5.6 Categories of sukuk under IFRS

Held for Trading Held-for-trading investments are sukuk held by a company for a short period of time. These sukuk are primarily bought and sold for short-term gains and are reported at their fair-market value at the end of the financial period. Gains and losses will be included in the 'unrealized holding gains or losses' in the income statement.

Available for Sale This is generally regarded as a default category. The primary difference between trading investments and available-for-sale investments is the changes in value of the sukuk. As indicated earlier, the changes in value of the former are dealt with in the operating income, while the changes in value of the latter are accounted for in 'other comprehensive income' (OCI). Thus, the unrealized gains or losses in OCI are the short-term available-for-sale fair-market adjustment.

Held to Maturity These are investments held by a company that intends to hold the investments to maturity. Such sukuk will be recorded at cost. Gains or losses are only recognised when the company sells the securities. Held-to-maturity investments in the case of sukuk are usually sukuk salam and sukuk istisna. These certificates are only redeemed upon maturity.

ACCOUNTING FOR SUKUK UNDER AAOIFI

The Originator

Under AAOIFI, the originator will record the sale of the asset and will also record the annual lease rental. Thus, the originator does not record any financial liability for the sukuk issued by the SPV. Finally, at the end of the maturity period, the originator records the repurchase of the asset as an acquisition of a new asset.

Sale and Lease Back

It is important to note that AAOIFI in its Sharia standard on sukuk specifically addresses the issue of buyback as follows:

> *It is permissible for a lessee in a Sukuk al-Ijarah to undertake to purchase the leased assets when the Sukuk are extinguished for its nominal value, provided he (lessee) is not also a partner, Mudarib, or investment agent.*

It is for this reason that most sukuk use the sukuk ijarah structure. This is primarily because sukuk ijarah allow the guarantee of a fixed predetermined return to the sukuk investors, provided the originator remains solvent to honour its obligations (i.e. to pay the lease rental and to repurchase the building on maturity date).

While AAOIFI has a Sharia standard on sukuk, it has not promulgated a specific standard on the accounting for sukuk. There was no discussion on the overriding concept of substance in both the *Statement of Financial Accounting No. 1: Objectives of Financial Accounting* and *Statement of Financial Accounting No. 2 (Amended): Concepts of Financial Accounting*. In 2010, when AAOIFI redrafted and combined the two statements, it emphasised both the substance as well as the legal form of the contract.

The Central Bank of Malaysia's Sharia Advisory Council's (SAC) stand is similar. The SAC states that 'substance' and 'form' are equally important. Further, 'substance' and 'form' must be consistent and shall not contradict one another. Should there be an inconsistency, the Sharia ruling prevails. Further, according to the SAC, Sharia places greater importance on substance rather than form.

The Sukuk Holder (Investor)

Sukuk are classified into three broad categories under AAOIFI's FAS No. 17. Sukuk are grouped as follows:

- For trading
- Available for sale
- Held to maturity

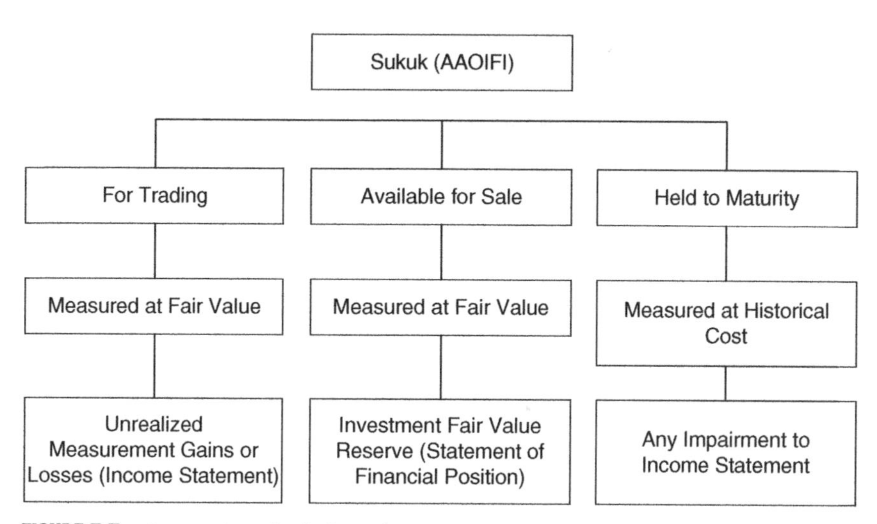

FIGURE 5.7 Categories of sukuk under AAOIFI

AAOIFI's classification is based on the well-known Sharia classification of trade and commodities for the purpose of zakat. Sukuk held for trading are acquired for the primary purpose of generating a profit from short-term fluctuations in price. Sukuk held to maturity are those investments an institution has the positive intent and ability to hold to maturity. Available-for-sale sukuk are those not in the two categories just described. Accordingly, these investments are neither held for trading nor held to maturity. The definition of each class of sukuk is similar to the definition under IFRS on investments.

At the end of each accounting period, sukuk held for trading and available for sale shall be revalued to fair value. The unrealised gains or losses on sukuk held for trading will be recognised in the income statement as 'unrealized remeasurement gains or losses' while the remeasurement at fair value of investments for 'available for sale' sukuk must be recognised in the statement of financial position under the 'investment fair value reserve'. However, sukuk held to maturity are measured at historical cost, unless there is a permanent impairment in value. If there is impairment, the difference shall be recognised in the income statement.

For disclosure, the value of sukuk, the percentage of sukuk acquired from each party issuing the sukuk, the type of sukuk (if material), the party guaranteeing the sukuk and the nature of guarantee, the contractual relationship between the issuer and the holders of a particular sukuk, and the classification of sukuk according to its maturity are all pertinent. Figure 5.8 summarizes the disclosure requirements.

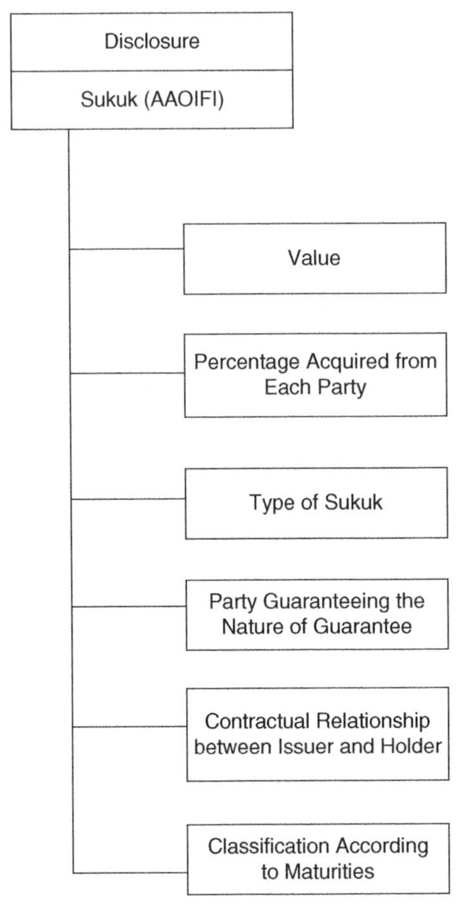

FIGURE 5.8 Disclosure of sukuk

WORKED EXAMPLE: SUKUK IJARA

The statement of financial position of Alif Enterprise (AE) for the year ended December 31, 2018, is as follows:

Assets	
Buildings	\$100 million
Cash	\$ 50 million
Financed by	
Share capital	\$120 million
Retained earnings	\$ 30 million

AE needs $100 million to finance its activities and wants to raise funds through issuing sukuk ijara. On January 1, 2019, AE sets up a special-purpose vehicle (SPV) and sells its office buildings to the SPV for $100 million.

The SPV then issues $100 million sukuk to investors (sukuk holders) and holds the office building in trust for sukuk holders. AE agrees to buy back the office building at $110 million on December 31, 2023. The SPV leases the office building to AE for $5 million annually.

AE makes a profit of $40 million each year. Assume all transactions are on a cash basis.

Required:

PART A: Discuss and describe with a diagram the process flow of the sukuk issuance.

PART B: Account for sukuk under IFRS in the books of the originator (AE).

PART C: Account for sukuk under AAOIFI's FAS in the books of the originator (AE).

PART A: The Process Flow

Essentially, ALIF ENTERPRISE needs to manage its liquidity by selling its office building to the SPV. It then leases it back from the SPV and promises to repurchase the building 5 years later. The SPV issued sukuk to investors or sukuk holders where each sukuk holder has a partial ownership in that particular office building. This is primarily why the term *asset-backed* sukuk is used. In other words, the sukuk holders' investment can be identified to the office building in AE.

AE received $100 million on the sale of the office buildings and will then pay a lease rental to the SPV of $5 million per annum. In 5 years' time, AE would pay the SPV $110 million to repurchase the office buildings.

The repurchase price of $110 million is fixed regardless of whether the value of the building changes. Thus, AE is fully exposed to all changes in the economic value of the building. Meanwhile, the sukuk holders are entitled to the $5 million of lease rental after deducting the trusteeship fee to the SPV for undertaking this trusteeship. The SPV would also charge its operating expenses against the rental income.

The preceding discussion would be clearer with a diagrammatic presentation of the process (Figure 5.9).

The following is the explanation of the complete process.

1. On January 1, 2019, AE (the originator) transfers the ownership of the office building to a special-purpose vehicle (SPV) for $100 million.

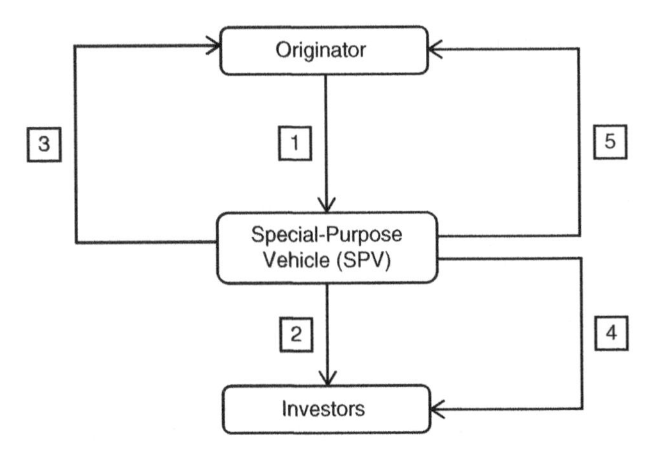

FIGURE 5.9 The process flow

2. The SPV issues sukuk certificates to investors at par value in an amount equal to the purchase price ($100 million). The sukuk holders thus acquire a beneficial interest in the office building of AE.

3a. The SPV leases the asset back to AE.

3b. AE pays periodic lease rentals to the SPV.

4. The SPV collects the lease rentals and distributes the amount to sukuk holders.
5. On December 31, 2023 (the maturity date), the SPV sells the assets to the originator for $110 million. This value was predetermined earlier at the point when the building was sold to the SPV. The SPV then distributes the amount to sukuk holders.

PART B: Accounting for Sukuk under IFRS

Given that the transaction is a financing transaction, the first step is to calculate the cost of finance (finance expense).

The total cost of financing will have to be spread over the 5 years. Over the 5 years, AE will be paying rental of $5 million a year and at the end of the period will pay another $10 million, thus giving a total of $35 million.

Given the annual interest of 5% and sukuk to be repaid in 5 years at $110 million, the internal rate of return on the loan is about 6.7477%[1].

Thus, Table 5.2 is relevant.

Tables 5.3 to 5.5 show the books of the originator (AE).

[1]This can be calculated using EXCEL or the financial calculator (see last page of chapter).

TABLE 5.2 Financing Cost over 5 Years

Year	Sukuk liability b/f	Finance expense on opening balance at approximately 6.7477%	Cash paid	Sukuk liability c/f
2011	100.00	6.75	5.00	101.75
2012	101.75	6.87	5.00	103.62
2013	103.62	6.99	5.00	105.61
2014	105.61	7.13	5.00	107.74
2015	107.74	7.26	5.00	110.00

TABLE 5.3 Journal Entries

Date	Entry	Amount
Jan. 1, 2019	DR Cash	100
	CR Sukuk	100
	Amount of financing raised through sukuk	
Dec. 31, 2019	DR Finance Expense	6.75
	CR Cash	5
	CR Sukuk	1.75
	Finance expense for the period	
Dec. 31, 2020	DR Finance Expense	6.87
	CR Cash	5
	CR Sukuk	1.87
	Finance expense for the period	
Dec. 31, 2021	DR Finance Expense	6.99
	CR Cash	5
	CR Sukuk	1.99
	Finance expense for the period	
Dec. 31, 2022	DR Finance Expense	7.13
	CR Cash	5
	CR Sukuk	2.13
	Finance expense for the period	
Dec. 31, 2023	DR Finance Expense	7.26
	CR Cash	5
	CR Sukuk	2.26
	Finance expense for the period	
	DR Sukuk	110
	CR Cash	110
	Redemption of sukuk	

TABLE 5.4 Income Statement of AE

Year to Dec. 31	2019	2020	2021	2022	2023
Op income	40.00	40.00	40.00	40.00	40.00
Financing expense	(6.75)	(6.87)	(6.99)	(7.13)	(7.26)
Net income	33.25	33.13	33.01	32.87	32.74

TABLE 5.5 Statement of Financial Position of AE

As of Dec. 31	2019	2020	2021	2022	2023
Building	100.00	100.00	100.00	100.00	100.00
Cash	185.00[1]	220.00	255.00	290.00	215.00
Total assets	285.00	320.00	355.00	390.00	315.00
Financed by:					
Share capital	120.00	120.00	120.00	120.00	120.00
Retained earnings	63.25[2]	96.38	129.39	162.26	195.00
Sukuk	101.75	103.62	105.61	107.74	—
Total	285.00	320.00	355.00	390.00	315.00

[1] 50 + 100 + 40 − 5 = 185
[2] 30 + 33.25 = 63.25

Notes to the Accounts On January 1, 2019, ALIF ENTERPRISE entered into a sukuk financing transaction by selling the building to an SPV for $100 million and subsequently leasing it back for 5 years at an annual rent of $5 million. ALIF ENTERPRISE will repurchase the building for $110 million on December 31, 2023, and because it retains all of the related risks and rewards, the transaction has been accounted for as a financing transaction. Thus, the building would not be derecognised from ALIF ENTERPRISE's statement of financial position. The effective cost of finance under the sukuk transaction is approximately 6.7477%.

Discussion: True and Fair View? Under IFRS, the originator of the sukuk would treat the transaction as if it was a bond issue. This is primarily because both the bond issue and the sukuk issue have the same economic consequences, and accordingly are given identical accounting treatment. The objective of the IFRS is to reflect on the economic substance of the transactions undertaken.

The notes to the financial statements regarding the issue of the sukuk are highly pertinent. ALIF ENTERPRISE provides the details of the sukuk issuance in the notes so that stakeholders know that although the office building is accounted for in the statement of financial position, the legal title to the asset is not with ALIF ENTERPRISE.

One question that has often been raised is whether reflecting the office building as the asset of ALIF ENTERPRISE is regarded as a misrepresentation of the truth. If one follows the *substance over form* argument, reflecting sukuk issuance as a bond issuance may well be apropriate. However, some may regard this as not reflecting the true state of affairs of ALIF ENTERPRISE, and this may be tantamount to a misrepresentation.

PART C: Under AAOIFI's Standard

Under AAOIFI, AE records the sale of the building for $100 million on January 1, 2019. AE also records the lease rental of $5 million annually. Note that AE does not record any financial liability for the sukuk issued by the SPV. Finally, at the end of the maturity period, AE records the repurchase of the building for $110 million on December 31, 2023, as an acquisition of a new asset.

Tables 5.6 to 5.8 show the books of the originator (AE).

TABLE 5.6 Journal Entries

1 Jan. 19	DR Cash	100
	CR Asset	100
	Disposal of asset to SPV	
31 Dec. 19	DR Lease	5
	CR Cash	5
	Lease rental to SPV	
31 Dec. 20	DR Lease	5
	CR Cash	5
	Lease rental to SPV	
31 Dec. 21	DR Lease	5
	CR Cash	5
	Lease rental to SPV	
31 Dec. 22	DR Lease	5
	CR Cash	5
	Lease rental to SPV	
31 Dec. 23	DR Lease	5
	CR Cash	5
	Lease rental to SPV	
	DR Asset	110
	CR Cash	110
	Purchase of asset from SPV	

TABLE 5.7 Income Statement of AE

Year to Dec. 31	2011	2012	2013	2014	2015
Op income	40.00	40.00	40.00	40.00	40.00
Lease rental	(5.00)	(5.00)	(5.00)	(5.00)	(5.00)
Net income	35.00	35.00	35.00	35.00	35.00

TABLE 5.8 Statement of Financial Position of AE

As of Dec. 31	2019	2020	2021	2022	2023
Building	—	—	—	—	110.00
Cash	185.00	220.00	255.00	290.00	215.00
Total assets	185.00	220.00	255.00	290.00	325.00
Financed by:					
Shareholders' equity	120.00	120.00	120.00	120.00	120.00
Retained earnings	65.00	100.00	135.00	170.00	205.00
Total	185.00	220.00	255.00	290.00	325.00

Notes to the Accounts When the buildings were sold on December 31, 2023, the entire sale proceeds of $110 million were distributed to the sukuk holders as the sukuk were redeemed on that date.

The SPV Regarding the sukuk financing transaction initiated by ALIF ENTERPRISE, the SPV acts as a trustee. Within such a transaction, legal title to the building is held by the SPV in trust, while the originator, ALIF ENTERPRISE, retains beneficial interest. As the SPV acts only as a trustee, its statement of financial position would not indicate the building and the cash flows arising from it. The SPV is thus accountable only for its trusteeship fee and its own operating expenses and dividends paid to its own shareholders.

Note that although the SPV owns the building, it is held in trust for the sukuk investors. Thus, the building is not included as an asset and the sukuk is also not recorded as a liability in the statement of financial position of the SPV. Accounting for SPVs is beyond the scope of this book.

CONCLUSION

The chapter discussed sukuk as a form of financing, distinguishing sukuk from conventional bonds. The various sukuk structures were discussed and the differences between asset-backed and asset-based sukuk were articulated. Finally, using both the International Financial Reporting Standards (IFRS) and the standards developed by the Accounting and Auditing Organization for Islamic Financial Institutions (AAOIFI), the accounting for sukuk was explained and demonstrated.

VOCABULARY

AAOIFI
asset-backed
asset-based
derecognised
IFRS
originator
sale and lease back
special-purpose vehicle (SPV)
sukuk ijara
sukuk istisna
sukuk mudaraba
sukuk murabaha
sukuk salam

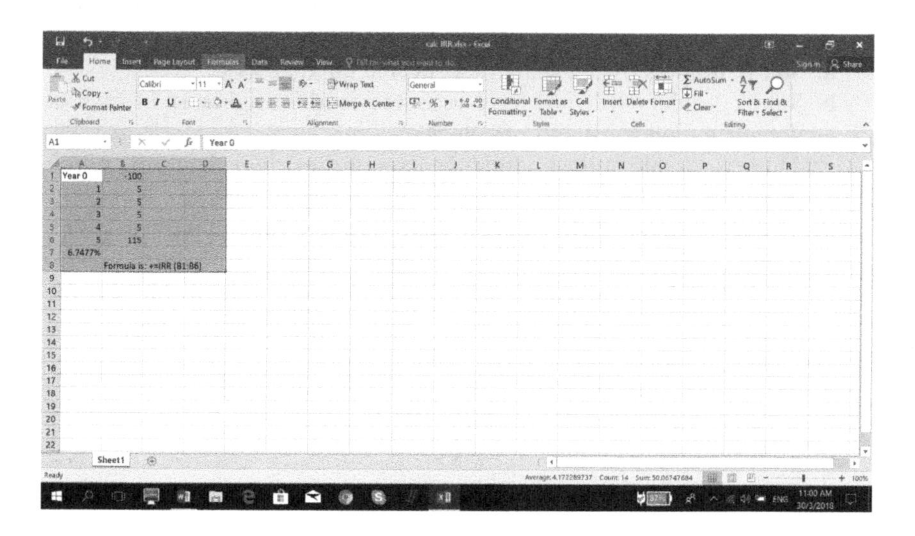

MULTIPLE-CHOICE QUESTIONS

1. Which of the following statement(s) is (are) TRUE?
   I. Sukuk are debt obligations due from the issuer to the investors.
   II. Sukuk are trust certificates.
   III. Sale of sukuk is basically the sale of a debt.
   IV. Funds raised using sukuk can be used for any purpose.
   V. Sale of sukuk represents sale of a share of a specified asset.
   a. I and II
   b. II and V
   c. II and III
   d. I and IV
2. Which of the following is (are) TRUE about an asset-based sukuk?
   I. It is when sukuk holders own a share of a specific tangible asset of the business.
   II. It is when sukuk holders will not have recourse to the originator in case of default in dividends and/or principal.
   III. It is structured to replicate conventional bonds.
   IV. It focuses on the risks of the assets.
   V. It is when sukuk holders will have full recourse to the originator.
   a. I and II
   b. II and III
   c. III and V
   d. III and IV
3. Which of the following is NOT a characteristic of an asset-backed sukuk?
   a. Sukuk holders own a share of a specific tangible asset.
   b. Sukuk holders will not have recourse to the originator in case of default in dividends and principal.
   c. There is no sale of the underlying asset of the originator to the sukuk holders.
   d. The bankruptcy of the originator will not have any impact on sukuk holders' rights to the cash flows from the asset.
4. Under AAOIFI, at the end of an accounting period, available for sale sukuk will be valued at its fair value. The unrealised gains or losses from the remeasurement will be recognised
   a. in the operating income.
   b. in 'other comprehensive income' (OCI).
   c. in 'investment fair value reserve'.
   d. in the statement of financial position.
   e. as an off-balance-sheet item.

5. Under IFRS, at the end of an accounting period, held-for-trading sukuk will be valued at its fair value. The unrealised gains or losses from the remeasurement will be recognised
   a. in the operating income.
   b. in 'other comprehensive income' (OCI).
   c. in 'investment fair value reserve'.
   d. in the statement of financial position.
   e. as an off-balance-sheet item.

DISCUSSION QUESTIONS

1. Define sukuk.
2. Why are sukuk becoming an increasingly important source of financing for companies? Discuss.
3. What are the differences between sukuk and bonds?
4. Mr Alex Lim, your neighbor who works in a conventional bank, wants to know what is meant by asset-backed and asset-based sukuk. According to him, a well-known Sharia scholar has always maintained that 85% of the sukuk issued throughout the world are non–Sharia-compliant. Discuss.
5. There are various types of sukuk structures. List and explain four of these.
6. The process of structuring sukuk requires a basic knowledge of the major Islamic finance products such as mudaraba, musharaka, ijarah, murabaha, and istisna. Discuss.

EXERCISES

1. LBJ Enterprise, a Malaysian-based company, requires $150 million for its expansion project in Indonesia. At its recent board meeting, the chairman proposed that the funds should be raised through issuing sukuk ijarah using an SPV. On January 1, 2020, LBJ sets up an SPV and sells its office building to the SPV for $150 million. The sukuk is for 5 years.

   The SPV then issued $150 million worth of sukuk to investors (sukuk holders) and holds the office building in trust for sukuk holders. LBJ agrees to buy back the office building at $175 million 5 years from the date the sukuk were issued. The SPV then leases the office building to LBJ for $5 million annually.

You are to assume the following:

- LBJ makes a profit of $200 million annually.

For each of the 5 years and using IFRS, you are required to provide the following:

a. The accounting entries in the books of LBJ
b. The income statement and the statement of financial position of LBJ

2. Using the information in Question 1, and on the basis of AAOIFI's standard on investments, you are required to provide (for each of the 5 years) the following:
   a. The accounting entries in the books of LBJ
   b. The income statement and the statement of financial position of LBJ
3. EXE Company purchased ijarah sukuk with a face value of $1,000 amounting to RM1 million on March 1, 2019, and classified it as '$1 million held for trading'. On December 31, 2019, the sukuk was quoted at $950. The rental income was 10% per year.

On the basis of AAOIFI FAS 17, you are required to:

a. Journalise all relevant transactions.
b. Show the extract of income statement for the year ended December 31, 2019.
c. Show the extract of the statement of financial position as at December 31, 2019.
d. Assume that EXE now regards the sukuk as 'available for sale'. How would the accounting entries differ?

4. AB Company invested in the following sukuk issued by the following companies:

	Cinetron Inc. (*Musharaka Sukuk*)	LimaTenzing Co. (*Ijarah Sukuk*)
Acquisition date	1 January 2014	1 January 2014
Types	Held-to-maturity	Held-to-maturity
Acquisition price per unit	$15	$12
Quantity	700,000 units	1,500,000 units
Maturity date	31 December 2020	31 Dec. 2019

Required:

a. Prepare journal entries to recognise the investment in sukuk in accordance with the requirements of AAOIFI FAS 17. The profit realised for sukuk invested in Lima Tenzing Co. on December 31, 2019, is $3 per unit.
b. Prepare the Investment in Fair Value Reserve account as at December 31, 2019.

ARAB Islamic bank has the following investments in sukuk:

Investments	January 1, 2019, acquisition cost $	December 31, 2019, fair value $
Sukuk I (held to maturity) – maturity date Dec. 31, 2020	120,000	120,000
Sukuk II (held to maturity) – maturity date Dec. 31, 2019	200,000	300,000
Sukuk III (held for trading)	250,000	265,000
Sukuk IV (available for sale)	2,000,000	2,750,000

Additional information:

Both Sukuk I and II pay an annual return of 5%. This income was not received by the bank at year-end.

For Sukuk III and IV, the bank received income as follows:

Sukuk III (held for trading)	$25,000
Sukuk IV (available for sale)	$40,000

Required:

a. Explain clearly what is meant by the terms *held to maturity, available for sale,* and *held for trading.*
b. Following the rules set out in FAS No. 17, record the journal entries for the sukuk held by Arab Islamic Bank during 2019.

CHAPTER 6

Accounting for Zakat

Learning Outcomes

At the end of this chapter, you will be able to:

1. Demonstrate an understanding of the concept, principles, and objectives of zakat.
2. Discuss the basic fiqh (jurisprudence) rules of zakat.
3. Calculate zakat base using both the net assets method and the net invested funds method.
4. Evaluate the different treatment of zakat in the income statement.
5. Understand how zakat is disclosed in the financial statements.

The central features of Islam are its five pillars: The declaration of faith (shahada), daily prayers, the giving of alms (zakat), fasting, and pilgrimage. This chapter focuses on zakat, the third pillar. The rich, endowed with wealth that ultimately belongs to God, have an obligation to spend it in the way of God and to redress any social injustice. This entails giving the poorer members of society some part of what is in excess of their needs. Zakat is essentially a tax that every Muslim whose wealth exceeds a certain nisab (minimum amount) has to pay. Accordingly, zakat may be regarded as a social security system in Islam. Further, zakat means purification and growth as it washes away the greed and the acquisitive orientation of the rich. Most important, Muslims believe that the giving of alms will not reduce one's wealth; if at all, it will increase one's riches further.

The following verse in the Quran attests to this:

> *The parable of those who spend their substance in the way of God is that of a grain of corn: it grows seven ears, and each ear has a hundred grains. God gives manifold increase to whom He pleases: and God cares for all and He knows all things (2:261).*

ZAKAT AND CHARITY

It is important to note that zakat is not charity. Charitable donations are voluntary, whereas zakat is a compulsory levy on wealth and income, once it exceeds a certain threshold (nisab). Charitable donations (sadaqah) can be given to any person.

On the other hand, the Quran is specific on whom the zakat beneficiaries are. The following eight categories (asnafs) are those allowed to receive zakat.

1. The poor
2. The needy
3. The amil (those employed to administer the funds)
4. Those whose hearts have been (recently) reconciled (to the truth)
5. Those in bondage
6. Those in debt
7. Those who fight for the cause of Allah
8. The wayfarer

Although sadaqah and zakat have different conditions of collection and distribution, most have regarded zakat as similar to charity.

ZAKAT AND TAX

In some countries, Muslims pay zakat as well as tax on their income. Tax is a fee levied by a government on a product or income in order to finance government expenditure on public goods and services. Accordingly, an individual or a corporation has to pay tax on the annual gains derived through work, business, investment, and other services. While zakat is obligatory on Muslims, as this is their obligation to God, income tax is a civil obligation as a citizen of a country. Failure to pay zakat is a debt to God and this debt is due forever until fully paid. Failure to pay tax will incur monetary penalty as well as a possible jail term for the defaulter.

The payment of tax does not discharge the duty to pay zakat. Moreover, tax is not deducted from the amount of zakat due. In some jurisdictions such as Malaysia, the amount of zakat paid by an individual to authorised collection centres can be deducted as a rebate from the income tax payable.

SOURCES OF ZAKAT

Typically, there are four main sources of zakat: Gold and silver, livestock, agricultural produce, and inventory. For each source, there are further detailed fiqh rules that vary amongst the schools of thought[1]. Gold and silver may also include cash and bank account balances as well as financial papers. For livestock, only cattle, sheep, goats, and camels are zakatable. Chickens, ostrich, and rabbits are not. Staple crops such as wheat and rice are liable for zakat but not cash crops such as rubber, cocoa, and palm oil.

The working capital of a business such as inventory, receivables, cash, and cash equivalents are also liable for zakat. Given that the focus of this book is on business zakat, the importance of the concept of 'working capital' in determining zakat is pertinent. This will be explained later.

The rate of zakat varies, depending on the category of wealth. For gold, silver, and profits on trade, the percentage is 2.5%. The same rate applies to assets consisting of cattle and other domestic animals. The rate for zakat on agricultural and farming produce is 10% if the land is irrigated by natural means (i.e. rain) but 5% if it is irrigated through artificial means requiring extra effort by the owner. If a mine or a treasure-trove is discovered, either by individuals or the state, the rate is 20%.

LIABILITY FOR ZAKAT

The Sharia specifies that liability for zakat falls solely on individuals. Accordingly, the issue of whether a company should pay zakat has generated considerable debate in the Islamic jurist community. The issue was resolved at the Zakat conference in Kuwait in 1985. At that conference, it was agreed that companies should pay zakat. Further, in the case of a company considered as a separate legal entity, the company's net current assets should be the basis for determining zakat. Specifically, companies have to pay zakat in the following cases:

1. The law requires the company to satisfy the zakat obligations as an entity.
2. The company is required by its charter or bylaws to satisfy the zakat obligation as an entity.

---

[1]The four schools of thought refer to the Shafie, Maliki, Hanafi, and Hanbali schools.

3. The general assembly of shareholders passes a resolution requiring the company to satisfy the zakat obligation as an entity.
4. Individual owners authorise the company to act as their agent satisfying the zakat obligation (SFAC 1, p. 29).

The Prophet did not approve the private dispensation of zakat as an individual should not be placed in a very embarrassing situation when receiving zakat from private citizens. Thus, on the one hand, the act of personally giving to a needy person will strengthen the bonds of brotherhood, but on the other, if such an act would put the receiver in a very uncomfortable position, the practice should not be undertaken. This is primarily because the giving and receipt of zakat must be accompanied with discretion and dignity. It is for this reason that the administration, collection, and disbursement of zakat by the state are advocated. Another reason is to prevent a situation where a giver cannot find a person in need of the zakat, mainly because a particular area has a large number of rich people who themselves are paying zakat. These situations justify the crucial role of government in an Islamic society. It is to safeguard the general interest of society against undue harm that the state has the authority to interfere.

DETERMINATION OF WEALTH FOR ZAKAT

Irrespective of whether a business has earned a profit, zakat is payable on its wealth. Zakat is, however, payable only on 'growing' capital, where 'growth' is defined as the realised and unrealised gains on fixed and current assets. This has led to the frequent suggestion that in an accounting system based on zakat, the significance of real assets should be emphasised. Accordingly, all transactions should be analysed in terms of their effect on assets, liabilities, and owners' equity, thus shifting the focus from a revenue expense approach to an asset-liability approach for income measurement purposes. In this way, the statement of financial position would become the main source of accounting information for determining zakat.

Wealth that is subject to zakat is classified into two categories of assets: capital assets and stock of inventories. In general, capital assets are fixed assets of a business such as tools and machinery, whilst stock of inventories (current assets) are for resale. Zakat is payable on cash, inventory, receivables, and marketable securities less all liabilities related to these items. Zakat is thus payable on net working capital. Both the realised and unrealised gains on current assets are liable for zakat. However, for distribution purposes, only realised gains on fixed and current assets can be distributed as dividends on the basis that further distributions would diminish the firm's ability to serve the community in future.

GENERAL CONDITIONS FOR LIABILITY TO ZAKAT

Essentially, assets would only be liable for zakat if the following conditions are satisfied:

1. Ownership is complete and the asset is either in the owner's possession without any restriction or it is held by another person but is under the owner's control.
2. The asset is growing or subject to growing.
3. The asset exceeds a minimum amount (nisab).
4. The asset exceeds basic personal and trade needs.
5. The asset is free of debt.
6. The asset has been held for one year.

Unencumbered Possession

The possession or ownership of the asset must be complete. Thus, the owner must possess the physical asset along with the ability to manage the assets. In other words, the owner must have control over the property, especially the power of disposal. Incomplete ownership may arise in two ways. A house that one owns but is being rented out would mean that one has the ownership but not the usufruct. Alternatively, one may have the usufruct but not ownership if a machine is leased from a third party.

Capable of Growth or Increase

As stated earlier, zakat is based on net working capital. It is important here to differentiate between the accounting concept of working capital and the theological concept of growing capital. Only in two situations may 'growing' capital be equal to net working capital. The first situation is when there is no long-term debt financing any current assets, and the second is when there is no short-term debt financing any fixed assets. However, such situations are rare because financing assets in this manner is perceived to involve a lack of prudence. Consequently, zakat is usually computed on net working capital.

Nisab

Nisab is the threshold beyond which zakat becomes payable. If the zakatable assets are less than the nisab, zakat is not payable. The nisab differs for different sources of zakat. For gold, silver, cash, and business working capital, the nisab is the monetary equivalent of 85 grams of gold or 595 grams of silver for each individual or company.

Exceeding Basic Personal or Trade Needs

What is deemed sufficient for basic needs differs between individuals and between businesses. This is where the spiritual and ethical dimensions come into play. Islam emphasises that in any action it is the individual's nobility of feelings, loftiness of objectives, and purity of intentions that are most important. Further, since Muslims regard all wealth as ultimately belonging to God, it is taken for granted that devout followers of Islam would naturally avoid understating their wealth to minimize the zakat they pay.

Free of Debt

The basic principle is that assets for which zakat are to be paid should be free from debts. Accordingly, if one has an asset that is worth $5,000 and there is a debt of $2,000 still outstanding on that asset, then the amount that is zakatable is only $3,000.

Haul and Zakat Rates

Haul is the fiscal period of zakat, which is one lunar year (354 days). Generally, Muslims pay their zakat in Ramadan (the fasting month) to obtain additional rewards from Allah. Businesses such as Islamic financial institutions, however, follow the Gregorian calendar, which follows the solar year. This is longer, at 365 or 366 days. Given that this is longer by 11 days, the rate for zakat is 2.5775% per solar year (365/354 × 2/5%). The rate, if companies follow the lunar year, is only 2.5%. Although it would be good for Islamic identity to follow the lunar year, companies are permitted to follow the Gregorian calendar.

The chapter focuses only on the calculation of zakat for companies. Accordingly, there are various other specific conditions that must be met by *trading* assets before zakat is due on such assets. These are discussed next.

SPECIFIC CONDITIONS OF ZAKAT ON TRADING ASSETS

Trading assets are only liable for zakat if these assets fulfil further conditions. Trading assets include items bought for resale as well as raw materials purchased for manufacturing and subsequent resale. In general, trading assets are acquired by way of purchase or exchange, or by way of discharge of a debt. Assets acquired by way of inheritance or donation would not be considered as trading assets. Such assets when sold for cash will give rise to a liability for zakat on the cash proceeds.

Intention to Trade

This means an intention to trade in the assets once these assets are acquired. The intention that matters is that the trading assets should become part of the assets held by the business.

Current Assets

Accounts Receivable Zakat is obligatory on accounts receivable. It is also obligatory if the debtors refuse to acknowledge the accounts receivable but there is evidence that these are due and collectible. If the debts are doubtful (either because the debtor refuses to acknowledge them and there is insufficient evidence to prove their existence, or because the debtor is insolvent or a procrastinator), zakat is payable only on the amount of the debt recovered when it is collected.

Accounts receivable must be after deducting bad debts and specific provision for doubtful debts. A general provision that is randomly based on percentage in the 'aging' debtors schedule is not deducted.

Inventory Zakat is to be paid on finished goods or on assets that are purchased for resale. Raw materials are not zakatable, as they are not in a tradable condition. Work-in-progress items are also not zakatable, as they are not in a tradable condition.

Prepaid Expenses Prepaid expenses are not zakatable, as these amounts are not under the full control of the business. The company does not have complete ownership of this asset.

Equity Investments: Trading Securities Equity investments are classified as trading securities or available-for-sale securities according to the company's intention as to the length of time it will hold each investment. Trading securities are those investments bought for the purpose of selling them within a short period of their purchase. These investments are considered *short-term* assets and are liable for zakat. However, *available-for-sale* equity investments are not liable for zakat (see explanation later in this chapter).

Dividends Receivable Only dividends received are zakatable. Dividends receivable are not zakatable.

Current Liabilities

Trade Creditors All trade creditors are deducted from current assets, as the liability arises out of trading operations.

Accruals Liability for normal operating expenses as in wages payable and utilities are also deductible. The basic rule is that only liabilities that are due in the year following the date of the financial statement (i.e. current liabilities) are deductible.

Tax Tax payable on the current year's tax may be deducted. Accumulated unpaid tax from previous years is not allowed because it should have been considered in the year it was incurred. The fact that the company has not paid the previous year's outstanding amount is irrelevant because the company may have used the money meant for tax for its own benefit and delayed paying the tax. Thus, any deferred tax liabilities should include only the current year's amount.

Others

Public Funds There is no zakat on public funds, or funds held for waqf (endowment) and charitable purposes, funds of charitable oragnizations, and property of nongovernmental organisations. These funds have no specific owner and are designated for spending on causes that benefit society in general. Accordingly, the basic rule is that funds intended for society's benefit are not zakatable. Thus, such amounts have to be excluded from current assets because there is no exact owner.

Unlawful or Suspect Funds (Prohibited Earnings) Unlawful income is not subject to zakat. However, if the income cannot be returned, then zakat has to be paid and the balance must be given to charity. Payments to charity cannot be considered as zakat.

Fixed and Noncurrent Assets

Property, Plant, and Equipment Fixed assets are movable or immovable assets that are not held for trading. Items acquired for use as fixed assets are not subject to zakat. These assets assist the business but are not stock in trade. Accordingly, such fixed assets are not subject to zakat. However, if a fixed asset is subsequently sold, zakat becomes due on the cash proceeds if the nisab is attained and the cash proceeds are still in hand at the end of the haul (the relevant financial year). On the other hand, an asset acquired for trading but subsequently converted to be used as a fixed asset is no longer counted as a trading asset.

Equity Investments: Available for Sale Equity investments not classified as trading securities are categorized as available-for-sale securities. Typically, these investments will not be sold in the near future. Accordingly, such investments will not be liable for zakat but the dividends received from such investments are zakatable.

Valuation of Trading Assets

Trading assets should be valued for zakat purposes at their market-selling price or cash equivalent value (and not at historical cost). This is primarily because the zakat base includes historical cost and any holding gains (losses). It is for this reason that some scholars have advocated the preparation of a current-value balance sheet for businesses operating in an Islamic economic system.

Payment of Zakat in Kind

Normally, zakat on business assets is paid in cash. However, it is permissible to pay in trade goods, especially in times of recession or if there is a lack of liquidity or if it can benefit the zakat beneficiaries.

Gains

Zakat is payable on the balance of each type of working capital at the end of a *haul*, including any gains from employing that type of working capital, such as business profits. This is the opinion of the Hanafis, and this is a safe compromise between the divergent views as to the different times when zakat is due on gains.

METHODS OF COMPUTING ZAKAT

The Accounting and Auditing Organization of Islamic Financial Institutions (AAOIFI), in its standard on Zakat (FAS 9), suggests two primary methods to determine the zakat base:

1. The net assets method
2. The net invested funds method

However, both methods produce the same results due to the equivalence of the assets and the liabilities side of the balance sheet. While the standard focuses on Islamic financial institutions, it can also be applied to other businesses.

The basic accounting equation is as follows:

$$FA + CA = SC + R + LTL + CL$$

Where

FA = Fixed assets
CA = Current assets
CL = Current liabilities
SC = Share capital
R = Reserves
LTL = long-term liabilities

From the above equation, we can derive the following:

$$CA - CL = SC + R + LTL - FA$$

The net assets method focuses on the left-hand side of the equation while the net invested funds method concentrates on the right-hand side of the equation. Thus, the basic calculation is (See Figure 6.1):

$$\text{Net assets} = CA - CL$$

$$\text{Net invested funds} = SC + R + LTL - FA$$

It is important to note that before the zakat base is determined, adjustments must be made for transactions that have not been accounted for in the preparation of the financial statements. For example, if there are bad debts that have not been accounted for, then the bad debts (and hence profit and loss) will be debited while debtors must be credited. Similarly, if there is depreciation that needs to be increased, then depreciation (and hence profit and loss) should be debited with the increase and the provision for

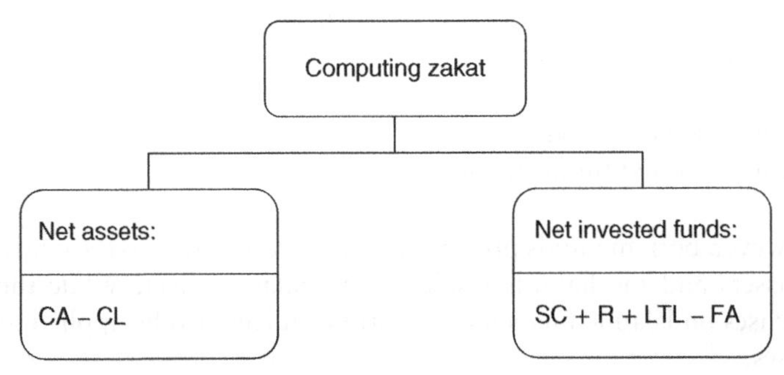

FIGURE 6.1 Computing zakat calculation

TABLE 6.1 Methods to Determine Zakat Base

Method I		Method II	
Net Assets Method		**Net Invested Funds Method**	
Current assets		Share capital	xx
Cash	xx	Reserves	xx
Net receivables	xx	Retained earnings	xx
Inventory (Finished goods)	xx	Net income	xx
Investments: Held for trading	xx	Long-term liabilities	xx
Deposits with other banks	xx		xxxx
	xxxx	LESS:	
LESS :		Net fixed assets	xx
Current liabilities		Investments: Available for sale	xx
Trade creditors	xx	Real estate	
Accruals	xx	Zakatable base (B)	xxxx
Minority Interest	xx		
Equity owned by public endowment	xx		
Equity owned by government	xx		
Equity owned by charities and NGOs	xx		
Zakatable base (A)	XXX		

Note: Zakatable base A should equal to Zakatable base B

depreciation should be credited. It is only after the adjustments have been done that the zakat base is determined (Table 6.1).

TREATMENT OF ZAKAT IN FINANCIAL STATEMENTS

A company, being an artificial entity, need not pay zakat. However, it is obliged to pay zakat in the following cases:

1. When the law requires it to satisfy the zakat obligation.
2. When it is required by its charter or bylaws to pay zakat.
3. When the general assembly of shareholders has passed a resolution requiring the company to satisfy its zakat obligation.

Zakat as an Expense

In the three situations just listed, *zakat* is treated as an expense of the business and is included in the determination of net income. Any unpaid zakat is treated as a liability and presented in the liabilities section of the balance sheet. This treatment complies with the definition of an expense as the gross decrease in assets or increase in liabilities or a combination of both, provided such a decrease in assets and increase in liabilities is not the result of distribution to or investment by shareholders.

Zakat as an Appropriation out of Profits

A company is not obliged to pay zakat as a corporate entity when none of the three conditions have been fulfilled. However, if some or all of the shareholders request the company to act as their agent in meeting the zakat obligation relating to their investment in the company, then the company must deduct zakat from the shareholders' share of distributable profits. Should there be insufficient distributable profits to meet the shareholders' obligations, the amount paid by the company shall be recorded as a receivable due from these shareholders.

Zakat Rate AAOIFI has suggested that if the accounting period is based on the lunar year (the Muslim calendar), the rate should be 2.5%. However, if it is based on the solar year (the Gregorian calendar), the rate should be 2.5775%.

Disclosure Requirements

According to FAS 9 (the standard on zakat developed by AAOIFI), the following should be disclosed in the notes to the financial statements:

1. The *method used* for determining the zakat base and the items included in this base.
2. Whether the company, as a holding company, pays its share of zakat obligations in its subsidiaries.
3. In the case where the company does not pay zakat, the amount of zakat that is due from each share.

The worked examples below illustrates zakat computation for a sole proprietor (Example I) and a company (Example II)

WORKED EXAMPLE I

Alim Inc. is a manufacturer of plastic containers. The statement of financial position as of December 31, 2017, is shown in Table 6.2.

Additional information:

1. The personal drawings of Alim for the year amounted to $20,000.
2. Alim also donated $2,000 to his favourite charity in November.
3. There is obsolete stock amounting to $500.

TABLE 6.2 Statement of Financial Position

	$		$
Current assets		**Current liabilities**	
Cash in hand	3,000	Trade creditors	500
Bank	1,500	Accrued expenses	2,000
Trade debtors	5,000		
Closing stock	4,500		
Work in progress	4,200		
Fixed assets			
Property, plant, and equipment	10,000	Capital	26,700
Real estate investments	10,000	Reserves	12,000
		Profit	3,000
	38,200		38,200

Required:

Determine the zakat payable by Alim.

Solution

Step 1: Calculate the current assets.

	$
Cash in hand	3,000
Bank balance	1,500
Trade debtors	5,000
Closing stock	4,500
Total current assets	14,000

Step 2: Calculate the current liabilities.

	$
Trade creditors	500
Accrued operating expenses	2,000
Total current liabilities	2,500

Step 3: Calculate the net assets (working capital).

Net current assets = 14,000 – 2500 = $11,500

Step 4: Adjustments

	$
Net current assets	11,500
Add/ less adjustments	
Add: Donation in last quarter	2,000
Add: Personal drawings	20,000
Less: Obsolete stock	500
Less: Work in progress	4,200
Net current assets	28,800

Step 5: Calculate the zakat base.

The zakat base is the net current assets after adjustments, and in this example it is $28,800.

Step 6: Multiply the net current assets due for zakat by 2.5%.

$$\text{Zakat payable} = (2.5\% \times 28{,}800) = \$720$$

WORKED EXAMPLE II

Table 6.3 shows the statement of financial position of AM Company as of December 31, 2017.

TABLE 6.3 Statement of Financial Position

	$		$
Current assets		**Current liabilities**	
Accounts receivable	100,000	Accounts payable	60,000
Inventory	70,000	Overdraft	5,000
Prepayments	10,000	Dividend payable	2,000
Cash & bank	54,000	Tax payable	5,000
Dividends receivable	1,000		
		Long-term loan	
		Term loan	200,000
Fixed assets			
Property, plant, and equipment	110,000	Share capital	100,000
Real estate investments	100,000	Reserves	60,000
		Profit	13,000
	445,000		445,000

The following have not been adjusted:

1. Inventory includes work in progress and raw materials valued at $10,000 and $5,000, respectively.
2. Prepayment is related to insurance and road tax.
3. Included in the bank is fixed deposit used to secure financing facility from Bank A amounting to $10,000.
4. Term loan payable during the next year is $25,000. This has not been reclassified.
5. One customer was declared bankrupt. He owed $5,000.

Required:

Calculate zakat payable using:

1. The net assets method
2. The net invested funds method

Solution

Step 1: Journalise the adjustments.

Journal entries for adjustments:

1	DR	Raw Material	10
	DR	Work in Process	5
	CR	Inventory	15

2		All prepayments will not be subject to zakat, as they do not satisfy the 'unencumbered possession'.	

3	DR	Fixed Deposit	10
	CR	Cash and Bank	10

4	DR	Term Loan	25
	CR	Current Liabilities	25

5	DR	Bad Debts (Profit and Loss)	5
	CR	Accounts Receivable	5

Step 2: Net current assets method.

a. Calculate current assets liable for zakat (use all adjusted figures).

Accounts receivable	100,000 – 5,000 =	95,000
Inventory	70,000 – 15,000 =	55,000
Cash & bank bal.	54,000 – 10,000 =	44,000
Total current assets		**194,000**

Note:
i. Dividends receivable are not zakatable.
ii. Prepayments are also not zakatable as company has 'no contro' over the asset.

b. Calculate current liabilities.

Accounts payable	60,000
Overdraft	5,000
Dividend payable	2,000
Tax payable	5,000
Loan payable	25,000
Total current liabilities	**97,000**

c. Compute the zakatable base (CA – CL)

Net assets = 194,000 – 97,000 = 97,000

Step 3: Net invested funds method.

a. Calculate the invested funds.

Term loan	200,000 – 25,000 =	175,000
Share capital		100,000
Reserves		60,000
Profit	13,000 – 5,000 =	8,000
Total invested funds		**343,000**

b. Calculate the fixed assets and other assets not liable for zakat.

Property, plant, and equipment	110,000
Real Estate investments	100,000
Fixed deposit	10,000
Raw materials	10,000
WIP	5,000
Dividends receivable	1,000
Prepayments	10,000
Total deductible assets	**246,000**

Step 4: Calculate the zakatable base (Table 6.4).

Invested funds – Total assets not liable for zakat

= 343,000 – 246,000 = **97,000**

TABLE 6.4 Calculating Zakatable Base

Net assets method	Net invested funds method
Current assets = 194,000	SC + R + PL = 343,000
Current liabilities = 97,000	FA + NCA + Others = 246,000
Net current assets = 97,000	Net invested funds = 97,000

Zakat payable is 2.5% × 97,000 = $2,425.

CONCLUSION

This chapter discusses the definition of *zakat* and the differences between zakat and taxation. The two methods of computing zakat, the net assets, and the net invested funds methods, were also elaborated. Finally, the presentation and disclosure requirements of *zakat* in the financial statements were discussed.

VOCABULARY

appropriation
cash equivalent
charity
disclosure
expense
general conditions
growing assets
net assets method
net invested funds method
prohibited earnings
specific conditions
tax
trading assets
unencumbered possession
unlawful earnings
zakat
zakatable base

MULTIPLE-CHOICE QUESTIONS

1. Which of the following is not a zakat beneficiary?
   I. The wayfarer
   II. The poor
   III. The needy
   IV. The soldiers
   V. The slaves
   a. IV and V
   b. IV only
   c. V only
   d. All are zakat beneficiaries.

2. Companies are obliged to pay zakat if they fulfil any of the following conditions.
   I. If the law is passed requiring the companies to pay zakat
   II. If they have not paid tax
   III. If the articles of association stipulate so
   IV. If the annual general meeting so decides
   a. I, II, III, and IV
   b. I, II, and III
   c. I, II, and IV
   d. I, III, and IV
3. AAOIFI suggests various methods to determine zakat. They include the following:
   I. Net invested funds method
   II. Net income method
   III. Net working capital method
   IV. Net assets method
   a. I, II, III, and IV
   b. I, II, and IV
   c. I and IV
   d. II and IV
4. Which of the following statements are TRUE?
   I. Equity investments that are held for trading are liable for zakat.
   II. Wages payable are not liable for zakat.
   III. Dividends received and receivable are not zakatable.
   IV. Works in progress are not zakatable.
   a. I, II, and III
   b. II, III, and IV
   c. I, II, and IV
   d. III and IV
5. Which of the following statements are TRUE?
   I. Zakat is treated as an expense if the managing director so decides.
   II. Zakat is treated as an expense if the annual general meeting makes this its resolution.
   III. Zakat is treated as an expense if it is stated in its charter or by laws.
   IV. Zakat is treated as an appropriation if the law requires the company to satisfy its zakat obligations.

a. I and II
b. II and III
c. I, II, and III
d. I, II, and IV

6. The zakat rate on wealth based on the solar year is
   a. 2.5575%
   b. 2.7555%
   c. 2.5577%
   d. 2.5775%
7. What is the zakat rate on wealth based on the lunar year?
   a. 2.500%
   b. 2.550%
   c. 2.5700%
   d. 2.7700%
8. Zakat is payable only on 'growing' capital. Growing capital is
   a. a fixed asset that can be expanded.
   b. the realised gains on fixed assets.
   c. the realised and unrealised gains on fixed assets.
   d. the realised and unrealised gains on fixed and current assets.
9. Growing capital will be equal to net working capital
   a. when there is no long-term debt financing any current assets.
   b. when there is no short-term debt financing any current assets.
   c. when there is no long-term debt financing any fixed assets.
   d. when there is no medium-term debt financing any fixed assets.
10. Which of the following statements are TRUE?
    I. The rate of zakat varies depending on the category of wealth.
    II. The rate of zakat is fixed at 2.5% irrespective of the category of wealth.
    III. Only liabilities that are due in the current year are deductible.
    IV. The rate for zakat on fixed assets is 2.5%.

    a. I and II
    b. I and IV
    c. I, II, and III
    d. I, III, and IV

DISCUSSION QUESTIONS

1. Discuss the limitations of conventional financial statements when computing zakat.
2. What are the two methods of computing zakat, and how do these differ?
3. Some scholars have suggested that zakat can be used as a tool for poverty eradication. Discuss.

EXERCISES

1. The following is the statement of financial position for MNC Ltd as at December 31, 2018.

Fixed assets		$	$
Vehicles		600,000	
Furniture & fittings		2,900,000	
Buildings		12,100,000	**15,600,000**
Current assets			
Stock	(Note 1)	4,100,000	
Trade debtors		1,100,000	
Fixed deposits		500,000	
Cash at bank		95,000	
Other debtors and prepayment	(Note 2)	5,000	5,800,000
Current liabilities			
Trade creditors		2,000,000	
Short-term loan		400,000	
Taxation		2,500,000	
Proposed dividends	(Note 3)	500,000	5,400,000
			16,000,000
Financed by:			
Share capital		5,000,000	
Reserves		7,450,000	
Shareholders funds			12,450,000
Long-term loan			3,550,000
			16,000,000

Notes to the account:

1. This includes raw materials of $71,000 and work-in-progress of $29,000.
2. This includes deposits for utilities as follows:

Electricity	$1,000
Telephone	$1,800
Water	$ 500
Miscellaneous	$ 200

3. This is only a proposed provision for dividends for the year.

Additional information:

The percentage of Muslim shareholders is 58%.

Required:

Calculate zakat payable by MNC Ltd. using:
i. the net assets method
ii. the invested funds method

2. The following table shows the statement of financial position for Jims Shams Company as a June 30, 2020.

Assets	$
Cash and balances with banks and agents	155,000
Deposits and placements with financial institutions	2,010,500
Investments: Held for trading (Note 1)	1,420,500
I Investment: Held to maturity	490,200
Investments: Available for sale	250,500
Stocks	3,800,300
Tax recoverable	9,200
Bills receivable (Note 2)	127,300
Fixed assets	350,000
	8,613,500
Liabilities	
Accounts payable	7,350,000
Accruals	50,500
Bills payable	65,500
Shareholders' funds	
Share capital	500,000
Reserves	647,500
	8,613,500

Additional Information at the end of the year:

1. A total of $400,000 value of held-for-trading securities of M Berhad has been treated as a long-term investment where the company has no intention to liquidate and the company intends to become the major shareholder of M Berhad.

2. Ten percent (10%) of the bills receivable is nonrecoverable and must be written off. This provision has not been provided in the preceding statement of financial position.

Required:

Determine the amount of zakat payable by Jims Shams Company for the financial year ended June 30, 2020, based on the two recommended methods in AAOIFI's FAS 9.

3. BM Company is a small construction company involved in housing development. The following is the statement of financial position as at December 31, 2019.

Fixed assets		**$**	**$**
Land and real estate		1,000,000	
Equipment and machinery		500,000	
Vehicles		300,000	
Furniture and fittings		200,000	2,000,000
Noncurrent assets			
Investments: Available for sale		500,000	500,000
Current assets			
Inventories	Note 1	1,800,000	
Houses under construction		2,700,000	
Raw materials		500,000	
Equipment for construction	Note 2	500,000	
Trade receivables	Note 3	1,500,000	
Deposit paid	Note 4	350,000	
Cash at bank		2,140,000	
Cash in hand		10,000	9,500,000
Current liabilities			
Trade payables		1,200,000	
Notes payables		500,000	
Advanced deposit received	Note 5	300,000	

		$	$
Current liabilities			
Non–trade payables		1,000,000	
Short-term trade financing		500,000	
Wages payable		500,000	
Overdraft		50,000	(4,050,000)
			7,950,000
Financed by:			
Ordinary share capital @ $2 per share		2,000,000	
Share premium		750,000	
Reserves	Note 6	100,000	
Retained earnings		1,900,000	4,750,000
Long-term liabilities			
Term loan		2,950,000	
Deferred taxation	Note 7	250,000	3,200,000
			7,950,000

Notes to the accounts:

1. Inventory consists of completed residential accommodation.
2. Market value of equipment for works is $60,000. The equipment for construction is not intended for sale.
3. On January 1, 2020, two of the customers have been declared bankrupt and the company's auditor has assessed that the probability for the amount due to be paid is extremely minimal. The total amount involved is $200,000.
   In addition, the company also provided general provision on doubtful debts that amounted to 10% of outstanding trade receivables.
4. This is a deposit paid to various utility providers.
5. Advanced deposit is the amount received from clients who booked their preferred residential units in advance.
6. The reserve is meant for charity, for education of staff and for the needy.
7. The deferred taxation includes tax payable for the year of $50,000.

Additional information:

a. The zakat rate is 2.5%.
b. The company pays zakat on behalf of its shareholders and assumes that all shareholders are Muslims.

Required:

Calculate zakat payable by the company using the
i. net assets method.
ii. net invested funds method.

CHAPTER 7

Islamic Commercial Contracts

Learning Outcomes

At the end of this chapter, you will be able to:

1. Explain why commercial contract law is important for business and accounting.
2. Describe the different systems of law in the world.
3. Explain the origins and development of Islamic commercial law and its revival.
4. Define and explain the differences between Sharia and fiqh.
5. Categorize and explain the components of the Sharia.
6. Describe the pillars and conditions of Sharia contracts and explain the rationale for these pillars and conditions.
7. Identify prohibited elements in contracts.
8. Classify contracts according to their legal validity.
9. Compare and contrast sale, lease-based, and investment contracts used in Islamic finance.

INTRODUCTION: LAW AND THE BUSINESS ENVIRONMENT

Students of accounting may be wondering what a chapter on commercial law is doing in an accounting textbook – perhaps a misprint that should have gone into a law book? Rest assured that this is not the case.

Accounting is mainly concerned with businesses, and businesses in every civilized society are operated under a set of laws we can loosely term 'commercial law'. These laws prescribe the terms and conditions of various types of business contracts. It also involves situations where there are no specific contracts between parties but legal responsibilities exist, e.g. in case of the tort law of negligence.

Commercial laws set out rules by which, if and when the transacting parties are in dispute, the courts (judge or Qadi) will judge the case according to these rules. Ignorance of the law exposes the business to many risks, which might lead to the disintegration of the business or heavy fines or even imprisonment of the managers and officers of a company, even a Sharia committee of an Islamic bank![1]

Commercial law affects many areas of the business, e.g. in selling and buying operations, rental operations, borrowing and lending money, relationships between owners and managers, and relationships between customers and employees (another related area known as employment/industrial law). Contract and related laws affect even nonprofit organisations such as waqf and zakat organisations.

Commercial law in the form of partnership law, companies law, and business registration laws affect even the formation and running of businesses themselves.

The focus of this chapter, however, will be on how commercial law affects accounting, in particular, how Islamic law affects Islamic accounting. Some of the specific laws affecting accounting are partnership law, companies law, agency law, carriage law, sale of goods acts, consumer credit acts, law of contracts, financial legislation governing deposits and loans, tax laws, etc.

Although accounting standards have increasingly taken over the role of accounting regulation from acts of parliament and decrees, the law of the land has legal precedence over accounting standards even when accounting standards are incorporated into the law. For example, in the Malaysian scenario, the accounting standards enacted by the Malaysian Accounting Standards Board (which basically adopts the International accounting standards) are enacted into law by the Financial Reporting Act of 1989 for registered companies. However, the Islamic Financial Services Act (IFSA 2013) has given the power of enacting accounting standards for Islamic financial institutions to the Central Bank of Malaysia (Bank Negara Malaysia), which is the regulator of Islamic banks in the country.

[1]See for example, section 29 of the Islamic Financial Services Act 2013 of Malaysia, which stipulates that Islamic financial institutions under the act are required to comply with Sharia standards issued by the regulator in accordance with the advice of the Sharia Advisory Council, Bank Negara Malaysia. This requirement to comply with the Sharia standards issued by the regulator also is imposed on the directors of the financial institution, the chief executive officer, senior officers, and members of the Sharia committee of the financial institutions. Any person who fails to comply with any standards specified, commits an offence and shall be liable for imprisonment for a term not exceeding eight years or to a fine not exceeding 25 million ringgit or both. (Miskam and Nasrul 2013).

DIFFERENT SYSTEMS OF LAW IN THE WORLD

There are basically two systems of law; secular law and several religious laws, in effect throughout the world. The secular laws in effect throughout most of the globe are the common laws of England, which are in effect in the UK and its former colonies (known as common-law countries) and the USA. These former colonies include Muslim countries such as Malaysia, Brunei, Pakistan, Nigeria, etc. These laws came from the evolved practices of customs and laws of England including many local acts based on the UK Acts. These laws evolved by decisions of judges presiding over many cases. Hence, common law uses similar previous cases as precedent or tries to evolve new rules by differentiating the facts of the case at hand. Hence, common law is ever evolving. Even statutory laws passed by parliaments, which are theoretically superior, can be modified by case law under this system, whereas in the civil law system (see below), the law code and statute are the ultimate source of law.

The other system of law is the civil law (Roman law/Continental) system derived from continental Europe derived from the code of Justinian (a Roman emperor), which also incorporates Napoleonic, Germanic, Canonical (relating to church-ordained law – canon law) and also incorporates ideas from Western philosophy of legal positivism and natural law theory. The core principles of this law are codified into a referable system, which forms the source of this law. Many of the countries of the Middle East colonized by countries other than Britain have this system of law incorporated into their national legal systems after colonization, replacing the Sharia law to a large extent. The most extreme case was Turkey after Attaturk, which adopted the French code, forcibly ditching the Hanafi Sharia fiqh code enshrined in the *Majallah* of the Ottoman period.

The other nonsecular systems of law are:

(i) Sharia law (sometimes referred to as fiqh), which is derived from the Quran and Sunnah and the classical fiqh texts and Ijtihad (derivations of new rules by Jurists) and
(ii) In Europe and other parts of the globe, the Church (especially the Roman Catholic church) uses canon law for its own organisation and procedures basically dealing with ecclesiastical matters.
(iii) In Israel, Jewish law from the Torah and Talmud is implemented in addition to secular sources of law and
(iv) In India, Indian law recognises certain elements from Hindu scriptural law and customs, e.g. joint Hindu family as well Muslim family law (although in a distorted Anglo-Muhammadan law format).

Sharia law, although comprehensive, covering criminal, family, commercial, and international matters, has largely been confined to family law in most Muslim countries, i.e in the area of marriage, divorce, custody, and succession, except in a few countries such as Iran and Saudi Arabia, which more or less implement the criminal laws of Islam as well as commercial and family laws. However, other than the Gulf countries, most Muslim countries have opted for secular laws derived from either common law or civil law systems in all areas except family, despite calls for implementation of Sharia laws in many parts of the Muslim world.

THE ORIGINS AND DEVELOPMENT OF ISLAMIC COMMERCIAL LAW AND ITS REVIVAL

Islamic commercial law is derived from the Quran and Sunnah and Arabian commercial customs Islamized by the Prophet (saw) and his Companions (r.a.) and elaborated by fiqh scholars over the ages, especially the Imams of the four Sunni schools and the imams and scholars of the Shia school. Although in *muamalat* (law of transactions) much of the law is the same between Sunni and Shia branches of Islam (especially those prohibited elements), this book shall mainly discuss the Sunni school of law enshrined in various fiqh books of the four Sunni schools of the Imam Malik, Abu Hanifa, Muhammad Idris As Shafiee, and Ahmad bin Hanbal. Islamic commercial law is known as fiqh muamalat, or law of transactions. However, this law includes marriage contracts (munakahaat). However, fiqh muamalat in modern terminology refers to Islamic commercial law, especially the Islamic law of contracts: Sale, partnership, rental (ijarah), wadiah (safe custody), Wakalah (agency), etc.

Islamic commercial law was used from the birth of Islam through the age of various Islamic *Khilafah* and kingdoms and finally under the Ottoman (*Usmaniyah*) *Khilafah* in Turkey, in which it was codified in the *Majallah* following the Hanafi school. However, after successive waves of colonization and especially after the enlightenment period, colonial law (mainly British common law and French civil code) replaced much of Islamic commercial law in Muslim lands.

However, an Islamic revival through Islamic economics, banking, and finance has rekindled a demand for Islamic commercial law. Although the laws found in the classical *fiqh* books are rather out of date, the principles are intact and continue to be of relevance; Islamic law has an inbuilt mechanism of evolution to stay tuned to the times and places in which it is implemented through the process of *ijtihad* (continuous exertion to find a legal solution) and *fatawa*, a legal decree by Islamic scholars (derived from the sources using the methodologies enshrined in the discipline of *usulul fiqh* – Islamic jurisprudence), which is necessitated by a new situation.

This has created a demand for *fiqh* scholars to man the Sharia committees of Islamic banks and other organisations. In recent years, a huge number of books on Islamic commercial law on various subtopics including waqf, Islamic banking, and Islamic jurisprudence (*Usulul fiqh*) have been freshly written or translated from the Arabic classics.

SHARIA AND FIQH: DEFINITIONS, DIFFERENCES, ORIGINS, AND OBJECTIVES

The word *Sharia* is often used interchangeably with *fiqh*, both terms referring to Islamic law. However, to clarify, the Sharia, which literally means 'a path towards a watering hole', refers to Islamic Sharia, which is the Law given by Allah, the Creator, to Muslims through the Quran, which is the scripture of the Muslims and the Hadith or the traditions of the Prophet Muhammad (peace be upon Him).

The Islamic creed asserts that since Muhammad is the final Prophet of God to walk the earth, the Sharia, which is contained in the Quran, and his Hadith are permanent until the Day of Judgement and no other religious law can modify or abolish it. Sharia as revealed is the Will of the Lawmaker, i.e. Allah, under which Muslims must lead their lives. Although the Sharia contains many legal principles, the detailed rules are fewer in number.

Fiqh (meaning 'to understand'), a term for Islamic Law used synonymously with Sharia; however, it refers to the human understanding, interpretation, and the elaboration of the Sharia. It is the attempt by the human mind to understand the Divine will in the Sharia. Fiqh is derived by interpretation of the Sharia through a methodology embodied in a body of knowledge known as 'Usulul Fiqh' (Islamic jurisprudence) to derive detailed rules from the principles and elaborate and extend rules contained in the Sharia to meet the changing needs of society through time and place without going against the Sharia principles. These *usuli* principles help to constrain the introduction of irrational opinion to produce rules according to one's own desires or one's school of thought. The process of deriving new rules from the Sharia should be undertaken by Sharia scholars, judges, and experts who are well versed in the Quran, Hadith, Arabic, and the precedents set by the Companions of the Prophet (saw), his household, and earlier scholars known as the *salaf*.

Over the first 300 years of Islam, the fiqh has evolved into the four main Sunni schools of thought or mazahib (singular: mazhab) and various Shia schools, mainly the Isna ashari, the Zaydi, and Ibadi. Although in area of creed there are some differences between the Shia and Sunni fiqh, in fiqh muamalat, especially in commercial transactions, there are only a few minor differences. This chapter will henceforth concentrate on only the Sunni fiqh, as it is the fiqh of the majority of Muslims in the world.

COMPONENTS OF THE SHARIA

Figure 7.1 shows that the Sharia of Islam consists of:

- *Aqidah*, which is the Islamic belief system or creed as well as the rules of worship or *ibadat*. Under aqidah, belief in God, angels, Prophets, Scriptures, Day of Judgement, and God's Decree is discussed and explained.
- *Muamalat*, or transactions affecting all relationships between human beings. This not only includes commercial relationships but also marriage, charitable gifts, laws of inheritance, and criminal law, i.e. punishments for crimes such as robbery, theft, murder, adultery, etc., which are covered under hudud (penal code) and *tazir* (lighter sentences).
- *Akhlaq*, i.e. moral and ethical code, considers and cultivates good character and behaviour such as honesty, sincerity, prudence, respect, helpfulness, kindness, mercy, love, and compassion and avoiding greed, pride, dishonesty, hypocrisy, miserliness, and other immoral behavior.

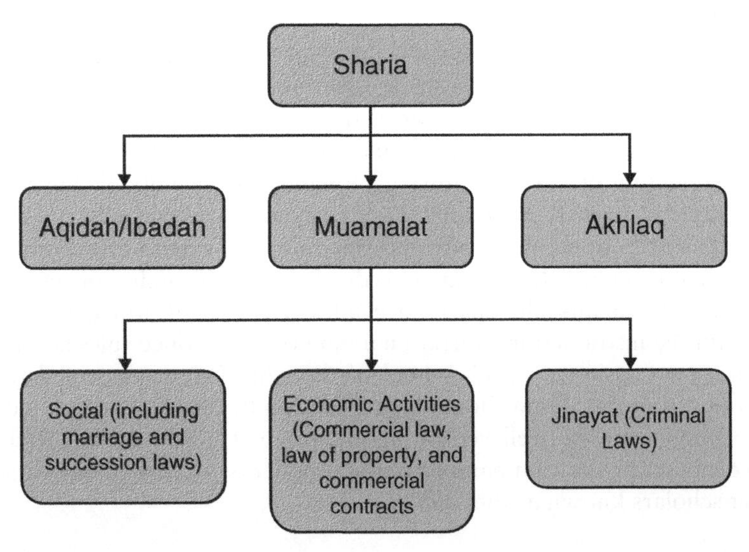

FIGURE 7.1 Components of Sharia

ISLAMIC CONTRACTS: PILLARS AND CONDITIONS

Most commercial law comes under the law of contracts known as *fiqh al uqud*. A contract is an agreement between two or more parties to perform certain actions. In Islam all contracts are sacred, as it is the command of the Quran to fulfil contracts. In Islam, contracts cover a broader area than commercial transactions. This includes social contracts, including marriage contracts, charitable contracts (gratuitous contracts) such as gifts, endowments, *tabarru* – contribution and *waad* (unilateral promise), which are used in commercial transactions and commercial contracts such as sale, lease, partnership, agency, and guarantee. Islamic finance, where most of the Islamic contract is applied, currently uses both the commercial as well as the gratuitous contracts and certain other supporting contracts. We shall look at the principles of Islamic contract law first and then some associated principles before looking at some of the specific Islamic commercial contracts.

Principles of Contract Laws in Islam

The basic principles of contract law in Islam are surprisingly similar to common-law contracts in English law. The basis of transactions in Islamic law is the contract or *aqd* (plural; *uqud*)

A contract in Islam can be defined as *an offer and acceptance by two or more parties on a specific subject with mutual consent*. A contract is more than a promise or *wa'ad,* which has its own place in contract law. A contract gives rise to mutual obligations, which can be subject to enforcement by the Sharia courts if either party fails to fulfil any terms of the contract.

The pillars of Islamic contracts can be divided into three categories:

1. The contracting parties
2. The offer and acceptance (ijab and qabul)
3. The subject matter of the contract

In addition to the pillars, there are several conditions related to the 'pillars', for example, the consideration or the inducement given by one party to another for the other party to part with something of value.

All the conditions and pillars of the contract are made to ensure justice and fair play between the parties. Please bear this in mind as you learn the pillars and rules of contracts; otherwise, it can get boring!

Contracting parties

The contracting parties must have the legal capacity to contract. What this means is that the parties to the contract must have:

1. **Sanity**: all parties to the contract must be sane. If all or both or any one of the parties are insane, the contract cannot be concluded. In case of temporary insanity, the contract cannot be concluded when the parties are insane but valid if the contract is concluded when either party recovers sanity even if for a temporary period.
2. **Puberty:** The contracting parties should have reached puberty or in case physical characteristics of puberty do not appear in spite of advancing age, the parties are considered to be legally mature when they reach the age of 15, 17, or 18 according to various scholars. Since the ages prescribed by the scholars are arrived at by ijtihad and not through textual proof in the Quran or Hadith, the legal authority of a country set the age of puberty or legal majority. Normally, contacts made by children are not valid unless the child is discerning (able to know right and wrong) and has the permission of their guardians. The discerning age is taken to be six or seven years old. The scholars have divided contracts into three types with their own conditions for examining their validity in case of minors.
   a. Purely beneficial dealings: E.g. accepting a gift or charity; valid and does not require permission from guardian.
   b. Harmful dealings: E.g. divorce, extending loans, or being a guarantor; this is not allowed even if a guardian gives permission.
   c. Dealings which may result in harm: Trading or renting is allowed if the child is discerning and the guardian approves or the child approves after he comes of age.
3. **Maturity (rushd):** Refers to the ability of the person to run his own affairs. According to jurists, maturity refers to whether the person can enter into good and proper dealings with wealth from a worldly viewpoint. If a person can deal with wealth without misusing or wasting it then he is considered mature. Puberty is not the same as maturity. Puberty can be reached without maturity. In this case, a guardian must take care of his wealth until he reaches maturity. There must be more than one party and the contract cannot be concluded by one legal proxy (representative or agent) for both parties excepting contracts of marriage (by a father).

Offer and acceptance

Mutual consent in any contract is a requirement of the Quran (An Nisa; 4:29):

يَا أَيُّهَا الَّذِينَ آمَنُواْ لاَ تَأْكُلُواْ أَمْوَالَكُمْ بَيْنَكُمْ بِالْبَاطِلِ إِلاَّ أَن تَكُونَ تِجَارَةً عَن تَرَاضٍ مِّنكُمْ وَلاَ تَقْتُلُواْ أَنفُسَكُمْ إِنَّ اللّهَ كَانَ بِكُمْ رَحِيمًا

> *4:29 O You who have attained to faith! Do not devour one another's possessions wrongfully – except by way of trade based on your mutual consent – and do not destroy one another: for, behold, God is indeed a dispenser of grace unto you!*

Offer and acceptance signifies mutual consent. However, since consent is an internal and intangible matter, the statement (sighah) of offer and acceptance is considered as external proof of the contract. One party must offer, i.e lay out the terms, and the other party must accept without varying the terms. Offer and acceptance can be done orally or written or by a sign of acceptance according to custom.

Conditions of Offer and Acceptance:

1. In a verbal expression the past tense is preferred; thus instead of 'I sell you this thing', it should be 'I sold you this thing' and the acceptance will be 'I bought from you this thing'. Sounds strange, doesn't it? However, most jurists agree that either the past, present, or future tense can be used according to the intention, custom, and circumstance of the parties.
2. The offer can be in written form even if the parties can speak.
3. Sometimes the offer can be made by nonverbal expression or action, for example, picking up something in a shop and paying for it.
4. The acceptance must conform to the offer, which can be explicit or implicit. Explicit acceptance to an offer for sale of a house for $100,000 is by saying, 'I accept to buy your house for the stated amount'. An implicit acceptance is saying, 'I accept your offer to buy the house for $105,000'. In English law this would not be valid, as varying the terms in any direction more or less is considered a counteroffer, but in Islamic law this is not considered a counteroffer since if a person is willing to sell a house for $100,000 he will surely agree to sell it for $105,000. However, if the acceptance is for less than the price offered, there is no implicit acceptance but it is a counteroffer and the seller will have to accept or reject the counteroffer.
5. The offer and acceptance must be clear and unambiguous. The offer and acceptance to be clear must conform with words and terms that are customarily used in the type of contract.
6. **Connection of offer and acceptance:** This is something unique in Islamic law, although it becomes increasingly untenable in contemporary times due to environmental changes. This is known as majlis al-aqd; i.e. both the offer and acceptance must be in the same session. In earlier periods, it was the same place and time. However, in contemporary times, the scholars say same session must be same time but not place. For example,

I can send an offer by fax or email and the other party can only accept it when it arrives.

In English law, once the offer is accepted, the contract is executed and the acceptance cannot be taken back or rejected subsequently. However, in Islamic law, a legal term called '*Khiyar al majlis*' which means 'option of the meeting' allows the contract to be revoked before the persons leave the place of contract. This means a person can change his mind any time before he leaves the place of the contract.

Subject Matter of Contracts:

1. Suitability of subject matter:
   a. The property must have a value to each party in the contract. For example, dead animals cannot be sold to a Muslim because they cannot be consumed.
   b. Ownership of subject matter: The subject matter must be owned by the seller. Stolen goods or ambiguity such as future harvest or fish in the ocean or birds in the air cannot be sold.
   c. The subject matter must not be forbidden by the Sharia: E.g. one cannot sell liquor to a Muslim; it is forbidden to rent a building to carry out gambling or prostitution.
2. The subject matter of the contract must be known to both parties.
   a. This means that the identity of the subject matter must be known to both parties to avoid ambiguity and conflicts later. For example, in a sale, the object of the sale can be evidenced physically before or at the time of the contract. This can also be done through a sample. For example, a sample of grains (taken from the actual grain store) can be shown as representative of all the grains to be sold. If the subject matter is well known by people or standardized in the market, the genus, type, and amount can be identified by description, e.g. Type 2B pencil or Honda Accord 2.4 Model 2018 black. There is an exception in the case of charitable contracts; e.g. if a person undertakes to give a gift of pencils, he can give any type of pencil, e.g. 2B, HB, etc., as these charitable contracts do not usually lead to disputes.
   b. In the case of contracts involving exchange of property, *the subject matter must be capable of being delivered to the party concerned after the contract is concluded.* Thus, you cannot sell a horse which has escaped captivity. In a contract for services, the services must be capable of being performed. Thus, a contract for the services of a doctor is not valid if the services are paid for only if the patient is healed, as the outcome is uncertain, as the treatment may not result in cure.
3. If the subject matter of a contract is tangible, i.e. it can be seen or touched, then the subject matter must be present or existing at the time

of the execution of the contract. Thus, you cannot sell a lamb which is still in the womb of the sheep or wheat from a plot of land which is still not ready for harvest. The purpose of this ruling is to ensure that there is no ambiguity (*gharaar*)or uncertainty in the contract. For example, in the preceding examples, if the lamb is born dead or the harvest of the plot of land is destroyed by bad weather, one party to the contract will suffer financial damage. The exceptions to this are in the contracts of salaam (future delivery contract) and istisna'a (construction or manufacturing contracts. Under the exceptions, additional safeguards such as price, genus, type, amount, and time of delivery must be specified to mitigate *gharaar*.

In a contract for services, it is not necessary for the subject matter to exist as long as the service can be performed as contracted. For example, Avis can hire out a particular car for next week, even though the car is not available when the contract is executed as long as the car or an equivalent will be available next week when the customer needs the use of the car.

PROHIBITED ELEMENTS IN CONTRACTS

Forbidden subject matter and forbidden elements

In a contract of sale, it is illegal to make a contract for the sale of goods which are forbidden by Sharia, e.g. liquor, pork, and drugs. There is a fatwa in Malaysia that even tobacco is haram to be bought or sold, as it can eventually lead to death.

In a contract for services, it is illegal to contract to do something prohibited in Islam, e.g. prostitution, cheat or defraud others, or steal.

In addition to prohibited subject matter, the contracts cannot include elements of *riba, maysir,* and *gharar.*

Riba, to put it simply, is interest or any additional amount of money given for a loan or for extension of time for repaying a loan. The prohibition of *Riba is* the basis of Islamic banking and finance.

Maysir refers to gambling. Highly speculative contracts such as futures and derivatives which are not regulated as well as gambling contracts, e.g. buying a lottery ticket, or contracts which have an element of gambling such as insurance contracts are forbidden.

Gharar refers to ambiguity or uncertainty or contingency in a contract. In contracts of exchange, the contract cannot be contingent on an outcome. For example, you cannot sell something and receive payment if only something happens such as in insurance. Further ambiguity such as not clearly mentioning the item, for example, a contract for the sale of a house without mentioning where and what type of house, is not valid, as is a contract for future delivery without specifying the date of delivery or specification of what exactly is to be delivered. *Gharar* also refers to subject matter which is uncertain of being delivered, for example, birds in the air and fish in the sea or unharvested wheat which is still growing in a plot of land.

Investment contracts such as commenda and partnerships have their additional rules.

Intentional and nonintentional prohibited elements in contracts

1. Deception *(Taghrir)*
   These are false or misleading statements or deeds which induce one party to undertake the contract based on the impression that it is in his interest to enter into the contract, whereas in actual fact, it is not.

   If a person makes a false statement to sell his goods, but the other party is not injured in any way, the seller will be punished on the Day of Judgement but the contract is still valid. However, if the contract results in a loss to the purchaser, it is the right of the purchaser to retain or cancel the contract. For example, a financial adviser sells unit trust units, saying that they are riskless, and the client suffers a loss.

   If the deception is by deed, for example, if a person does something to the subject matter to show it in a better condition, which is in contradiction to the reality, the contract is not binding – for example, putting very good fruit on top of a pile and rotten fruit at the bottom of the pile and selling the fruit from both the top and bottom of the pile without the customer knowing about this, or selling a car with defects which are not noticeable by the buyer and without warning by the seller.
2. Inequality (Ghubn)
   a. This is inequality in price and subject matter of the contract which is not known at the time of the contract. This is divided into excessive inequality *(Ghubn fahish)* and insignificant inequality.
   b. If the inequality is insignificant, this is not prohibited in most cases and the contract will be valid except in a small of number of contracts, e.g. in cases of conflict of interest or accusation, such as a trustee for orphans giving a small discount to his relatives when selling the property of orphans.
   c. Excessive inequality due to deception will enable the buyer to cancel or retain the contract according to most schools of thought.
   d. Excessive inequality will nullify the contract (whether due to deception or not) when it involves property of endowments or state or property of minors or insane or foolish persons.

When is inequality excessive or insignificant? The scholars have devised various standards to measure scale of inequality such as using a general % selling price or % selling price for each category, e.g. business goods 5%, animals 10%, and land 20%. Others have insisted on 1/3 or 1/6 of the price.

3. Duress (*Ikrah*)

Duress is forcing someone to do things which he does not want to do or dislikes, but is forced to do against his will, to remove a greater harm. Duress, according to the majority of scholars, leads to the nullification of the contract, as duress causes nonexistence of consent and choice. In fact, the compelled person does not want to conclude a contract, but rather he wants to be rescued from the situation. They also agree that even if free consent is given after the removal of the duress, the contract is still not valid. However, the Hanafi school holds that consent, if given after the duress is removed makes the contract valid.

To be accepted under the Sharia, duress must fulfil three conditions, i.e.

a. The duress must be from a person who can implement the threat,
b. The compeller (*mukrih*) must be serious in his threat, and
c. It must be a serious threat, i.e difficult for the threatened party to bear such as threats of murder, injury to an organ of the body, damage to the whole property of the person compelled, or permanent imprisonment.

4. Ghalat (*Mistake*)

A mistake is an assumption which comes to the mind of a person but is not in conformance with reality; i.e it is not true. It is contradicting reality but *without intention.*

A mistake in a contract is when one discovers after the execution of the contract that the subject matter was not what was contracted for. If there has been a mistake in the subject matter, this could be due to two things: mistakes in essence and mistakes in attribute.

If the mistake in the subject matter is a mistake in essence of the subject matter, for example a gold ring instead of a silver ring was given, then the contract is invalid.

If the mistake in the subject matter is a mistake in attribute of the subject matter, then it depends on whether the person was present when the contract was made and the attribute could have been observed.

If the person bought the goods without looking at them then he has the right to choose to invalidate the contract or to validate it. However, if the purchaser was present at the time of contracting and the attribute was observable, e.g. color or size, then the contract is valid and binding.

For example, if he purchased a table said to be 10 feet long but he took a table of size 8 feet, then the contract is still valid and the purchaser does not have any right to cancel the contract.

However, if the attribute is not observable, e.g. origin of manufacture, then the purchaser has the option to cancel due to error or retain the contract as valid.

CLASSIFICATIONS OF CONTRACTS ACCORDING TO LEGAL EFFECTS

There are many different classifications of contracts in Sharia. Some scholars opine that there are three classifications, whereas others say there are five major classifications. We will not delve into all these classifications but only one, which is very important: That is classification according to the legal effects and soundness of the contract.

Under this classification we find there are three types of contracts: Valid (*sahih*), invalid (*Batil*), and imperfect (*Fasid*).

Valid (*sahih*) Contracts

A valid contract is one which fulfils all the pillars and conditions of the Sharia and does not contain those attributes which make it unlawful. Hence, the contract becomes lawful to execute and suitable for the purpose for which it was executed. For example, if a sale contract is executed by parties who have legal capacity to contract, there is proper offer and acceptance and for subject matter that is not prohibited, identified properly, existed at the time of contract, and can be handed over after the execution as well as meets the conditions of the contract such as not having any duress, inequity, mistake, deception, or major inequality, then the contract is valid. However, it must be remembered that certain contracts can have exceptions in that certain conditions may not be met but yet Sharia validates them. As an example, in *salam* a contract which is a payment in advance for deferred delivery, the subject does not exist at the time of execution of the contract. However, in this case, the scholars have come up with additional conditions to mitigate the effect of the absent conditions. Thus, in *salam,* the price, quantity, specifications of the subject matter, and time of delivery must be agreed in advance to mitigate *gharaar* or ambiguity.

Invalid (*batil*) Contracts

An invalid contract is a deficient contract which makes the contract illegal and of no legal effect. It is prohibited in the Sharia. For example, a contract to sell pork to a Muslim is not a valid contract. There are differences of opinion among the different mazahib or schools of thought in the Sharia, as to what makes a contract invalid.

According to the Hanafis, a contract is invalid if one of the pillars of contracts, i.e. offer and acceptance, subject matter, and legal capacity of the parties, does not exist. However, the majority of the jurists do not differentiate between the absence of a pillar, condition or attribute of a contract, thus according to them if any of these aspects of a contract is missing, then the contract is invalid. This means that, for example in a contract of sale, if all three pillars exist but there was deception (a condition, not a pillar), then the contract would not be invalid but imperfect to the Hanafis; but most other jurists would deem the contract to be invalid.

Imperfect (*fasid*) Contracts

Imperfect contracts are contracts in which some conditions are absent (or negative conditions are present) but the pillars of the contract, i.e offer and acceptance, legal capacity, and subject matter, are okay. For example, a contract of sale of a nonfungible (nonidentical or noninterchangeable) item in which deferment is a condition is a *fasid* contract but not invalid. This is so because a sale must result in change of ownership at the time of sale except for fungibles in a salaam contract and specified nonfungibles in a istisna'a contract (contract of manufacture/construction).

FINANCIAL CONTRACTS UNDER THE SHARIA

So far, we have studied general theory of contracts in Islamic law. In this part of this chapter we will study some important financial contracts in Islam, a few more specific rules and conditions of these contracts, and how these contracts are used in Islamic banking, which will take us to the next chapter, where we will study how these contracts are applied to accounting following Sharia standards and accounting standards of the Accounting and Auditing Organization for Islamic Financial Institutions.

Figure 7.2 gives a comprehensive listing of commercial and noncommercial contracts in Islam. Some of the contracts are not recognised as Sharia-compliant in Pakistan and in the Arab world, e.g. Bai'al inah (essentially buy and sell back to the same person at a higher price) as well as bai ad dayn (sale of debts at a discount). These will not be discussed, although they are used extensively in Malaysia and Southeast Asia to the chagrin of purists (especially academics!). Of course, we are not covering every contract in the figure, but if your interest is piqued, do a Google search and find out more about these contracts. Just note that even the noncommercial contracts such as hibah (gift) and Qard (interest-free loan) have their uses in Islamic finance.

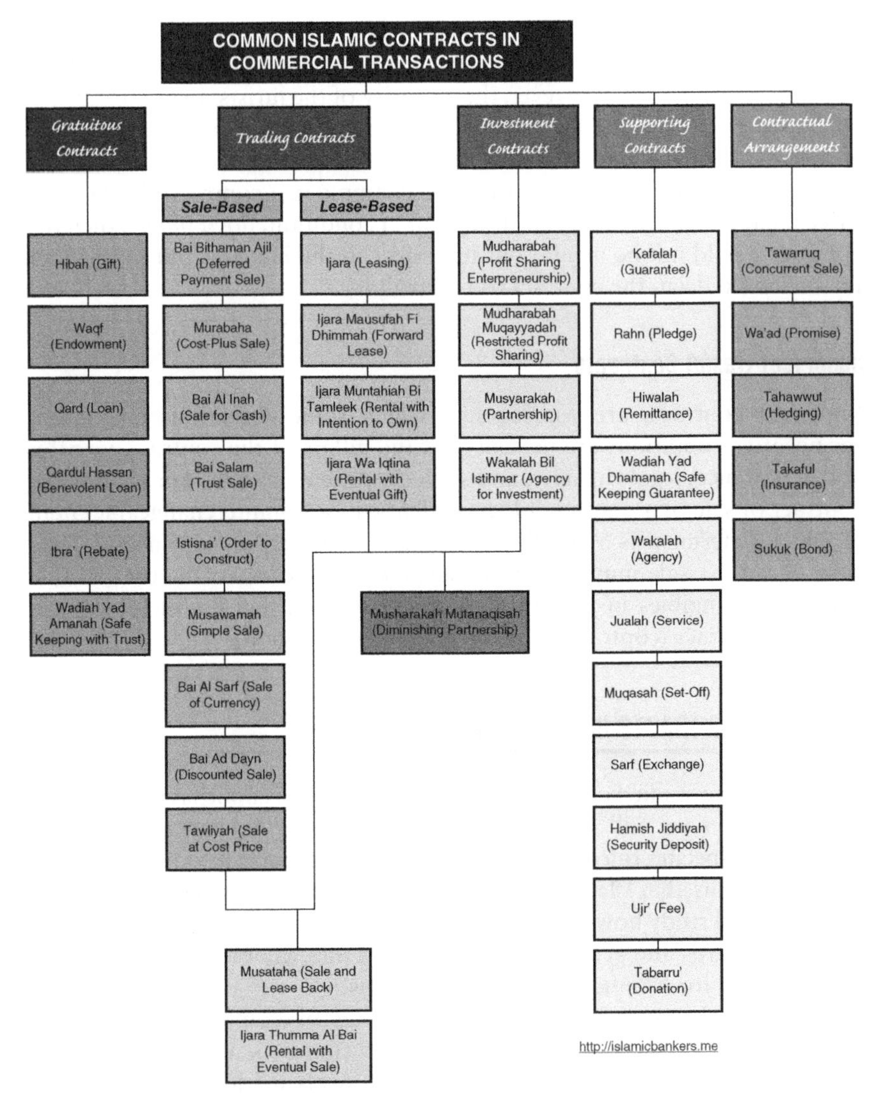

FIGURE 7.2 Islamic Financial Contracts
Source: http: Islamicbankers.me

We will go through some of the important contracts in Figure 7.2 from the top left-hand corner, down, and then to the right. The contracts discussed are not in the order of importance but are used in commerce.

- *Hibah* is a unilateral gift contract. One person promises or gives another person a gift. This is a charitable contract and some of the conditions and pillars of Islamic contracts need not exist. For example, consideration – there is no reward or exchange for this contract and it is not binding on the giver. An example would be a gift of books or money to a public library. However, in Islamic banking it is used to give some return to depositors, e.g. current or savings account, in wadiah (safe custody) contracts, at the exclusive discretion of the bank. Thus, the depositor cannot demand any return. I personally feel that from a fairness point of view, the banks should give a small return to such depositors if the bank is profitable, as the bank uses the depositors' money to make some of the profits. However, Islamic banks do give *hibah* to their depositors for competitive reasons.
- *Waqf (plural awqaaf)* is a permanent endowment (for religious or charitable purposes. A person through a waqf deed gives an amount of money or property such as a mosque or religious school building, in which he states the objectives and the beneficiaries of the waqf. He must also elect a nazir or mutawalli (trustee) to take care of waqf after his death. Many countries have Ministries or Waqf Boards to oversee the administration of waqfs. In Islamic history, awqaf have a great heritage in the Middle East, Africa, Turkey, and the Indian subcontinent funding parks, animal hospitals, and universities (such as the first University Al-Azhar and in a separate waqf – grazing land for the Rector's donkey!). In contemporary times a modified version, the cash waqf, is developing in countries such as Malaysia where the public jointly contributes cash amounts to an entity which manages the waqf for stated charitable and religious purposes. The essential condition for waqf is that the capital or corpus must be maintained (it cannot be sold, inherited, or gifted) and only the income (or the corpus itself, such as a mosque) can be used. In Pakistan, Takaful (Islamic insurance) companies are set up as waqf.
- Qard is a loan of money or any interchangeable (fungible) object to another person with a promise by the other person to pay back (or return the object) within an agreed period or on demand, without any addition. Islam prohibits the lender from charging interest, i.e. any sum above the original amount (principal) given to the borrower including charging extra for extension of the loan period. The term *Qard Hasan* (a goodly loan or benevolent loan) is used to described an Islamic loan without interest. It is useful to differentiate the term *dayn* from *qard*, as sometimes these terms are wrongly used interchangeably. *Dayn* is a debt incurred

as a result of either a loan or other transactions such as a credit sale and gives rise to a liability which is to be settled as per agreement and cannot be demanded otherwise. Thus *dayn* is a liability in the borrower's or buyer's books. All Qard leads to a dayn but not all dayn is Qard. Qard Hasan is used in the Middle East Islamic banks as the underlying contract for a noninvestment deposit such as current or savings account[2]. It is also used in the Takaful industry in Malaysia.

- *Ibra* is not strictly a contract but is the discount or rebate given for early repayment of a qard or loan. The Quran encourages the forgiving loans partially or in total for those who are unable to pay their debts. In Islamic finance, *ibra*, which technically is at the discretion of the bank, is given as a rebate for early settlement of a debt.
- *Wadiah Yad Amanah* is a safe custody/safekeeping contract whereby a person deposits a property with a depository (say, a bank) and the depository becomes a trustee for safekeeping. Normally unless the depository uses the property or is negligent, he becomes a guarantor for the return of the property in case the item is stolen or lost. Otherwise, he is a trustee (amanah) to keep it safely with the same care as his own goods and return it to the owner on demand. *Wadiah Yad Dhammanah*. Another type of contract used by Islamic banks in Southeast Asia is a contract for safe custody of money with a guarantee to return on demand, if the bank uses it or it is stolen from the bank. In some countries, the bank charges a commission or fee for safekeeping while in Southeast Asia, they offer some return as a gift if the bank makes a profit with the money.
- The Sale Contract. In Islamic law, a sale is a mutual exchange contract whereby one party transfers the ownership of property to another party either in exchange for another property or cash or deferred payment. There are many different kinds of sale contracts in Islam: sale on the spot, i.e for cash and immediate delivery; sale for deferred price, i.e. credit sale (bai al muajjal); murabaha sale, i.e. sale with markup on cost disclosed to the buyer; murabaha to the purchase orderer; bai as salaam, i.e sale for payment in advance for deferred delivery; and bai al istisna'a, which is a contract to manufacture or construct property and sell it to the customer.

The conditions for a 'normal' sale include all the pillars and conditions, i.e legal capacity, agreed price, halal nature and existence of subject matter, and capability of delivery. Here I would like to expand on certain

[2]Recently, Islamic banks in Malaysia have shifted for wadiah contracts to Qard contracts for current and savings accounts.

different types of sale contracts, which are mentioned above and are increasingly being used in Islamic finance.

Murabaha Contracts

In this contract, a seller buys a product and then sells at the cost plus a markup which is disclosed to the buyer. Thus,

$$\text{Selling price} = \text{cost} + \text{markup}$$

The selling price is either paid on the spot (i.e. cash on delivery) or can be deferred or can be paid in instalments which in total must not exceed the agreed initial selling price. This is important, as adding any additional 'profit' for extension of the instalment period (i.e. credit period) is regarded as riba or interest and is thus prohibited. However, a rebate known as *'ibra* can be given as a discount for early payment.

A modification of this is murabaha to the purchase orderer. In this case, the ultimate buyer gives an 'order' to the seller to purchase a particular product which costs, say, \$X and agrees to pay the seller in addition a markup of, say, \$Y. Meanwhile the buyer promises the seller that he will buy the product once it is purchased by the seller through a *wa'ad* contract, which is a promise by one party to do something in the future.

The Islamic banks saw this contract as an opportunity in home and car financing and this has become the main financing device of the Islamic bank. Any person requiring finance, e.g. to buy a car, goes to the bank and requests the bank to buy it for him. The bank buys the car, adds a markup, depending on the amount and term of the financing required, and sells it to the customer, who pays by instalments. Once delivered, the car becomes the property of the customer, although it could be collateralized.

The structure of a murabaha is illustrated in Figure 7.3.

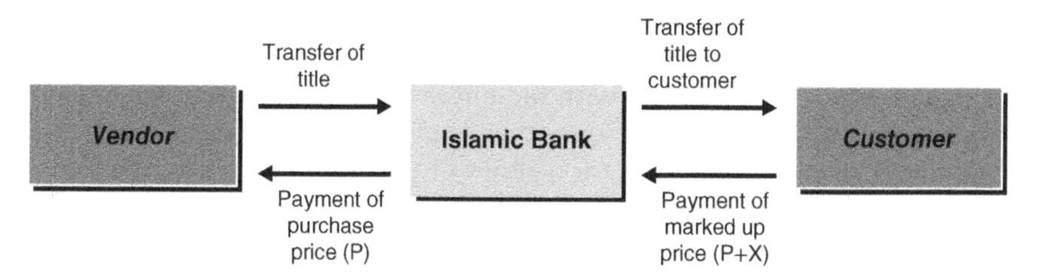

FIGURE 7.3 Structure of a murabaha contract

Bai As Salam

This is a contract where the buyer of a specified commodity and price pays the price in advance to the seller for delivery in the future. Normally this contract is prohibited because of the absence of the subject matter at the time of contracting. However, Islam makes an exception for the public interest provided the elements that make the contract ambiguous are mitigated by fixing the price, the specification of the commodity, and the time of delivery in addition to some other conditions. In Islamic banking this contract is used in conjunction with a parallel salam contract to provide financing to a commodity producer while selling the future product at a markup to another party who needs the commodity at a future period at a fixed price. In Figure 7.4 the salam contract is on the left and parallel salam on the right.

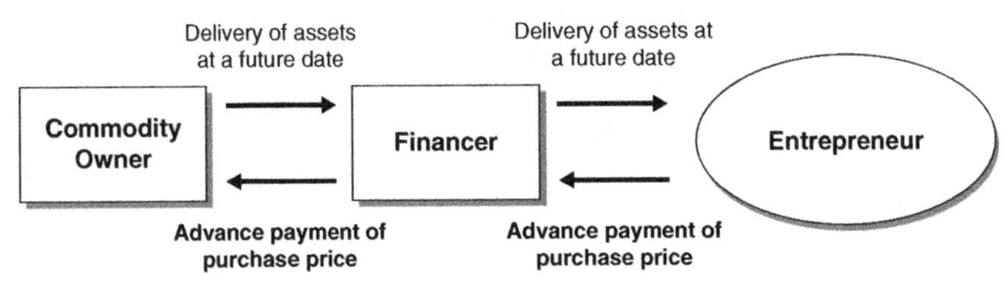

FIGURE 7.4 Salam and Parallel Salam

Bai al Istisna'

Istisna is a variation of salam. It is the payment for commissioned manufacture or construction. A buyer can contract to have goods manufactured and delivered at a later date, in accordance to specifications. Unlike salam, payment is at delivery or according to manufacturing or construction progress. The payment can also be made in instalments. Thus, this instrument can be used to finance construction or manufacturing projects. Islamic banks have also used and modified this to a 'back-to-back' istisna where two contracts are made up, one with the manufacturer and one with the ultimate buyer. The Islamic bank uses this contract to finance the purchase of ships or airplanes. The bank contracts with the buyer to supply the item for a fixed future payment schedule. On the other leg, the bank contracts with the shipbuilder to supply the ship for a series of progress payments which can extend for more than the period of manufacture.

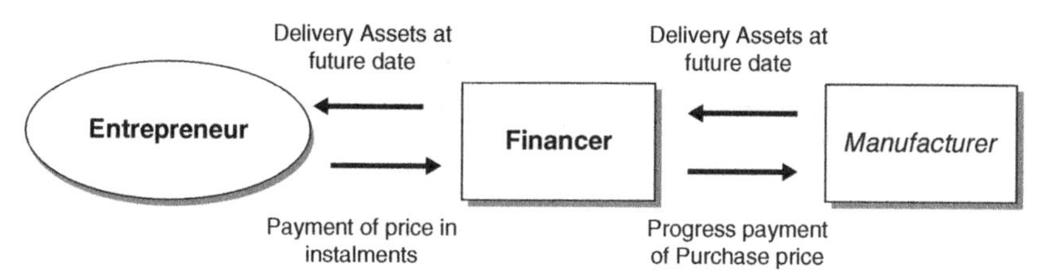

FIGURE 7.5 Structure of an Istisna contract – (Project Finance)

Ijarah

Ijarah is renting or leasing of the benefits (or usufruct) of assets. Here the bank purchases the asset and leases it to the lessee. The owner takes the risk of ownership and gets a rental payment, while the lessee uses the asset. The ownership resides with the bank. However, certain modified ijarah contracts can result in transfer of ownership to the lessor at the end of the lease period. Such ijarah contract is termed *ijarah muntahia bittamleek* wherein there is an option to acquire ownership of the asset at the end of the lease. The buying option can be pre-agreed at the inception of the contract. This is known as an *Ijarah wa iqtina* (lease and sell) contract.

Investment/Partnership Contracts

Mudaraba Mudaraba is a labor-capital partnership, wherein an investor (sahibul mal) puts up an amount of capital for a specific period of time with an entrepreneur (mudarib) who conducts business with the amount. The investor contributes the capital while the entrepreneur contributes the labor or expertise. The investor is not allowed to interfere with the management of the business. However, he can specify the type of business or investment the entrepreneur can undertake. When the entrepreneur determines the type of business or investment, the contract is a restricted mudaraba. If there

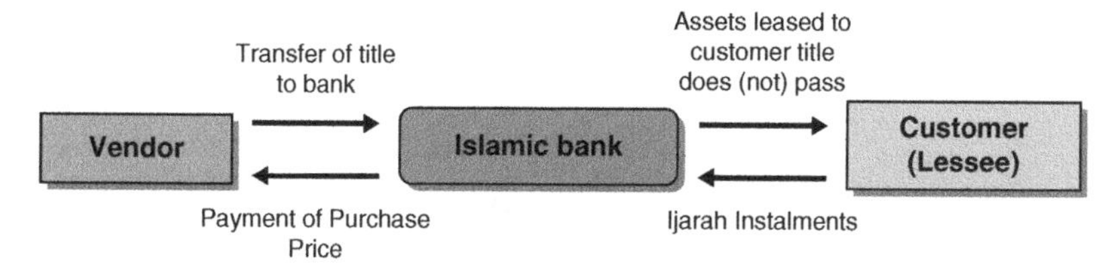

FIGURE 7.6 Structure of a Ijara Muntahia BiTamleek (lease to own)

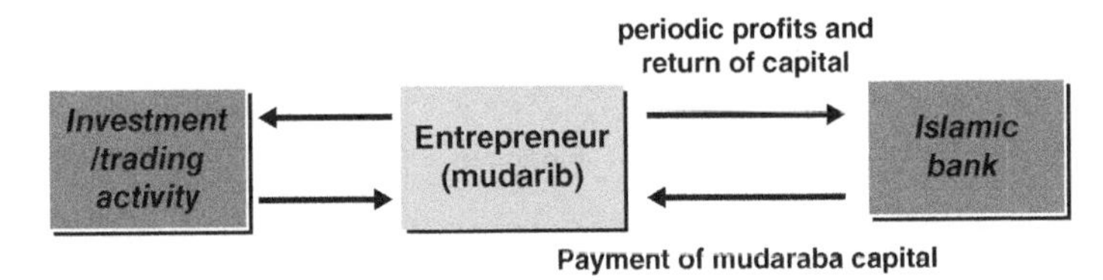

FIGURE 7.7 Structure and pillars of a mudaraba contract

is no such specification, it is an unrestricted mudaraba. The profit sharing ratio between the entrepreneur and the investor is predetermined. At the end of the period, any profits are shared in the agreed ratio. In case of losses, the investor bears the entire loss; the entrepreneur loses his labor, as he is not paid a salary.

Pillars of Mudaraba:

1. Rabbul Mal or Sahibul Mal – Owner of capital, fund provider
2. Mudharib – Entrepreneur
3. Ra'sul Mal – Capital
4. Al-Amal or Mashru' – Business venture or projects
5. Ribh – Predetermined share of profit
6. Sighah – Ijab (offer) and Qabul (acceptance)

The Islamic bank adopts a two-tier mudaraba contract. In the case of investment accounts, the depositor is the investor while the Islamic bank is the entrepreneur or manager of the fund. The bank itself then becomes the investor when it places money with the entrepreneur who runs the actual business. In case of profit the bank and the entrepreneur share the profits. From the bank's share of the profit, a pre-agreed share is given to the depositor. In case of loss, the bank passes on the whole loss to the depositor. The bank's overhead expenses are not charged to the investment accounts, as the bank is only entitled to a profit share and is not entitled to a salary.

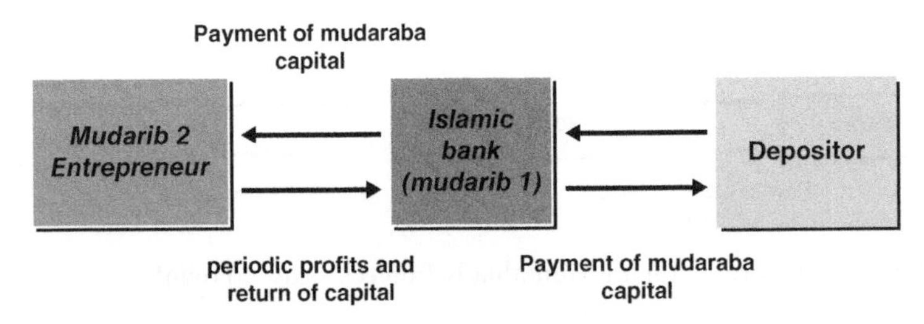

FIGURE 7.8 The structure of a two-tier mudaraba contract

Musharaka This is plain partnership financing. Here the bank becomes a full partner of the entrepreneur, who also contributes capital. The bank shares profits of the business with the entrepreneur in a pre-agreed ratio that is not necessary in the ratio of the capital. However, in case of loss, the losses are shared in the ratio of the capital, not the profit sharing ratio. In case the bank does not play an active part in the business, then the entrepreneur may charge management salary or expenses to the business account. Unlike the case of mudaraba, where the bank cannot interfere in the running of the business, the bank has executive powers in musharaka contracts.

A variant of the musharaka contract that is used to finance the acquisition of assets is the *Musharaka Mutanaqqisa* or reducing partnership contract. In this contract, initially the customer and the bank are partners. Over a period of time, the customer gradually increases his share of ownership (and, consequently, the bank's share gets reduced until it becomes nil) by paying instalments, which include a portion to purchase a portion of the bank's share and a portion representing the rental payment (if the customer is using or occupying the asset).

Supporting Contracts *Wakalah* is an agency contract when one party (principal) contracts another party (agent or wakil) to undertake specific tasks for the benefit of the principal. This contract is used both in Takaful, where the Takaful operator (Islamic insurance operator) is appointed as a wakil on behalf of the policy holders to run the takaful operations, as well as in Islamic banking, i.e commodity murabaha where the customer appoints the bank as an agent to buy or sell commodities on his behalf.

Kafalah is a contract of indemnity whereby one party undertakes to guarantee or indemnify the other party for a particular purpose. E.g., Islamic banks can enter into *kafalah* contracts with their customers to guarantee the payment of a certain sum of money to a third party in the event the customer is unable to pay.

Jualah is a contract to encourage healthy competition. For example, a person can make a jualah contract with a sports team to give them $1,000

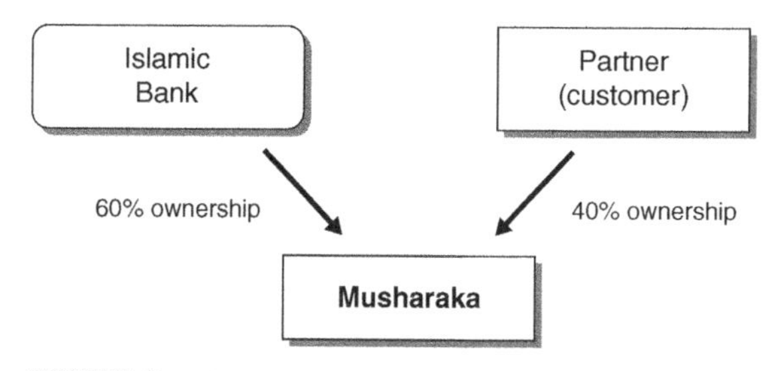

FIGURE 7.9 The structure of musharaka contract

if they win a game. Here jualah should be distinguished from gambling. In gambling, both parties getting the contingent reward must pay an upfront amount and must also benefit if the bet turns out to be in his favor with loss to the other party. Jualah can be used with mudaraba and wakalah to reward partners or agents for superior performance.

CONCLUSION

In this chapter we have learnt that commercial law is an important component of business and impacts accounting greatly. There are mainly two systems of secular law in the world, continental Roman law and the common-law system of England. Islamic commercial law is part of the broader Sharia law, which is sourced from the Quran (the Islamic Scripture) and Hadith (the traditions of the Prophet Muhammad (peace be upon Him). Sharia consists of both Sharia principles and detailed rules of fiqh, which are the interpretation of the Sharia by Islamic scholars grouped into five main mazahib, or schools of legal thought, under various Imams. The main Sunni schools are Hanafi, Shafi, Maliki, and Hanbali; each school is focused on a different part of the Muslim world while the Shii school is mainly followed in Iran and Uzbekistan, although followers exist on the Indian subcontinent as well.

The main components of the Sharia are aqidah/ibadah (belief and rituals), muamalat (transactions), and akhlaq (moral character and behaviour). Islamic commercial law falls under muamalat, which also includes inheritance and marriage laws as well as criminal law.

Islamic commercial law is made up of general law of contract (fiqh al uqud), which includes principles (pillars) and conditions that are meant to achieve fairness and clarity and avoid fraud, ambiguity, and inequity and ensure mutual consent between the contracting parties. The main prohibited elements in Islamic contracts are riba (usury/interest), gambling, and gharar (ambiguity/uncertainty and fraud) as well as contracting for goods or services that are prohibited in Islam such as alcohol and pork, and illicit activities such as prostitution and gambling.

The pillars of Islamic contracts include legal capacity of the contracting parties such as maturity, sanity, and puberty. While essential conditions of Islamic contracts are suitability, value and ownership of subject matter, existence and legality of subject matter.

Prohibited elements in contracts include deception, inequality, mistake, and duress. Contracts with prohibited elements may lead to contracts that are invalid (batil) or fasid (imperfect contracts). The latter can be made valid by the action of the parties or removal of the invalid condition in most cases.

Valid (sahih) contracts are those that result if all the pillars and essential conditions are satisfied.

We have also looked into specific contracts applied in Islamic finance including sale (including sale with deferred payment or delivery) and sale at disclosed markup and contracts for sale of goods that need to be manufactured. We also discussed briefly Ijarah (leasing) and investment contracts along with supporting contracts of indemnity and agency. Further, trust and safekeeping (amanah and wadiah) contracts, debt contracts including giving of rebates were also discussed along with their applications in Islamic finance.

In the next chapter, inshaAllah, we will discuss the application of some these contracts to accounting in Islamic banking.

VOCABULARY

Gharar
Ijarah
Istisna'a
Maisir
Mudaraba
Murabaha
Musharaka
Riba
Salam
Sukuk
Tawarruq/Commodity
Wadia
Wakalah

MULTIPLE-CHOICE QUESTIONS

1. Which of the following systems of law are not religious based?
   a. Hindu family law
   b. Canon law
   c. Sharia
   d. Roman law

2. The legal system practiced currently in Turkey is mainly based on
   a. Sharia as codified in the Majallah.
   b. common law of England.
   c. Continental European law.
   d. Canon law.
3. The following are Islamic legal schools of thought except:
   a. Shafi.
   b. Mazhabi.
   c. Maliki.
   d. Hanafi.
4. What is the difference between Sharia and fiqh?
   a. Sharia is based on the Quran, while fiqh is based on Hadith.
   b. Sharia consists of legal rules and fiqh consists of legal principles.
   c. Sharia consists of mostly legal principles and fewer legal rules, whereas fiqh is the derivation of detailed legal rules based on the discipline of usul al fiqh. Both are based on the Quran and Hadith.
   d. Sharia is based on the Hadith and fiqh is based on the Quran.
5. The components of Sharia include the following, except:
   a. Aqidah/Ibadah.
   b. Aqeeqah.
   c. Muamalat.
   d. Akhlaq.
6. The Muamalat component of the Sharia includes:
   a. Commercial transactions only.
   b. Commercial and marriage contracts.
   c. Commercial, family, charitable, and hereditary laws.
   d. Commercial, marriage, and charitable contracts as well as hereditary and criminal laws.
7. The following are the pillars of the Islamic contracts *except*:
   a. Legal capacity of contracting parties.
   b. Offer and acceptance.
   c. Suitable, known, and existing subject matter, with some exceptions for existence.
   d. Consideration.
8. Which one of the following contracts is imperfect (fasid) and NOT batil?
   a. A trustee of an orphan's property sells it at a small discount to his relatives.
   b. Ahmad rents out his property to a lottery franchise.

c. John sells a painting to Ali, misrepresenting it as a da Vinci when it is actually a Picasso. The Picasso is of slightly lesser value then the da Vinci.
d. George, a gangster, forces Abdullah to sell his apartment to his boss for half the actual value under the threat of burning down his apartment.

9. Which of the following is NOT a condition of the subject matter of the Islamic contract of sale?
   a. The subject matter must exist at the time of contracting except for salam and istisna contracts.
   b. It must be owned by the seller.
   c. The subject matter must be halal, i.e. permitted by the Sharia.
   d. The subject matter must be of high value.
10. Which of the following makes mudaraba different from a musharaka contract?
    I. Capital contribution
    II. Loss sharing
    III. Profits shared in pre-agreed ratio
    IV. Management participation
    a. I, II, and IV
    b. I and IV only
    c. All the above
    d. II and IV only

DISCUSSION QUESTIONS

1. What are the two systems of secular law in the world?
2. Is there any other religious law in the world besides the Sharia? What are these, and where are they practiced?
3. Explain the differences between Sharia and fiqh.
4. Categorize the Sharia into the main components and give a brief explanation of each.
5. What do you think are the main objectives of Islamic contracts? Derive these from the pillars and rules of Islamic contracts.
6. What is the difference between Qard and Dayn?
7. What are the pillars of Islamic contracts. State and explain briefly.
8. Explain the prohibited elements in Islamic contracts.

9. What elements make an Islamic contract defective or invalid besides the prohibited elements in question 8?
10. Differentiate between mudaraba, musharaka, and murabaha.

EXERCISES

1. Search the website of an Islamic bank in Malaysia and one bank in Bahrain and list the deposit and financing products. What are the underlying contracts in these products? Are the underlying contracts the same in the Malaysian and Middle East banks?
2. Categorize the following contracts as valid, invalid, or imperfect.
   a. An Islamic bank provides financing to build a Masjid.
   b. Rajoo Islamic bank provides interest to its depositors.
   c. Ali signs up for a family takaful policy (similar to life insurance).
   d. An Islamic bank in country X enters into an istisna contract to finance the building of a prostitution center. Prostitution is legal in the country.
   e. An Islamic bank provides murabaha financing for a car already owned by Ahmad.
   f. An underaged boy enters into a loan agreement with his friend.
   g. Kathija is forced to sell her car for $10,000 (less than the market value) to Kevin by Nathan, who is a paraplegic using a wheelchair.
3. Restructuring the mudaraba contract: Hussain enters into a mudaraba agreement with Hasan, who will be the mudharib. The terms of the agreement are as follows:
   a. Hasan gets $4,000 monthly salary, whereas Hussain gets 5% of his capital amount every year in addition to any profits, even in the case of losses.
   b. Hussain provides 70% of the capital; Hasan provides the rest.
   c. Hussain and Hasan share the profits and losses equally.
   d. Losses are shared by Hussain and Hasan in the capital contribution ratio.
   e. Hussain will take an active part in the management of the mudaraba.

   Discuss the above scenario from the fiqh point of view of a mudaraba contract. If you are called to advise the partners regarding compliance with the Sharia, how will you restructure the contract to be according to mudaraba principles? What other option is available if the partners do not want to make too many changes to their contract?

CHAPTER 8

Application of Islamic Financial Contracts to Accounting

Learning Outcomes

At the end of this chapter, you will be able to:

1. State three Islamic financial contracts that are used in the Islamic financial services industry and why these contracts are mainstream.
2. Apply murabaha contract rules to accounting under AAOIFI standards.
3. Explain the meaning of urboun and undertake the accounting entries required for it.
4. Discuss the difference between interest and tawid and journalise the transaction.
5. Explain the time value of money, compounding, and discounting concepts.
6. Define effective rate of profit, internal rate of return, annuity, amortised cost, and the effective profit rate.
7. Compute present and future values of a single cash flow and annuities in Excel.
8. Construct an amortisation table using Excel.
9. Apply IFRS standards to account for murabaha financing transactions.
10. Explain ibra and compute ibra under both AAOIFI and IFRS accounting.
11. Extract the balance sheet and profit and loss account (income statement) for murabaha financing transactions under AAOIFI and IFRS.
12. Journalise the transactions required for murabaha financing initiation, instalments, early redemption, and termination under both AAOIFI and IFRS.

Islamic banking was initially premised on the partnership contracts of mudaraba and musharaka. Unfortunately, due to practical problems, mainly *agency costs,* these contracts proved untenable, and thus, the murabaha contract of sale tends to dominate the Islamic banking industry up to this day, while the mudaraba contract is used to mobilize savings and investment account deposits for Islamic banks and is rarely used in financing – i.e. giving 'Islamic credit' to customers. On the financing side, the contract of murabaha sale and ijarah (leasing) is used. Recently, reverse murabaha or commodity murabaha (also known as tawarruq) is being used to mobilize deposits. This is an Islamic account, mimicking a fixed-deposit account, giving a prefixed return to the depositor. The following example shows an announcement for these Islamic banking products for retail customers.

MASHREQ AL ISLAMI LAUNCHES PERSONAL FINANCE FOR RETAIL CUSTOMERS

The new products are available under three Islamic concepts, goods murabaha, service ijarah (manfa), and tawarruq, and are available to all customers across the UAE. These products cater to the needs and those customers seeking Sharia-compliant banking personal finance and are available to both UAE nationals and expatriates.

Through Murabaha (Figure 8.1), customers will be able to buy personal products such as furniture or a car. On the other hand, service ijarah (manfa) will provide funds to customers who are looking to finance services such as a holiday or education, while tawarruq is a contract adopted for a cash-lending facility for those looking for Sharia-compliant personal finance.

There are two reasons that murabaha, reverse murabaha (tawarruq), and ijarah became mainstream for Islamic financing:

1. They are the nearest in operation to the conventional banking instruments, which give a fixed return. Murabaha is akin to an interest-based loan, ijarah to conventional leasing, and tawarruq to a fixed-deposit account.
2. The profit-sharing contracts are not popular in Islamic banking (although they form a greater share of financing in the Middle East and Pakistan) because users of such financing enjoy perks (known as agency costs) and invariably show losses, which the Islamic bank has to bear. Further, in order to be successful in the current less-than-honest business environment, they incur high monitoring cost such as auditing and financial reporting and supervision. Another reason is the return has not been high (because of prudential regulations such as penalizing investments in properties) and the depositors are not prepared to take risk for a meager return.

Personal **Finance for Expatriates**

BENEFITS

- High Finance amount
- Comfortable repayment tenor
- Competitive fixed profit rate
- Quick and easy processing

HOW IT WORKS

Personal finance is a Sharia'h Compliant Islamic lending; based on three Islamic principles.

1. **Goods Murabaha:** A sale contract of a tangible asset for a profit mark-up over and above the cost of the asset and an agreed mode of payment (payment can be spot or deferred but often defined in form of Instalments). In Murabaha the seller has to reveal the cost to the buyer. The bank buys an item and sells it to the customer on a deferred basis. The price includes a profit margin agreed by both parties

2. **Service Ijarah (Manfa'):** Under the "Ijarah" agreement, the bank will buy and pay for the services from the provider as requested by the customer and lease the nominated services to him. The customer will enjoy the benefits of the services and in return will pay the rent over a specific period

3. **Tawarruq:** It is also known as Reverse Murabaha or Monetization, where the bank buys a commodity in the market on behalf of the customer and sell it to the customer on deferred payment. The customer can apply for a Personal Finance based on one of the above-mentioned principles.

FIGURE 8.1 Use of Financial contracts at Mashreq al Islami Bank for personal financing
Source: modified from Bank Mashreq Al Islami website (http://www.mashreqal islami.com/en/personal/finance/personal_finance_expatriates/index.aspx)

Murabaha and ijarah have been explained in Chapter 7 on Islamic commercial law. Here we want to explain *tawarruq* briefly: Tawarruq is a mechanism to provide Islamic financing where a depositor requires a fixed return or a customer requires cash, which he will repay in instalments.

Three separate contracts are used in tawarruq: The contract of Wakalah (agency), the contract of murabaha sale, and musawammah (simple sale).

What happens is essentially five steps:

1. The customer who needs cash goes to an Islamic bank and makes a promise to buy certain commodities from the bank, should it acquire it and sell it to him on murabaha. The bank then goes to a commodity trader and buys the commodity and immediately sells the commodity to the customer at markup (murabaha sale).
2. Now the customer owns the goods for which he has contracted to pay for in instalments.
3. However, since he needs cash, he does not take delivery of the commodity he has bought but appoints the bank as an agent to sell the commodities to the market.
4. The bank sells the commodity to the market on behalf of the customer and credits the proceeds to the customer's account.
5. The customer pays the bank in instalments.

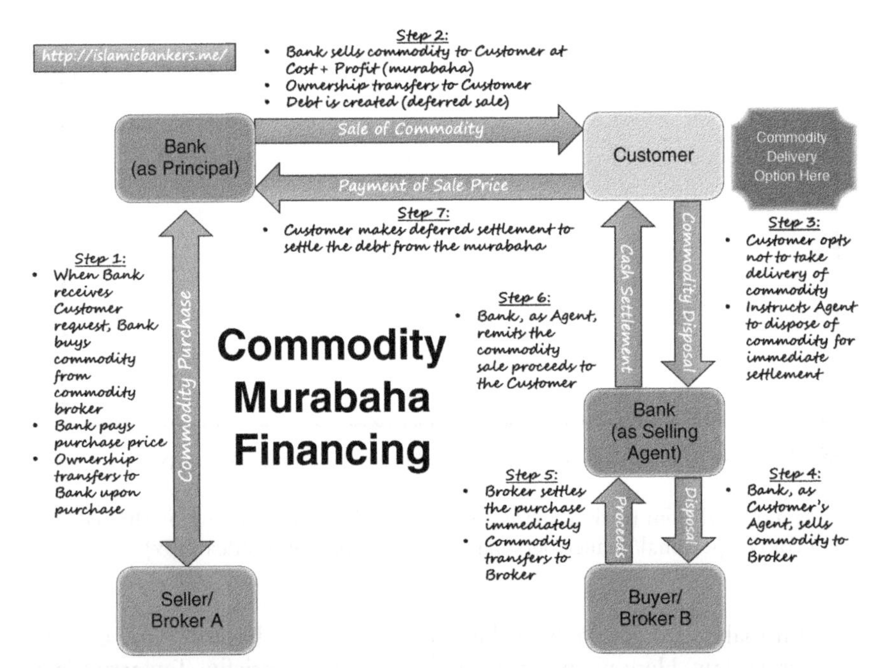

FIGURE 8.2 Tawarruq/ commodity murabaha flows for cash financing of customer
Source: https://islamicbankers.me/

In the case where the customer wants to deposit the money for a fixed return, he appoints the bank as the agent to buy the commodity on his behalf at the time he deposits his funds, after which he immediately sells the commodity to the bank on a murabaha basis, which the bank will pay at a later date. Meanwhile, the bank sells the commodity to the market and gets cash for its financing operations.

AAOIFI AND IFRS ACCOUNTING STANDARDS

From a study of accounting principles, you should have learned that there are many methods of accounting that give different results. Hence, accounting standards have been developed over the years to standardize accounting to achieve consistency and comparability across organisations and even countries.

There are national and international accounting standards for conventional accounting. Currently, the International Financial Reporting Standards (*IFRS*) set by the *International Accounting Standards Board* are increasingly being applied by businesses in most parts of the world including those in the finance industry.

However, because of the different objectives of Islamic finance, as well as the need to comply with the Islamic commercial law (usually termed *Sharia compliance*), there needs to be a different set of accounting standards, as the IFRS did not specifically cater to the requirements of Islamic financial transactions.

Because of this, in the early 1980s when Islamic banks were developing, the concerned Islamic banks and international banks, which had Islamic financing operations, with the support of the Islamic Development Bank in Jeddah and the Bahraini government started an organisation that developed Sharia, auditing, and accounting standards for Islamic financial institutions. This organisation is currently known as Accounting and Auditing Organizations for Islamic Financial Institutions. AAOIFI has issued 27 Islamic accounting standards. Unfortunately, many nations have committed to converge their national accounting standards to the IFRS including for the Islamic finance industry. This has resulted in the loss of support for AAOIFI accounting standards. However, AAOIFI standards are still used in a couple of jurisdictions and AAOIFI standards are a logical place to start, as this is more in line with the Sharia requirements of Islamic finance and Islam.

ACCOUNTING FOR MURABAHA FINANCING TRANSACTIONS UNDER AAOIFI STANDARDS

To recall, murabaha contract is a markup sale where the seller sells the goods to the buyer for the actual cost of the goods plus a profit markup.

FIGURE 8.3 Murabaha to the purchase orderer

Thus,

$$\text{Murabaha selling price} = \text{Cost} + \text{Markup (profit)}.$$

This profit is disclosed to the seller and the selling price can be paid on the spot or deferred to a later date or paid in instalments. In Islamic banking, the price is paid in instalments.

However, as Islamic bankers are financiers and not in trading, they do not want to stock up and take the risk of unsold goods. As such, they secure the order from the customer first and then purchase the goods from the vendor and then proceed to sell the goods to the customer who requires financing. This is known as murabaha to the purchase orderer. We will now account for this transaction. To clarify, these are the steps in the transaction (Figure 8.3):

1. The customer orders the bank to purchase the identified goods, while promising (this may be binding or nonbinding) to buy the goods from the bank, giving it some profit.
2. The bank buys and pays for the goods, from the vendor.
3. The bank executes a murabaha contract of sale to the customer and delivers the goods.
4. The customer pays for the goods on an instalment basis to the bank.

ISSUES TO BE CONSIDERED

Five other considerations need to be looked into before we can start the actual accounting process, i.e. customer deposit, calculation of murabaha selling price, profit recognition, late payment, and early settlement:

1. *A deposit is typically required.* In order to reduce the risk of nonperformance (i.e. the customer does not keep his promise to buy the products that he ordered from the bank after it purchases it for him),

usually the bank requests the customer to pay a *deposit* when he orders the goods with a promise to buy it from the bank. This deposit is normally *urboun* (see below), which is a nonrefundable deposit, should the customer not proceed with the purchase. How do we account for the deposit?

> **URBOUN**
>
> It is the amount paid by the client (orderer) to the seller (i.e. the original purchaser) when the former purchases an asset from the seller. If the customer proceeds with the sale and takes the asset, then the urboun will be part of the price; otherwise, the urboun will be for the seller.

2. *The murabaha selling price is calculated.* This involves two phases.
   a. Calculate the cost of financing, which is the actual amount financed by the IFI (Islamic Financial Institution)

   $$\text{Cost of financing} = \text{Equipment cost} - \text{Deposit from customer}$$

   Remember, equipment cost must include all associated costs such as delivery, taxes, insurance (or takaful), etc.

   b. Calculate markup.

   This is the actual profit for the entire period of the murabaha contract:

   $$\text{Markup (profit)} = \%\ \text{markup on cost of financing} \times \text{Period of murabaha contract.}$$

   c. Calculate murabaha selling price.

   $$\text{Murabaha selling price} = \text{Cost of financing} + \text{Markup}$$

3. *Profits must be recognised.* The markup portion of the profit is for the whole period of the contract. Following the prudence concept in accounting, we do not recognise the whole profit in the first financial year, as the risk of realisation is much greater than a cash sale. Hence, we need to allocate this profit over the period of the contract to give a fairer method of recognition.

   The AAOIFI provides several ways to do this:
   a. Recognise the profit equally over the period.
   b. Recognise the profit according to the instalments received or receivable.
   c. Any other reasonable method.

d. There are really no Sharia problems in the method used to recognise profits unless there is early redemption.
e. Under IFRS, profit is recognised using the effective profit rate on the amortised cost (which we will discuss later). This has the effect of recognising more profits in the earlier years of the murabaha and less profits in the later years, a pattern consistent with interest recognition on loans where the higher the balance of the principal, the higher the interest recognised. In a conventional loan, the instalments received are broken down into payment of the interest portion and the principal portion.
f. Under AAOIFI we can also recognise profits in such a way to mimic interest recognition in a conventional loan using a double-declining balance method or reducing balance method, which is used in depreciation calculations.

4. *The murabaha instalments are usually due every month*. In conventional banking, if one is late in paying instalments, interest is charged to the customer, which is then compounded, if there is further delay. This cannot be done by Islamic banking since it is riba. However, the scholars have allowed the banks to collect a fine called tawid to encourage customers to pay on time. This amount is normally given to charity to avoid Sharia issues.
5. *Normally the murabaha contract is for a fixed term – say, 3 or 5 years*. However, the customer may choose to settle the debt earlier than the agreed term. This is known as early redemption. In conventional banking, this is not a problem. Usually the interest is calculated to the point of time the customer wants to redeem. Hence, only the balance of the principal amount of financing needs to be repaid (in some instances, the bank charges a fine or additional interest). However, in Islamic banking, the murabaha selling price includes profit to the end of the initial term of the contract. Hence, if the customer redeems early, he technically has to pay the full balance of the murabaha price still unpaid. When compared to conventional banking this seems unfair, as the financing is for a shorter term. However, from an Islamic point of view the transaction is a sale resulting in a debt, which has to be paid. In the Sharia, one is encouraged to forgo part of the debt which is known as ibra, which is basically a discount on the balance of the murabaha price to take into account the unexpired period of the contract. Although the ibra is voluntary on the part of the bank, in Malaysia, it is now written into the murabaha contract in the interest of fairness to the customer.

Now we are ready to start the accounting for murabaha contracts.

ACCOUNTING ENTRIES

Let us look at the journal entries required for the preceding transaction flows:

1. Order from the customer. On placement of order, the customer deposits money into the bank account. On the part of the bank, this is a liability, as the bank has not performed any services to earn the money as such.

DR Cash CR Deposit Payable	with the amount of deposit

2. Purchase of equipment by the bank. Suppose the customer orders a car, then the bank buys the car from the vendor and pays for it; thus:

DR Equipment CR Cash	with the total amount paid for the equipment (cost of financing + deposit received)

3. Murabaha sale of equipment to the customer.

DR Murabaha Financing	with the murabaha selling price
CR Equipment	with the **cost of financing**
CR Unearned Profit	with the total murabaha profit (markup)

4. To write of the deposit liability as it is used to reduce cost of financing.

DR Deposit Payable CR Equipment	with the amount of the deposit received from customer.

5. To record instalments received. This requires two double entries: One to recognise the cash received and reduce the debt. The other to recognise profit.

DR Cash CR Murabaha Financing	with amount of instalment received
DR Unearned Profit CR Profit and Loss Account (Income Statement)	with the amount of profit recognised

6. To record overdue instalments.

DR A/C Receivable CR Murabaha Financing	with amount of instalment overdue
DR Unearned Profit CR Profit and Loss Account (Income Statement)	with the amount of profit recognised in the overdue instalment

7. To record fine on overdue instalments received. This amount will be given to charity when received.

DR A/C Receivable CR Charity Payable	with amount of tawid or fine.

8. To record overdue instalments received. Remember the profit has already been recognised earlier.

DR Cash CR Accounts Receivable	with amount of overdue instalment received (**including tawid**)

9. To record tawid paid to charity.

DR Charity Payable CR Cash	Tawid received paid to charity

10. To record termination of murabaha contract. This requires two double entries: One to recognise the cash received and reduce of the debt, the other to recognise profit.

DR A/C Receivable CR Murabaha Financing	with the balance amount of instalment
DR Unearned Profit CR Profit and Loss Account (Income Statement)	with the amount of final profit recognised

11. To record final instalments received.

DR Cash CR A/C Receivable	with amount of final instalment received

12. To record early termination and settlement with rebate.

(a)

DR Cash CR Murabaha Financing	with the settlement amount received
DR Unearned Profit	with the outstanding balance in the account
CR Profit and Loss Account (Income Statement)	with the final amount of profit recognised
CR Murabaha Financing	with the rebate amount given

Table 8.1 shows the summary of journal entries.

FINANCIAL STATEMENT PRESENTATION OF MURABAHA FINANCING

Figure 8.4 shows extracts from the 2016 Annual Report of Bank Islam Malaysia which is prepared under IFRS, all amounts receivable as a result of Islamic financing (including Murabaha Financing) are shown on the face of the balance sheet, under financing and advances. However, in the notes to the accounts, the breakup according to each contract is shown (this is required by the central bank of Malaysia, not by IFRS). However, no such breakup (from various Sharia contracts) is shown in the income statement of Bank Islam Malaysia for income from various Sharia contracts.

Under AAOIFI standards, however, both the balance sheet and income statement (profit and loss account) show the murabaha financing balance and the profit earned from murabaha financing clearly. The notes to the financial statements from the Bahraini Islamic Bank follow AAOIFI standards (Figure 8.5 shows how these are presented).

Note: Although AAOIFI standards use the term *murabaha financing*. Bahrain Islamic Bank uses the term *Financing Assets in its Balance Sheet*

TABLE 8.1 Journal Entries

No.	Transactions/Events	DR	CR.
a	Customer deposit received	Cash	Deposit Payable
b	Purchase of asset by bank	Equipment	Cash/Creditors
c	murabaha sale	Murabaha Financing (Financing cost + Profit)	Equipment Account at financing cost and Deferred profit Account with profit
d	Write off deposit payable	Deposit Payable	Equipment
e	Instalment receipt and	Cash	Murabaha Financing
	Recognition of profit as each instalment is received	Deferred Profit	Profit and Loss
f	Instalment overdue (with the amount of instalment)	A/C Receivable	Murahaha Financing
	Recognition of profits in the overdue instalment	Deferred Profit	Profit and Loss
g	Amount of tawid or fine for late payment	A/C Receivable	Charity Payable
h	Collection of tawid and overdue instalment and payment of tawid to charity	Cash Charity Payable	A/C Receivable Cash
i	Termination of murabaha contract:		
	Balance of selling price unpaid	A/c Receivable	Murahaha Financing
	Final profit earned on the contract	Deferred Profit	Profit and Loss
	Redemption amount paid by customer	Cash	A/C Receivable
k	Rebate for early payment	Deferred Profit	Murabaha Financing

with a subitem; murabaha in the notes (leaning towards the IFRS presentation), while in previous years' annual reports, it was shown as murabaha receivables directly in the balance sheet,

All the income from Islamic financing is summarized in one line in the statement of income (profit and loss account) However, it is broken up by type of contract in the notes to the financial statements of Bahrain Islamic Bank (figure 8.5 below).

9. Financing, Advanced and Others

(a) By type and Sharia contract

Group and Bank 31 December 2016	Bai* Bithaman Ajil RM'000	Murabaha RM'000	Bai Al-Dayn RM'000	Bai Al-Inah RM'000	At-Tawarruq RM'000	Ijarah Muntahiah Bit-Tamleek RM'000	Ijarah Thumma Al-Bai RM'000	Istisna* RM'000	Ar-Rahnu RM'000	Total RM'000
At amortised cost										
Cash line	–	–	–	37,899	1,199,021	–	–	–	–	1,236,920
Term financing										
House financing^	4,484,247	–	–	–	9,503,014	–	–	59,088	–	14,046,349
Syndicated financing	–	–	–	196,129	1,045,889	–	123,189	–	–	1,365,207
Leasing financing	–	–	–	–	–	90,610	902	–	–	91,512
Bridging financing	–	–	–	–	–	–	–	82,313	–	82,313
Personal financing^	–	–	–	42,177	11,197,744	–	–	–	–	11,239,921
Other term financing	2,086,188	933,316	–	4,063	7,106,669	–	–	1,503	–	10,131,739
Staff financing	83,743	5,087	–	–	98,821	–	–	14,218	–	201,869
Credit cards	–	–	–	9,004	450,388	–	–	–	–	459,392
Trade bills discounted	–	741,037	180,010	–	–	–	–	–	–	921,047
Trust receipts	–	5,169	–	–	–	–	–	–	–	5,169
Pawn broking	–	–	–	–	–	–	–	–	85,315	85,315
Investment Account Platform*	–	–	–	–	5,690	–	–	–	–	5,690
	6,654,178	1,684,609	180,010	289,272	30,607,236	90,610	124,091	157,122	85,315	39,872,443
Allowance for impaired financing, advances, and others										
– collective assessment allowance										(554,971)
– individual assessment allowance										(128,198)
Net financing, advances and others										39,189,274

FIGURE 8.4 Notes to the financial statements of Bank Islam Malaysia 2016

Notes to the Consolidated Financial Statements

31 December 2017

3. Cash and Balances with Banks and Central Bank	2017 BD'000	2016 BD'000
Cash on hand	13,042	12,829
Balances with CBB, excluding mandatory reserve deposits	3,654	3,877
Balances with banks and other financial institutions	17,765	12,737
	34,461	29,443
Mandatory reserve with CBB	35,205	33,765
	69,666	63,208

The mandatory reserve with CBB is not available for use in the day-to-day operations.

Balances with banks and other financial institutions include an amount of BD 2,512 thousand which is not available for use in the day-to-day operations.

4. Placements with Financial Institutions	2017 BD'000	2016 BD'000
Commodity Murabaha	53,519	43,511
Deferred profits	(5)	(27)
	53,514	43,484
Wakala	27,331	20,321
	80,845	63,805

5. Financing Assets	2017 BD'000	2016 BD'000
Murabaha (note 5.1)	455,501	396,917
Musharaka (note 5.2)	106,321	109,539
	561,822	506,456

5.1 Murabaha	2017 BD'000	2016 BD'000
Tasheel	206,855	225,868
Tawarooq	195,474	136,348
Altamweel Almaren	64,912	48,174
Letters of credit refinance	27,229	29,198
Motor vehicles Murabaha	9,625	13,058
Credit cards	17,992	15,894
Others	58	70
	522,145	468,610
Qard fund	71	65
Gross receivables	522,216	468,675
Deferred profits	(52,695)	(45,781)
Provision for impairment	(14,020)	(25,977)
	455,501	396,917

Nonperforming Murabaha financing outstanding as at 31 December 2017 amounted to BD 34,436 thousand (2016: BD 30,951 thousand). The Group considers the promise made in the Murabaha to the purchase orderer as obligatory.

The composition of the Murabaha financing portfolio net of deferred profit and before provision for impairment by sector is as follows:

	2017 BD'000	2016 BD'000
Commercial	95,128	73,780
Financial institutions	32,693	16,214
Others including retail	341,700	332,900
	469,521	422,894

The Group exposures of Murabaha financing portfolio is concentrated in the Middle East.
www.bisb.com

FIGURE 8.5 Notes to the financial statements of Bank Islam Bahrain

Notes to the Consolidated Financial Statements
31 December 2017

18. Capital Adequacy (Continued)
To assess its capital adequacy requirements in accordance with the CBB requirements, the Group adopts the Standardised Approach for its Credit Risk, Basic Indicator Approach for its Operational Risk, and Standardised Approach for its Market Risk. The capital requirements for these risks are as follows:

	2017 BD'000	2016 BD'000
Risk weighted exposure:		
Total Credit Risk Weighted Assets	571,069	527,820
Total Market Risk Weighted Assets	10,702	12,226
Total Operational Risk Weighted Assets	86,085	66,722
Total Regulatory Risk Weighted Assets	667,856	606,768
Investment risk reserve (30% only)	353	227
Profit equalization reserve (30% only)	374	374
Total Adjusted Risk Weighted Exposures	667,129	606,167
Capital Adequacy Ratio	19.40%	20.30%
Tier 1 Capital Adequacy Ratio	17.41%	18.33%
Minimum requirement	12.5%	12.5%

19. Income from Financing

	2017 BD'000	2016 BD'000
Income from Murabaha financing	23,483	20,143
Income from placements with financial institutions	1,093	341
Income from Musharaka financing	6,580	6,300
Income from Ijarah Muntahia Bittamleek	9,351	8,097
	40,507	34,881

20. Income from Investment Securities

	2017 BD'000	2016 BD'000
Dividend income	513	739
	513	739

21. Income from Investment in Real Estate

	2017 BD'000	2016 BD'000
Loss on sale	(39)	(843)
Rental income	371	362
Impairment charge	(119)	(82)
	213	(563)

22. Other Income

	2017 BD'000	2016 BD'000
Recoveries from previously written off financing	1,883	3,499
Foreign exchange gain/(loss)	489	(1,001)
Others	368	2,046
	2,740	4,544

FIGURE 8.5 (*Continued*)

Previously, the information in note 19 (Figure 8.5) was detailed in the main income statement; however, with the intent to conform with IFRS wherever possible, even Bahraini Islamic Bank has modified AAOIFI requirements.

WORKED EXAMPLES

Illustration 1: Simple Murabaha Accounting under AAOIFI

Ali needs financing to buy a house for $100,000. The Islamic bank sells him a house at a markup of 10% per annum constant rate of return with a financing period of 5 years. Instalments are paid yearly.

Required:

a. Calculate the markup, murabaha selling price, the yearly instalment, and the profit recognised per year.
b. The journal entries in the bank records for initiation and recording of the receipt of the first instalment and recognition of profit *if profit is recognised when the instalments are received* and all instalments are received on schedule.
c. Show the extract of the balance sheet at the beginning and end of the first year and profit and loss account at the end of the same year.
d. Draw a graph showing on the axis the profit recognised per year and the years on the x-axis.

Answer:

a. Cost of financing = $100,000

Markup = 10% × 5 years × $100,000 = $50,000

Murabaha selling price = (Cost + Markup) = $150,000

Yearly instalment amount = $150,000/5 = $30,000

Profit recognised per year = $50,000/5 instalments = $10,000 per instalment.

b. Initiation of contract

	Dr	Cr
Dr Equipment	$100,000	
Cr Cash		$100,000

Bank pays cash to developer to purchase the house.

	Dr	Cr
Dr Murabaha Financing	$150,000	
Cr Equipment		$100,000
Cr Deferred Profit		$ 50,000

The bank sells the house to Ali at markup.

	Dr	Cr
Dr cash	$30,000	
Cr Murabaha Financing		$30,000

First instalment received at the end of the year.

Dr Deferred Profit $10,000*
Cr Profit and Loss account $10,000

Profit recognised on receipt of first instalment.

c. Balance sheet:

	Beginning of Year	End of Year
Murabaha financing	$150,000	$120,000 (150,000 – 30,000)
Less: Deferred profit	50,000	40,000 (50,000 – 10,000)
Net book value	100,000	80,000

Profit and loss account at the end of the year (after first instalment).

Profit from Murabaha Financing	$10,000

Illustration 2: Murabaha Profit Recognition Using Double-Declining Method

As explained earlier under 8.4(c), if we use a reducing balance method such as double declining of effective profit rate method, we would see that profit recognised is high in the beginning years and lower in the subsequent years. This would give a pattern of profit recognition akin to a conventional interest-based loan, as, although the interest rate remains the same, the principal (the amount lent) becomes less and less, as the instalments are used to pay both principal and interest. This happens due to the interest rate being applied to the remaining principal every period and not to the original amount of the loan.

So now let us now explain to you what the double-declining method is and how it is used to calculate the profit recognised using the data in the previous illustration.

If the period of financing is n (which can be months or years or quarters), then the double-declining method rate is $2 \times 1/n$; thus, in the previous illustration where the period of financing is 5 years, then $n = 5$ and the double declining rate is $2 \times 1/n = 2/5 = 40\%$ per year.

We need to use this rate to multiply the total profit to get the first amount of profit recognized in the first period, and subsequently, we use this rate on the remaining profit at the beginning of the subsequent period. We can construct an amortisation (in this case profit recognition) table to calculate the amount of profit to be recognised each year (Table 8.2).

TABLE 8.2 Amortisation Table

Profit amortisation table using double-declining balance method, $r = 40\%$

	Beginning year balance of profit to be recognised	Profit for the year recognised @ 40% of beginning balance	End of year balance of profit yet to be recognised
Yr 1	50,000	20,000	30,000
Yr 2	30,000	12,000	18,000
Yr 3	18,000	7,200	10,800
Yr 4	10,800	4,320	6,480
Yr 5	6,480	6,480	0

Year 5 profit to be recognised is actually 40% × 6,480 = 2,592, but since this is the last year we take all the remaining, yet to be recognised profit.

As you can see from the table above, the profit recognised per year declines every year.

PROFIT RECOGNITION USING EFFECTIVE PROFIT RATE METHOD UNDER IFRS

In this section, we will explain how to:

1. Calculate the *effective profit rate* method used to recognise profit.
2. Value that the murabaha financing as presented in the balance sheet at the *fair value at amortised cost.*
3. Construct an amortisation table.

To calculate the effective profit rate (or interest rate as it is called in conventional finance), we need to use either a compound interest table or an Excel formula.

We will use the Excel formula (you can also use a financial calculator, but we will not cover this in this book).

The concept of an effective interest rate depends on the concept of *time value of money*, which is a controversial concept in Islam. Time value of money implies that a dollar received today is worth more than a dollar received in a future time. If we have the option of receiving $1 million today or $1 million 5 years from today, this concept says that $1 million received today is worth more than the $1 million that will be received 5 years from now. In the inflation-ridden world of today, this is easy to understand – we will not be able to buy the same amount of goods and services with

$1 million received 5 years from now as compared to $1 million received today due to inflation.

However, even in the absence of inflation, there is a possible opportunity cost forgone (the cost of the next best alternative use of the money). Let us say that I have $1,000,000 and perhaps the best investment I can make is to buy and sell land, which can make me 10% a year. So in 5 years, my $1,000,000 will compound to $(1 + 0.1)^5 \times 1{,}000{,}000 = \$1{,}610{,}510$. So I am forgoing an opportunity to make $610,510 in 5 years. The time value of money is used as a benchmark to measure this. The act of calculating the future value of an investment at a rate of i% per year compounded is called *compounding*.

To illustrate the difference between a simple and a compound return, let us take $1,000 at a simple rate of return of 10%. In this case, the $1,000 @10% per annum will give us $100 profit for one year. So an amount of $1,000 will yield a simple return of $100 × 2 years = $200, which, together with the investment, will give us a future value of $1,200. Here, we assume we do not reinvest the $100 profit from the first year. However, compounding assumes we reinvest the $100 return from the first year together with the original amount in the second year:

Compounding $1,000 @ 10% per annum for two years will give:

$$\$1{,}100 \text{ (total value at end of the first year)}$$
$$+\ 1{,}100 \times 10\% = \$1{,}100\ +\ 110 = \$1{,}210.$$

The extra $10 difference from a simple return of $200 is because we have reinvested the earnings from the first year along with the principal for another year.

Hence, we can say, the future value of $1,000 @ 10% per annum (p.a.) = $1,210. This is the same thing as saying that investing $1,000 compounded at 10% profit rate per annum gives us $1,210 in two years. In mathematical notation, this is said to be the future value or FV, hence, $FV(1000)_{0.1} = 1{,}210$.

Related to this is the concept of discounting, which is the opposite of compounding. In compounding, we move forward in time to get the future value of and amount invested today, while in discounting we move from the future to the present. Hence, the present value (PV) of $1,210 received in two years' time discounted at 10% p.a. profit rate is worth $1,000 today. We can write this as $PV(1{,}210)_{0.1} = 1{,}000$. Figure 8.6 should make this clear.

The calculations get more complex as the number of periods and the number of cash flows get more and more. Consider Figure 8 where there are different amounts of cash flows for five years.

To overcome this complex problem, we can use formulae and compound interest and discount tables to simplify.

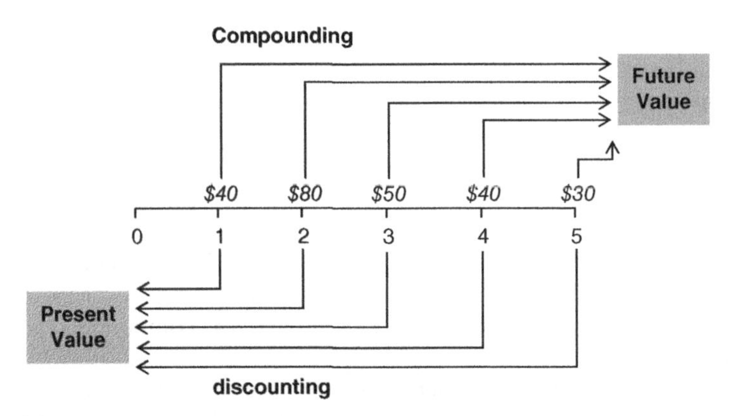

FIGURE 8.6 Different cash flows over different time periods

The formula for calculating a future value (FV) of, say, an amount (PV) at 10% per annum compounded profit in n years' time is given by the formula

$$FV = PV(1 + 0.1)^n,$$

while the present value of an amount FV n years from now is given by

$$PV = FV \times 1/(1 + 0.1)^n \text{ or } FV \times (1 + 0.1)^{-n}$$

However, even with the given formula it is difficult to calculate the PV or FV manually. This can be made easier by financial calculators or using the future value of $1 and present value of $1 financial tables, which are available.

The problem becomes more acute when we have to, in addition to calculating the future value of a single amount invested at the initial period (time period 0, in Figure 8.6) or present value of a single payout as we did above, calculate the PV or FV of a series of cash flows of the same amount over a number of periods, as in the calculation of FV or PV of a loan amount, which is usually repaid over several periods at the same amount of the instalment every period. This series of equal cash flows over several periods is known as an *annuity*.

ANNUITY

Annuity is the receipt or payment of the same amount of money each period for a number of time periods.

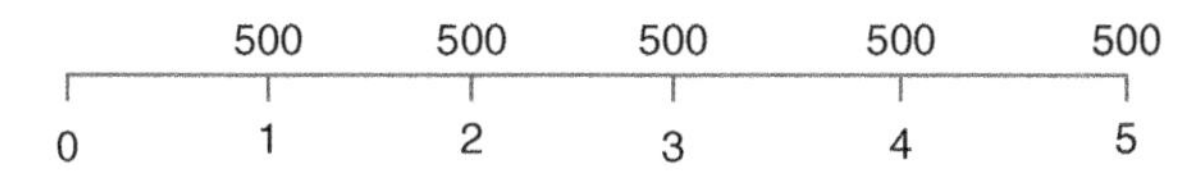

FIGURE 8.7 Cash flow timeline for annuity of \$500 for 5 years

This can be seen in the timeline in Figure 8.7, which consists of a payment of \$500 per month.

If we were to calculate the PV of the above cash flows, we would have to do it like this, if the discount rate was 10% per period:

$$\text{PV}\,(500)\,5\rceil\!\lfloor 0.1 = 500 \times (1+0.1)^{-1} + 500 \times (1+0.1)^{-2} + 500 \times (1+0.1)^{-3} + 500 \times (1+0.1)^{-4} + 500 \times (1+0.1)^{-5} = 1{,}895$$

Fortunately, there is both a table and a formula for calculating the PV or FV or an annuity, which are given below:

$$\text{PVA} = PMT\left[\frac{1-(1+i)^{-n}}{i}\right]$$

thus, plugging in the variables,

$$\text{PVA} = 500[\{1-(1+0.1)^{-5}\}/0.1] = 1{,}895$$

We can use this formula to calculate the instalments for murabaha financing or the present value of a series of constant cash flows, i.e. an annuity.

We can also easily compute this by referring to the table of present value of annuity of \$1 table for 5 periods and profit rate 10% (Table 8.3). You can download this and various other financial tables from the Internet.

Table 8.3 gives the discount factor of 3.79079 for an annuity of \$1 at 10% for 5 years. This means the present value of an annuity of \$1 for 5 years at 10% is \$3.79079. To get the present value of an annuity of \$500 per period, we simply multiply this factor by the amount of the annuity, i.e., \$500; thus,

$$500 \times 3.79079 = \$1{,}995$$

We now explain how the effective rate of profit is calculated using an Excel formula =IRR, which is the formula to calculate the internal rate of return of a series of cash flows. The internal rate of return is the discount

TABLE 8.3 Present Value of Ordinary Annuity

Period = 5

Profit rate
$i = 10\%$

PRESENT VALUE OF ORDINARY ANNUITY
(annuity in arrears -- end of period payments)

Periods	RATE PER PERIOD															
	%	0.50%	0.75%	1.00%	1.50%	2.00%	2.50%	3.00%	4.00%	5.00%	6.00%	7.00%	8.00%	9.00%	10.00%	11.00%	12.00%
1	9751	0.99502	0.99256	0.99010	0.98522	0.98039	0.97561	0.97087	0.96154	0.95238	0.94340	0.93458	0.92593	0.91743	0.90909	0.90090	0.89286
2	99252	1.98510	1.97772	1.97040	1.95588	1.94156	1.92742	1.91347	1.88609	1.85941	1.83339	1.80802	1.78326	1.75911	1.73554	1.71252	1.69005
3	2.98506	2.97025	2.95556	2.94099	2.91220	2.88388	2.85602	2.82861	2.77509	2.72325	2.67301	2.62432	2.57710	2.53129	2.48685	2.44371	2.40183
4	3.97512	3.95050	3.92611	3.90197	3.85438	3.80773	3.76197	3.71710	3.62990	3.54595	3.46511	3.38721	3.31213	3.23972	3.16987	3.10245	3.03735
5	4.96272	4.92587	4.88944	4.85343	4.78264	4.71346	4.64583	4.57971	4.45182	4.32948	4.21236	4.10020	3.99271	3.88965	3.79079	3.69590	3.60478

Discount
factor = 3.79079

(100,000)	30000	30000	30000	30000	30000
0	1	2	3	4	5

FIGURE 8.8 Cash flow over time period

or profit rate at which a series of cash inflows or outflows at different time periods equals the initial investment.

If we look back at Illustration 1, we can rearrange the murabaha financing given to Ali as a series of cash inflows of $30,000 per year with an initial investment of $100,000, which is the cost of financing given to Ali.

See the cash flow over time period in Figure 8.8.

We want to find the effective profit rate, i.e. at what profit rate per annum will present value of the total amount of $150,000 paid to the bank over the five years equal the cost of financing of $100,000.

Using the Excel formula (Figure 8.9), we get 15.2382% effective profit rate per annum.

Please note the formula shaded in the window is =IRR(D3:I3,0.1). D3:I3 is simply showing the computer the range of cells having the cash flows and 0.1 is the guess rate of 10% to start the computer to calculate. You can give any percentage in decimals, such as 0.08 for 8%, and Excel will produce the same results.

The lower range of numbers in cells E7:I7 is the present value of the instalments of each period discounted by 15.2382% to the initial period. The cell D7 contains the =sum formula to add all the discounted value of the instalments. We can see that this is =$100,001; with a rounding error of $1, it is = $100,000. This is to prove to you that the 15.2382% IRR is correct, subject to the rounding error.

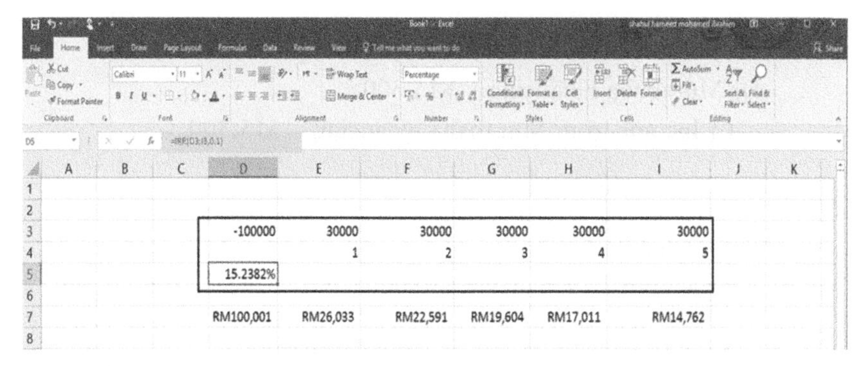

FIGURE 8.9 Illustration 1 using Excel formula

TABLE 8.4 Amortisation Table

Amortisation table of murabaha financing at 15.3% p.a. effective rate					
	a	b	c	d	e
Year	Financing cost	Profit @15.3%	Financing cost + profit	Yearly instalment	Balance of financing cost = a + b − d
1	100,000	15,300	115,300	30,000	85,300
2	85,300	13,051	98,351	30,000	68,351
3	68,351	10,458	78,809	30,000	48,809
4	48,809	7,468	56,276	30,000	26,276
5	26,276	3,724	30,000	30,000	0

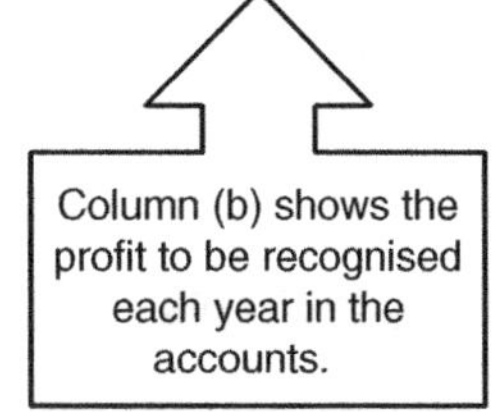

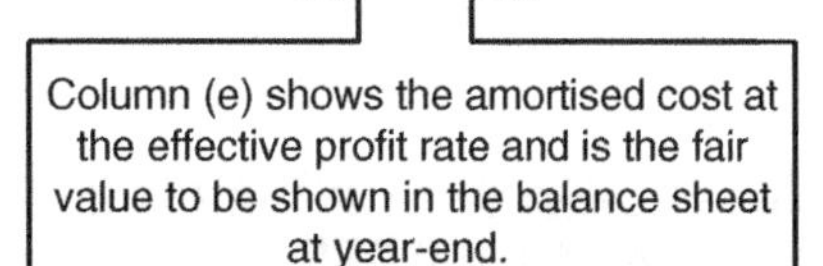

Finally, we shall calculate the profit accrued in each period by constructing an amortisation table using the effective rate of profit but rounded up to 15.3%. Thus, we have the amortisation table in Table 8.4.

Thus, for example, the journal entry for the first year after initiation is:

Dr Murabaha Financing	$100,000	
Cr Equipment		$100,000

When profit is recognised when instalment is due, the entry is:

Dr Murabaha Financing $15,300
Cr Income from Murabaha Financing $15,300

When an instalment is received:

DR Cash $30,000
Cr Murabaha Financing $30,000 (The balance in the Murabaha Financing account after this is 100,000 + 15,300 –30,000 = 85,300, which is shown in the balance sheet.)

At the end of the financial year,

Dr Income from Murabaha Financing $15,300
Cr Profit and Loss account $15,300

The balance sheet at the end of Year 1 will be:

Murabaha Financing $85,300

And the Profit and Loss account will show:

Income from Murabaha Financing 15,300

Note: As compared to AAOIFI , there is no deferred profit account, as the murabaha financing is not shown at the balance of the murabaha price but at the amortised cost, i.e the fair value. The balance of the murabaha price is in a memorandum records in the accounting system and not part of the ledger.

COMPREHENSIVE ILLUSTRATION OF MURABAHA ACCOUNTING UNDER AAOIFI AND IFRS

The Islamic Bank of Bahrain (IBB) finances Sadiq Al Maghribi for him to purchase power generation equipment for his electricity generation plant on January 1, 2016, through a murabaha contract. The purchase price of the equipment is Bahraini Dinars 50 million. Sadiq pays a deposit of BD 10 million to IBB as urboun. The murabaha contract is for 5 years and the markup is BSD 10 million. The murabaha price is repayable in five equal yearly instalments on December 31 of each year. Sadiq paid the instalments on time every year until December 31, 2018. At the beginning of the fourth year, Sadiq requested to terminate the contract with payment of the balance.

The bank agreed to give him a rebate of the full balance of the remaining unearned profit. The bank accrues the profit equally over the term of the contract and follows AAOIFI accounting standards.

You are required to:

a. Calculate the murabaha selling price.
b. Calculate the yearly instalment.
c. Calculate the profit earned each year.
d. Calculate the rebate (ibra) given in the beginning of the fourth year.
e. Calculate the redemption amount Sadiq needs to settle with the bank at the beginning of the fourth year.
f. Show the extract of the income statement and the balance sheet of Bank Saderat in respect of the transaction at the beginning of the transaction and the end of 2016.
g. Show the journal entries for the termination of the murbaha.
h. Please repeat (c), (d), (e), and (f), if the bank follows IFRS accounting standards. Show the amortisation table as your working.

Answer:

a. Murabaha sale price = (50 – 10(deposit) + 10 markup) = 50 million dinars.
b. Murabaha instalments = 50/5 = 10 million dinars/year.
c. Murabaha profit earned per year under AAOIFI = 10/5 = 2 million dinars per year.
d. Rebate (ibra) given at the beginning of the 4 year = (Total murabaha profit 10) – (profit recognised until the end of 3 years [2 × 3] 6) = 10 – 6 = 4 million.
e. Settlement (Redemption) amount is = 50 million (total price) – 30 million (amount paid for three years) – 4 million (discount/rebate) = 16 million.
f. Balance sheet and income statement under AAOIFI standards.

Extract of balance sheet for Bank Islam Bahrain as at 31st December

	Beginning 2016	End 2016	2017	2018	2019
Murabah Financing	50m	40m	30m	20m	–
Less unearned Income	–10m	–8m	–6m	–4m	–
Net Receivable	40m	32m	24m	16m	–

Extract of balance sheet for Bank Islam Bahrain as at 31st December

Profit from Murabah	–	2m	2m	2m	

g. Termination entries on early redemption under AAOIFI at beginning of year 4:

Dr Cash	16 m	
Dr Deferred Profit	4 m	
Cr Murabaha Financing		20 m

Under IFRS, we have to first calculate the effective profit rate using Excel internal rate of return =IRR function.

The cash flows are the same as before, i.e. –40 m (amount of financing) and 10 million each as instalment payment; thus:

BIB financing of Sadiq Al Maghribi: Cash flows

Cash flow in BD (millions)	−40	10	10	10	10	10
Year	0	1	2	3	4	5

Using the =irr function in Excel, the internal rate of return for the cash flows is 7.93%, as can be seen in the Excel spreadsheet in Figure 8.10.

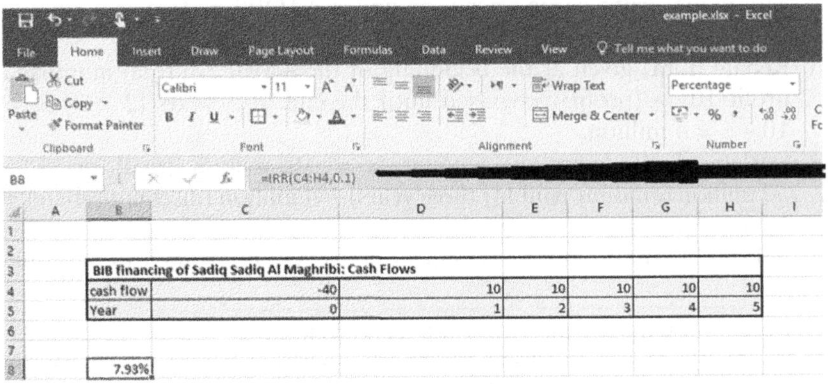

FIGURE 8.10 Excel illustration for Sadiq Al Maghribi

Using this rate of 7.93%, we must construct an amortisation table as shown below in Table 8.5. Column D shows the fair value as the amortised cost of financing at the given profit rate.

Rebate given in the beginning of the fourth year under IFRS is (Selling price) 50 – (Instalments paid) 30 – (Balance of financing cost)17.848681 = 2.151391 million.

TABLE 8.5 Amortisation Table for comprehensive example under IFRS

BIB Amortization table for Murabaha financing of generator project of Sadiq al Maghra (in BD (Millions)

Year	Cost (A)=	(B) effective profit @ 7.93%x A	(C) Repayment	(D)amortized cost = A + B – C
2016	40.000000	3.172	10	33.172
2017	33.172000	2.63054	10	25.80254
2018	25.802540	2.046141	10	17.848681
2019	17.848681	1.4154	10	9.264081
2020	9.264081	0.735919	10	0

Finally, the redemption or settlement amount 17.848681 million, i.e. the fair value at the beginning of the third year, represents the remaining amount of the original cost of financing.

Finally, the extract of the balance sheet and profit and loss account for Bahrain Islamic Bank for the murabaha transaction under the IFRS is as follows:

BIB Balance Sheet and Profit and Loss account 31st December re: Murabaha Transaction Sadiq Al Maghribi

	1/1/2016	2016	2017	2018
Murabaha Financing (FV) at Amortised cost	40,000,000	33,172,000	25,802,540	17,848,681
Income statement				
Profit from Murabaha		3,172,000	2,630,540	2,046,141

VOCABULARY

AAOIFI (Accounting and Auditing Organization for Islamic Financial Institutions)

compounding

discounting

early redemption

effective profit rate

effective rate of interest

ibra
IFRS (international financial reporting standards)
irr (internal rate of return)
markup/profit
murabaha
murahaba selling price
murabaha to the purchase orderer
tawid

MULTIPLE-CHOICE QUESTIONS

1. Which of the following is correct, when ibra is recorded in the accounts?
   a. It shall be debited to the Murabaha Financing account.
   b. It shall be treated as a liability.
   c. It shall be taken out of the deferred profit account and credited to Murabaha Financing.
   d. It shall be credited to the Murabaha Payables account and debited to cash.
2. Which of the following is incorrect?
   a. The contract of murabaha requires that the markup (profit) must be recognised equally over the murabaha contract period.
   b. In murabaha financing, the selling price must be fixed without any hidden cost.
   c. The contract of murabaha allows for early redemption with rebate on the unearned income.
   d. Late payment charges levied by the bank are allowed by AAOIFI but should be given to the charity if directed by the Sharia committee and should not be compounded.
3. Identify the correct action of the islamic bank in the following case study: Mr. Bilal made a binding promise to an Islamic bank that he would buy a van from the latter through a murabaha transaction. Based on that promise, the Islamic bank collected urboun of US$500 from him, and bought a van from a vendor for US$30,000 in cash. After the van was delivered to the Islamic bank, Mr. Bilal decided not to buy it. The Islamic bank then sold the van to John in a forced sale, for US$29,800 in cash.
   a. The Islamic bank should return US$200 to Bilal
   b. The Islamic bank should return US$500 to Bilal.
   c. The Islamic bank should not return any money to Bilal.

   d. The Islamic bank should not return any money to Bilal but must pay US$200 to John as a gift to be thankful to John for being willing to buy the van.
4. Which is the most common contract for personal financing being employed by Islamic banks?
   a. Murabaha
   b. Musharaka
   c. Tawarruq
   d. Mudharaba
5. Identify the correct journal entries at the time of contracting the murabaha contract under the following scenario: An Islamic bank enters into a murabaha financing agreement for a plant at a cost of $300,000 and profit of $100,000. It has purchased the asset already.
   a. Debit: Murabaha Financing; Credit: Equipment and Deferred Profit
   b. Debit: Cash; Credit: Equipment and Deferred Profit
   c. Debit: Murabaha Financing; Credit: Cash and Profit with the appropriate amounts
   d. Debit: Murabaha Financing; Credit: Accounts Payable and Deferred Profit

Questions 6 to 10 are based on the scenario of Jordan Islamic Bank given below:

Jordan Islamic Bank gave murabaha financing to Ahmad to purchase a house that cost the bank 200,000 dinars over a 10-year period. The markup was a constant rate of return of 10% per annum. The instalments are to be paid equally over the 10 years. The bank recognises profit equally over the period. Ahmad paid the instalments regularly for the first 4 years and at the end of the fifth year he redeemed the financing. Jordan Islamic Bank agreed to give Ahmad 80% of the unearned deferred profit at the end of year 5, after taking the full profit for year 5.

6. Which of the following is the correct entry on receipt of instalments of year 1, including recognition of profit?

a. Dr Cash 40,000	Cr Murabaha Financing 40,000
Dr Deferred Profit 30,000	Cr Profit and Loss 30,000
b. Dr Cash 40,000	Cr Murabaha Financing 40,000
Dr Deferred Profit 20,000	Cr Profit and Loss 20,000
c. Dr Cash 40,000	Cr Murabaha Financing 40,000
Dr Profit and Loss 20,000	Cr Deferred Profit 20,000
d. Dr Murabaha Financing 40,000	Cr Cash 40,000
Dr Profit and Loss 20,000	Cr Deferred Profit 20,000

7. Which of the following is the correct extract of the balance sheet of Islamic Bank of Jordan at the end of the **2nd year after the second instalment is paid?**
   a. Murabaha Financing 200,000
   b. Murabaha Financing 320,000
   c. Musharaka Financing 320,000
   d. Murabaha Financing 400,000
8. Which of the following is the correct extract of the income statement of Islamic Bank of Jordan at the end of the **1st year?**
   a. Profit/(loss) from Murabaha Financing (20,000)
   b. Profit/(loss) from Murabaha Financing 20,000
   c. Profit/(loss) from Murabaha Financing 200,000
   d. Profit/(loss) from Murabaha Financing 40,000
9. Which of the following shows the correct balance of Deferred Profit account of Islamic Bank of Jordan at the end of the 5th year after the payment of the 5th instalment but before redemption?
   a. 80,000
   b. 120,000
   c. 100,000
   d. 200,000
10. Which pair of the following figures shows the redemption amount (assume the instalments for the 5th year have been paid separately before redemption) and the **total** profit taken in the 5th year?
    a. Redemption amount 120,000, Profit recognised for year 20,000
    b. Redemption amount 200,000, Profit recognised for year 40,000
    c. Redemption amount 200,000, Profit recognised for year 120,000
    d. Redemption amount 120,000, Profit recognised for year 40,000

DISCUSSION QUESTIONS

1. What are the reasons for the failure for mudaraba and musharaka contracts to become mainstream in the Islamic financial services industry?
2. Suggest ideas to make mudharaba and musharaka contracts mainstream in the Islamic financial industry.
3. You were introduced to urboun (a nonrefundable deposit) in this chapter. Use Google to find the meaning of another deposit termed *hamish al jiddiyah*, which is refundable. Explain the difference between urboun and hamish jiddiyah in your own words. Do not cut and paste or memorize.
4. After referring to the Internet or other references to obtain knowledge of hamish jiddiya, draft and discuss the journal entries to account for a

hamish jiddiyah deposit of $5,000 and its refund where the bank lost $1,000 due the customer not keeping his promise and the promise was binding. Use your knowledge of double-entry bookkeeping; do not copy from other resources.

5. Draw a diagram showing how a customer using tawarruq can place a deposit in a bank with a fixed return.
6. Do you think IFRS accounting standards are suitable for Islamic accounting, given that Islamic accounting has different social, religious, and economic objectives as opposed to the capitalist market nature of IFRS?
7. Research the Accounting and Auditing Organization and make a 10-minute presentation in class. Conduct a class discussion for 5 minutes after your presentation on whether AAOIFI should continue its work on accounting and other standards given that the world is converging to IFRS standards.
8. Explain the concept of time value of money. Search for references on the Islamic perspective on this concept and discuss why you agree or disagree with this concept.
9. Looking at the illustration in this chapter, discuss which accounting standard (IFRS or AAOIFI) is more beneficial to the customer if he wants to redeem his murabaha financing in the 5th year of an 8-year murabaha contract.
10. Using the definition of assets, liability, and equity, explain in your words the logic of the accounting entries under AAOIFI for a simple murabaha transaction with deposit but without early redemption, from beginning to end.

EXERCISES

1. Wan Rosli places a tawarruq deposit with Maybank Islamic for a period of 8 years. The murabaha selling price of $10,000 to the bank is based on a return of 5% per annum compounded. Using the PV of $1 table, calculate the amount that is placed in the bank.
2. Othman al Habshi needs $50,000 for his son's wedding. He decided to seek Islamic financing using tawarruq financing from Bank Islam of Yemen with a term of 10 years. If the bank uses a 7% compound rate a year and Othman intends to pay 10 equal annual instalments, calculate using Excel or a formula or relevant financial table, the amount of the instalment he has to pay per year.

   Hint: Use the =pmt Excel formula or the formula given in this chapter with the help of tables.

3. The Baghdad Islamic Bank sold on a murabaha basis a house to Imam Ghazali at a markup of 8% per annum constant rate of return to be paid over 10 years in equal annual instalments. The cost of the house was 50,000 dinars and Imam Ghazali paid 10,000 dinars as deposit. Baghdad Islamic Bank follows Islamic accounting Standards and recognises profits according to instalments due. Imam Ghazali paid the instalments for the first 2 years but was late in paying the 3rd instalment by one month (which he paid together with the tawid). The bank charged him ta'wid 10 dinar, which would be payable to charity. At the end of the 4th year, the Khalifa Harun Al Rashid gifted Imam Ghazali, a bounty for his magnum opus 'Ihya ulumuddeen' of 60,000 dinars. The Imam decided to redeem his house financing, keep a balance of 10,000 dinars for his expenses, and give the balance as sadaqah to achieve the pleasure of Allah swt. Baghdad bank gave him a full rebate on the unearned profits for the remaining period of the original murabaha contract, which was redeemed on the last date of the 4th year. Alhamdulillah, the Imam was able to give the intended amount of the sadaqah in Ramadhan as the moon was sighted on the last day the 4th year of the murabaha contract. How much sadaqah did he give?
4. Using the facts in E3, if the IFRS accounting recognition method is used, how much charity will Imam Ghazali be able to give? Explain the difference.
5. Using the data in the Comprehensive Illustration given in this chapter, record the entries in the **following ledger accounts** and close off the accounts each year until early redemption, under AAOIFI accounting standards only.

Murabaha Financing, Deferred Profit, Cash, Profit and Loss, Deposit Payable, and Account Receivable Accounts.

CHAPTER 9

Social Responsibility Accounting

Learning Outcomes

At the end of this chapter, you will be able to:

1. Demonstrate an understanding of the importance of sustainable development of businesses.
2. Discuss the development of corporate social responsibility (CSR).
3. Deliberate on the concept of accountability in Islam and its impact on sustainable development.
4. Evaluate the various sustainability reporting guidelines.
5. Assess the sustainability reporting framework from Islam's perspective.

Traditionally, a business organisation's primary objective is on its economic sustainability. Accordingly, profitability is the main focus. However, this is slowly but surely changing. Organisations and their stakeholders are becoming increasingly aware of the need for socially responsible behaviour. More important, there are benefits for companies that put social responsibility as one of its core values. Hence, the focus of companies now is broader. Many are familiar with the 3 Ps (profits, people, and planet) of a business and its relationship to sustainable development. Besides profits, companies are now focusing on people as well as the planet. Thus, the need to report on the social and environmental impacts of a business entity is paramount.

Essentially, corporate social responsibility (CSR) reporting or sustainability reporting is concerned with trying to present a comprehensive picture of the full extent of the organisation's interactions with its external environment. More specifically, the Global Reporting Initiative's Sustainability Reporting Guidelines (GRI, 2000–2011) states that sustainability reporting is

> *the practice of measuring, disclosing, and being accountable for organizational performance while working towards the goal of sustainable development [GRI 3.1, p. 43].*

It went on to state that

> *A sustainability report provides a balanced and reasonable representation of the sustainability performance of the reporting organization, including both positive and negative contributions [GRI 3.1, p 43].*

From Islam's perspective, justice (*adalah*) and benevolence (*ihsan*) are the basic ethos of individuals as well as corporations. Given this, the emphasis of providing information to particular groups of users such as investors, creditors, and others who have a purely financial interest in the entity would be anathema to Muslims and people with distinct religious beliefs. In fact, in Islam, the reporting of social and environmental information can be regarded as mandatory primarily because it is specifically provided for in the Quran. Thus, while CSR is looked at from a cost–benefit perspective in the Western world, in Islam CSR is natural, as it flows from the Quran. For example, there are no less than 40 verses in the Quran extolling Muslims to give regular charity. What is interesting is the fact that the charitable donations are written in the same verse as performing regular prayers. This shows how important CSR is to the *ummah* (community of believers).

The following verse attests to this:

> *And they have been commanded no more than this: to worship Allah, offering Him sincere devotion, being true (in faith); to establish regular prayer; and to practise regular charity; and that is the religion right and straight [98:5].*

DEVELOPMENT OF CSR

Social responsibility of corporations has been a hotly debated topic in the United States as well as continental Europe since the late 1960s. With it comes the criticism that conventional accounting is not able to give a true picture of the interaction between society and corporations. Consequently, in the early 1970s, the American Accounting Association (AAA) issued a series of reports on many aspects of the social responsibility debate (AAA, 1973; 1974; 1975). The reports discussed the accounting issues on reporting to employees and reporting about employees (employment reporting), as well as issues concerning the reporting of accounting information to trade unions for the purposes of collective bargaining. Thereafter, in 1975, the Accounting Standards Steering Committee (ASSC) in the United Kingdom published the Corporate Report (ASSC, 1975). The Report attempted to establish a program to develop accounting to become more responsive to wider social responsibility issues. More important, it was through the efforts of the Global Reporting Initiative (GRI) that CSR reporting was brought to its highest level.

The GRI promotes sustainability reporting as a way for organisations to become more sustainable. To date, it has produced various versions of the sustainability framework. The GRI launched the first version of the Guidelines in 2000. The second version, G2, was developed in 2002, while the third, G3, was introduced in 2006. In 2011, GRI published the G3.1 Guidelines. This is an update of G3, encompassing guidance on reporting gender, community, and human rights–related performance. In May 2013, GRI issued G4, the fourth generation of its guidelines where organisations are encouraged to provide only information that is critical to their business and stakeholders, thus ensuring that companies focus on sustainability impacts that matter. The International Organization for Standardization, in 2010, also issued ISO 26000, a standard on CSR reporting.

ISO 26000 also helps increase a company's understanding of its social responsibility through agreed definitions, principles, core subjects, methods for integration, stakeholder engagement, and communication. The standard is based on seven core principles of accountability, transparency, ethical behaviour, respect for stakeholder interests, respect for the rule of law, respect for international norms of behaviour, and respect for human rights. On the basis of these principles, the ISO has suggested that companies disclose seven categories of information: organisational governance, human rights, labor practices, environment, fair operating practices, consumer issues, and community involvement and development. Altogether, there are 36 significant issues in these seven subject areas. A company needs to identify the issues that are most relevant and significant for it to address through its own as well as through its dialogue with stakeholders. A full discussion of ISO 26000 is not attempted here, but suffice it to say that most of what has been suggested by the GRI has also been addressed in the standard. In January 2014, the International Organization for Standardization and the GRI jointly published a manual showing how the GRI Guidelines can be used in conjunction with ISO 26000.

ADVANTAGES OF CSR REPORTING

Besides being closely aligned with the teachings of Islam, CSR reporting has various advantages. These include, amongst others, increased information for decision making, more accurate product or service costing, improved image, ability to identify the company's market development opportunities, and most important, maintaining the organisation's legitimacy to operate. One cannot deny the important fact that companies do benefit from undertaking CSR activities, as sustainability issues are linked to profitability. Specifically in Islam, a verse in the Quran provides the specific benefits of those who give regular charity as follows:

> *The likeness of those who spend their wealth in the Way of Allah, is as the likeness of a grain (of corn); it grows seven ears, and each ear has a hundred grains. Allah gives manifold increase to whom He wills. And Allah is All-Sufficient for His creatures' needs, All-Knower [2:261].*

THE ISLAMIC WORLDVIEW

Given that different worldviews may lead to different economic objectives and socioeconomic behaviour, a discussion of the Islamic worldview will help clarify the framework with which CSR from an Islamic perspective may be developed. The Islamic worldview rests on the following philosophic concepts: *tawhid* (unity), *khilafah* (vicegerency), *rubbubiyyah* (perfect state), *adalah* (justice), and *tazkiyah* (growth and purification). In addition, concepts such as accountability, responsibility, equilibrium (balance), and *shura* (mutual consultation) will also be discussed.

Tawhid (Unity)

Tawhid is the foundation of the Islamic faith. It refers to the Unity of God and the belief that the universe has been consciously designed and created by God and did not come into existence by chance or accident. The doctrine of tawhid preserves the absolute monotheism of Islam where God's sovereignty is recognised. This dominates Islamic belief and practices and consequently affects how Muslims view religion. To Muslims, Islam is viewed as integral to the state, law, and society. This viewpoint differs from the modern Western perspective that regards religion as separate from the state. It is this tawhidic paradigm that recognises that ultimately accountability is to God. This brings a powerful statement to the importance of CSR.

Khilafah (Vicegerency)

As is generally understood, the purpose of social responsibility accounting is primarily to determine the effects that corporate actions have on the quality of life of society and hence the emphasis on accountability. The primary objective may be similar, but in Islam, CSR would have a wider focus. God puts a personal responsibility on all Muslims for what is done with the resources entrusted to them. The concept of khilafah (vicegerency) defines a person's status and role, specifying the individual's responsibilities to himself and his responsibility to the ummah. Four implications emanate from the concept of khilafah.

The first is universal brotherhood, where mutual sacrifice and cooperation are the social order. Such a social order allows the development of the entire human potential. Accordingly, from the perspective of business enterprises, competition is encouraged if it is healthy, raises efficiency, and helps promote the well-being of society. Competition that results in jealousy, ruthlessness, and destruction must be avoided.

The second implication of khilafah is that the individual is regarded as the trustee of God's resources. This leads to a totally different meaning to private ownership as understood in the secular world. Although private ownership is recognised in Islam, ownership is not absolute. The property owner recognises his responsibility of using his resources in a manner that will provide benefits not only to himself but, more important, to society. Thus, this has great implications on how CSR is viewed in Islam and its importance to Muslim societies.

The third implication of khilafah is the emphasis on a humble lifestyle. A lifestyle of extravagance may result in unnecessary pressure on resources, which, in turn, may lead to the inability to satisfy the basic needs of society.

Finally, khilafah also implies the concept of human freedom in Islam. An individual's freedom to act is not curtailed by any other individual but is constrained by the bonds of social responsibility. Hence, there is a qualification as to what individual freedom entails in Islam. Unlimited freedom goes hand in hand with unlimited responsibilities. Consequently, it is inconceivable that anyone would want unlimited freedom.

It is this concept of khilafah or trusteeship that links Islam to CSR. Given the fact that all resources are put in trust to us, we must manage it in accordance with divine laws (the Sharia), as we are ultimately accountable to God.

Rubbubiyyah (Perfect State)

Rubbubiyyah refers to God's arrangement for directing things towards a perfect state of human sustenance. Accordingly, Muslims believe that resources are adequate to sustain everybody to achieve God's perfect plan for the universe. It is in the context of this divine arrangement that human efforts take place. Because goods are adequately provided by God for every being, greed and self-interest should not exist. This contention may not be consistent with the basic tenet of neoclassical economic theory, that there is a scarcity of resources and that human wants are unlimited.

Adalah (Justice)

Adalah or justice is strongly emphasised in the Quran. The bonds of brotherhood would be a hollow concept if social justice and social responsibility did not exist. Islam's commitment to brotherhood and justice demands that all God-given resources are at the disposal of every individual. Accordingly, wealth should not remain concentrated on a few individuals.

There are three basic criteria for the attainment of social justice: Absolute freedom of conscience, complete equality of all men, and the permanent mutual responsibility of society and individuals. It follows that if the social behaviour pattern and the economy of Islamic societies are strictly in accordance with Islamic teachings, there cannot exist extreme inequalities of income and wealth. However, Islam recognises inequalities insofar as these relate to skills, initiatives, efforts, as well as risk. Justice is strongly emphasised in the Quran as in the following verses.

> *Be equitable, that is closer to piety; and fear Allah, Allah is well aware of all that you do [5:8].*
>
> *Say: 'My Lord has enjoined justice and righteousness; and be steadfast in your worship and invoke Him alone, and dedicate your faith sincerely to him' [7:29].*

Tazkiyah (Growth and Purification)

The concept of tazkiyah is similar to zakat; that is growth and purification. Muslims believe that the mission of all the Prophets was to perform the Tazkiyah of man in his relationship with God, with other men, and with society. This concept is of great importance in Islamic economic theory. Tazkiyah endorses the ideas of change and expansion, which, according to some authors, are absent from Christian canon law. It also requires an individual to expend his best efforts in order to achieve a better material life. However, material well-being must lead to social justice and the spiritual enhancement of society.

Accountability

Muslims believe that everything created by God has a purpose and it is this purpose that gives meaning and significance to man's existence. As such, man is accountable to God and his success in the hereafter depends on his performance in this life on earth. The following verses elaborate the notion of accountability in Islam.

> *To Allah belongs all that is in heavens and on earth. Whether you show what is in your minds or conceal it, Allah calls you to account for it [2:284].*
>
> *Soon will God observe your work, and His Messenger, and the believers: soon will you be brought back to the Knower of what is hidden and what is open: then will He show you the truth of all you did [9:105].*
>
> *And fear the Day you shall be brought back to God; then shall every soul be paid what it earned, and none will be dealt with unjustly [2:281].*

Given that the accountability concept is the pillar on which CSR rests, accountability will also be discussed later in the chapter.

Responsibility

Responsibility guides the Muslim mind in its creative and intellectual movement towards an understanding of life and the universe. It is a Muslim's belief that peace of mind in this world and his destiny in the hereafter are shaped by how well he fulfills his responsibility to work, strive, sacrifice, and do good in this life.

Equilibrium (Balance)

Pertinent to the discussion of CSR, accounting, and business is the concept of balance in Islam. Islam emphasises balance in anything that one does. For example, the following verse in the Quran explicitly deals with a Muslim's need to balance worldly affairs with the hereafter.

> *But seek with the wealth which Allah has bestowed on you, the Home of the Hereafter, nor forget your portion in this world [28:77].*

Specifically, on the issue of expenditure, the following verse from the Quran explicates the concept of balance.

> *Those who they spend are not extravagant and not niggardly, but hold a just balance between those extremes [25:67].*

The preceding concept, although very delicate, is of primary importance in the conduct of a Muslim's life and, hence, by implication, in the manner CSR is practised.

Shura (Mutual Consultation)

The process of *shura* (consultation) is fundamental to achieving the ideal Islamic society and is important in Islamic business organisations. Further, it was reported that the Prophet himself consulted his followers on matters pertaining to the state, politics, wars, and international relations. Evidently, the bonds of brotherhood will be further strengthened with *shura*. The following verse explicates the concept of *shura* in Islam.

> *Consult them in affairs (of moment), then when you have taken a decision, put your trust in Allah, for Allah loves those who put their trust in Him [3:159].*

Although *shura* is encouraged in Islam, no detailed descriptions have been given to its implementation. Thus, the basic concept of *shura* must be interpreted in light of the particular needs and circumstances of a particular situation. However, specific to corporate reporting, *shura* may be operationalised in the case of stakeholder engagement in social and environmental reporting. The Global Reporting Initiative has suggested that companies engage a dialogue with stakeholders in order for companies to know what stakeholders need with respect to disclosure on social and environmental issues. This is precisely what *shura* aims to achieve.

In summary, the concept of *tawhid* (unity) governs a Muslim's outlook in life, recognising that there is only one God and man's accountability is to Him. Additionally, an individual's relationship with other individuals mirrors his relationship with God. Both are equally important. The general theme of the Islamic social order is cooperation and mutual consultation (*shura*). *Khilafah* prescribes the Islamic social order formed on the basis of the principles of justice, equality, and brotherhood. Further, in Islam, individual freedom is constrained by its ethical limits. Thus, an individual's freedom of actions must be combined with a sense of responsibility towards others. Since social awareness and a concern for individuals are inextricably blended, working for the welfare of others is the most promising way of extending one's usefulness in pleasing God. The emphasis on the well-being of the community is implicit.

ISLAM AND CSR

In Islam, although the earning of profits is encouraged, non–profit-oriented objectives are equally important. In the context of corporate reporting, firms should accept the responsibility of competing objectives, striking a balance between the interests of employees, customers, investors, and the general public. Hence, a company's freedom to operate should be combined with a self-induced responsibility, and there should not be a conflict between a firm's private and social interests. It must be emphasised here that although Islam considers the profit motive as essential for the successful operation of a business, it also places moral restraints on the profit motive. Islam advocates the attainment of profit through fostering individual self-interest within a social context. Essentially, the basic basic pillar on which CSR from Islam's perspective rests is on the Islamic concept of accountability.

Accountability and CSR

The Quranic view of life divides man's functions into *hablumminallah,* his obligations to God (vertical dimension of accountability), and *hablumminannas*, his obligations to society (horizontal dimension of accountability). Implicit in the concept of brotherhood is the need to achieve socioeconomic justice. The Islamic concept of accountability can be interpreted as one that promotes both social justice and social accountability. Two essential principles underlie the concept of accountability in Islam: The precept of full disclosure and the concept of social accountability. Arguably, social accountability may, in some sense, constitute a subset of full disclosure. However, since social justice is important in Islam, the social accountability or CSR aspect is singled out.

In line with the above, one would expect a business operating in an Islamic environment to emphasise socially related information disclosure. What constitutes matters of social concern in Islam is specifically laid out in the Sharia. For example, monopoly practices and unfair trading practices, being specifically prohibited, should be issues that need to be disclosed. In contrast, these matters have not been the focus of social responsibility accounting in the West.

Further, in Islam, a person holds property in trust for God and there should be no conflict between private and social interests. In a corporate reporting context, such a concept suggests that the accountant's accountability focus is enhanced to include a wider audience, namely the public.

This may be contrasted with capitalist-oriented societies where the primary focus is on investors and creditors. Thus, one would expect a firm operating in an Islamic environment to be particularly concerned about the consequences of its own actions for the community. This is precisely what CSR is.

The Quran is so emphatic about the discharge of an individual's obligations that the question of positively articulating a Muslim's rights does not arise. The individual acknowledges the rights of others because this is a duty imposed on the individual. Being an integral part of society, a person must not be passive to the consequences of the exercise of the individual's own rights. Mutual sacrifice and cooperation should be the process by which human life can be enriched. Viewed from this perspective, one would therefore expect a business firm to regard itself as an integral part of the community. As such, the firm's success should be measured by how well it has met the needs of the society in which the firm operates.

The ultimate objective is the attainment of social and economic justice and the equitable distribution of income and wealth. Specifically, unethical business practices that are provided in the *Sharia* as having the potential to affect the well being of the community were not dealt with.

Full Disclosure and Social Accountability

As is generally understood, the purpose of social responsibility accounting is primarily to determine the effects corporate actions have on the quality of life of society and hence the emphasis on accountability. The primary objective may be similar but in Islam CSR would have a wider focus. Two essential principles flow from the Islamic concept of accountability: Full disclosure and social accountability. In line with this, it has been suggested that companies reporting in an Islamic economy would also provide a current value balance sheet (CVBS) and a value-added statement (VAS). The argument is that the need for greater awareness of the social impact of firm activities in Islam would render these two financial statements more relevant to the needs of Muslims.

The CVBS is important primarily in determining zakat. Zakat is a compulsory levy on wealth and income on Muslims whose wealth exceeds a certain threshold (*nisab*). It is often said that zakat represents the social security system of an Islamic society. Given this and the fact that zakat is calculated based on current values, one would expect a CVBS to be part of CSR reporting for Islamic-based organisations.

The VAS is important because it has a 'social dimension' to it since the distribution of wealth between the different sectors of society is, by definition, a matter of social interest. From an Islamic perspective, it is this distributional characteristic of VAS that supports accountability in Islam, a theme similar to that advocated in the Corporate Report of 1975. Most important, growth in an Islamic society should lead to social justice and a more equitable distribution of power and wealth.

The inclusion of the CVBS and the VAS may not totally satisfy the full disclosure and social accountability aspects of corporate reporting from an Islamic perspective. Given Islam's emphasis on safeguarding the welfare of the community, reporting on CSR issues is of primary importance. The last may have some similarities with the Global Reporting Initiatives' Sustainability Reporting Guidelines (GRI).

Environmental Reporting

The principle of *maslahah* (well-being of the masses) specifically provides that the community's interest is of primary importance. Thus, protecting the environment is implicit. In fact, one is indirectly harming others if one harms the environment. Caring for and protecting the environment are specifically provided for in the Quran as in the following verses.

> *Do not work corruption on the earth after it has been set right [7:85].*
> *Do not corrupt the land [11:85].*
> *Corruption has overtaken in land and sea for what the hands of the people have earned, that He may let them taste some of what they have done [30:41].*

Thus, an enterprise conducting its business in an Islamic environment must report on how they are addressing environmental issues. When businesses are forced to report on their environmental performance, these businesses would have no choice but to be environmentally responsible. This is because, as information on a company's environmental impact is made publicly available, they would be inclined to want to portray the image of an environmentally responsible organisation. There are about 500 verses in the Quran that relate to environmental issues and the manner in which such issues are to be addressed. Most important, in Islam, planting trees and preventing pollution are as good as feeding the poor and attending to the sick.

THE PROPOSED ISLAMIC CSR MODEL

As explained in the preceding section, the commonly known international guidelines that have been developed to enable corporations to report on sustainability issues is the framework on sustainability issued by the GRI.

The GRI promotes sustainability reporting as a way for organisations to become more sustainable.

The argument that there is a need for greater awareness of the social impact of firms' activities in Islamic societies would necessitate detailed descriptions of externalities and trading practices harmful to the public to be disclosed in the notes to the accounts. Accordingly, a reasonable conclusion one may reach at this point is that social responsibility accounting, as envisioned in the West, forms *part* of Islamic accounting. Given that Islam advocates the reporting of the economic, social, and environmental issues, a starting point to develop the CSR model from Islam's perspective is to look at what the GRI framework has suggested companies should report in their annual or sustainability reports.

The Global Reporting Initiative Framework on Sustainability

The GRI framework provides companies with guidelines on the reporting of an organisation's economic, environmental, and social performance. Specifically, the framework provides the principles in defining the report content so as to ensure the quality of reported information.

There are three categories of information that companies should disclose: Economic, social, and the environment. This is sometimes referred to as the 3Ps of a business – profits, people, and the planet. Items to be reported under 'economic' include issues pertaining to customers, suppliers, employees, providers of capital, and the public sector. The 'social' has four subcategories: Labour practices, human rights, society, and product responsibility. On the environment, the GRI specifically include the usage of materials, energy, water, impact on biodiversity, measurement of emissions, effluents, and waste, suppliers, products and services, compliance, and transport.

As explained earlier, the GRI's emphasis on sustainability reporting focuses on the economic, social, and environmental performance indicators (both qualitative and quantitative) of companies. This is shown in Figure 9.1.

Economic Performance Indicators From the perspective of Islam, in addition to the list of economic performance indicators suggested by the GRI, information on the amount of *zakat* paid by the company, the number of Muslim shareholders and their shareholdings, whether the company is a monopoly in the provision of particular goods and services, whether the company (in the case of listed companies) is listed as a halal (permitted) counter and whether the company or any of its subsidiaries are engaging in haram (forbidden) activities should also be disclosed.

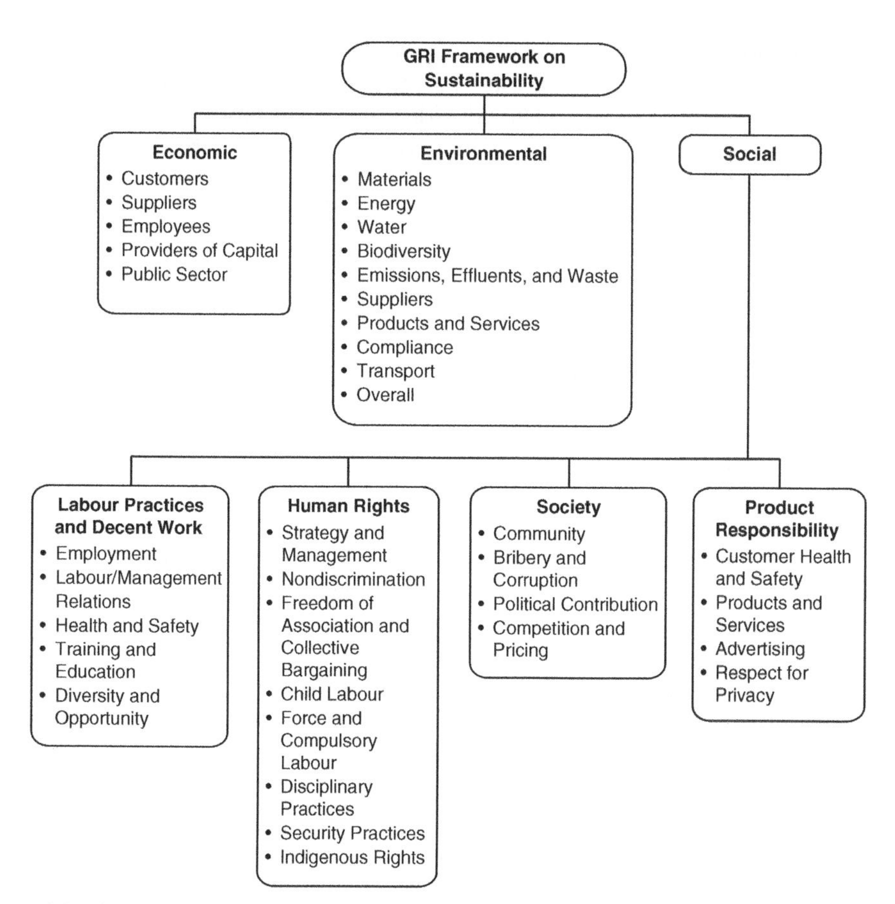

FIGURE 9.1 GRI framework on sustainability

Further, ideally, Islamic business enterprises should not engage in any transactions pertaining to interest. However, should an Islamic business enterprise engage in interest-bearing transactions, that fact should be specifically disclosed. A firm following strictly the tenets of Islam in its conduct would also disclose activities that may be categorised as having the possibility of impairing social and economic justice, such as the hoarding of necessary goods, fraudulent business practices, and price manipulation.

Full disclosure in such cases would include the steps that would have to be taken to ensure that such activities are not continued, how the income (if any) from such activities was to be dealt with, and why the company undertook such activities. It is unlikely that such disclosures would happen voluntarily but that fact is not an argument against disclosure per se.

Social Performance Indicators Finally, the social dimension of sustainability, according to the GRI, emphasises an enterprise's impacts on the social systems in which it operates. The GRI identifies key performance measures pertaining to labour practices, human rights, as well as broader issues concerning the consumers (as in product responsibility), community, and other stakeholders in society. However, from Islam's perspective, social performance indicators may enjoy less of a consensus than environmental performance indicators.

In particular, in Islamic corporate reporting, social performance indicators should include (amongst others) whether employees from the higher echelons in the company perform the congregational prayers with lower and middle level managers; whether Muslim employees are allowed to perform their obligatory prayers during specific times of their working day, and whether there is a proper place of worship for the employees. Specifically, under 'product responsibility', whether a product is forbidden (*haram*) or allowed (*halal*) in Islam should be clearly indicated. For example, the selling of food that contains alcohol or pork derivatives, however minute its content, should be reported. Thus, a responsible business enterprise should ensure that such information is disclosed, not only in its annual reports but also provided on the product itself.

The focus on the three categories of information as proposed by the GRI that companies should disclose may appear adequate. However, from Islam's perspective, there are other reports that companies need to prepare in order to discharge their social accountability. In particular, committed Muslims would like to see a CVBS as well as a VAS.

Environmental Indicators Specific to environmental issues, the list of environmental performance indicators provided by the GRI appears comprehensive. Accordingly, one would not expect there to be differences between environmental performance indicators disclosed by secular and Islamic business enterprises. The importance of including environmental information in the CSR reporting framework was discussed in an earlier section.

While the GRI framework already discussed is a good starting point, CSR from an Islamic perspective would require more than what the GRI has to offer. Other information about the company's discharge of its social responsibilities would include the items in Figure 9.2.

The Current Value Balance Sheet (CVBS)

The use of current values relates to the justice and equity aspects that Islam emphasises with regard to the payment of zakat. Zakat constitutes one aspect of social accountability in Islamic societies and the current value

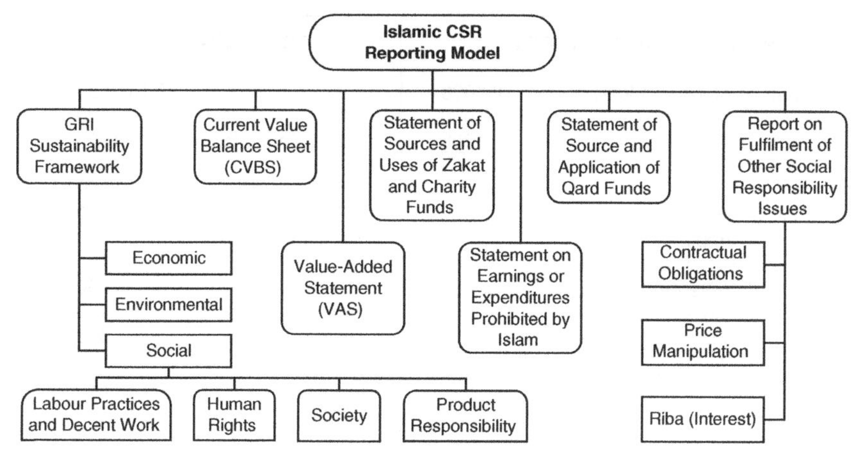

FIGURE 9.2 Islamic CSR reporting model

balance sheet (to determine zakat) supports the Islamic principle of justice to a greater extent than the historical cost balance sheet. Thus, a CVBS disclosed in the 'notes to the account' will enable committed Muslims to determine their zakat obligations. Thus, not only should the amount of zakat be disclosed in the annual report, one should also ensure that interested stakeholders can determine the amount of zakat from the financial statements of the organisation – hence the importance of the CVBS.

The Value-Added Statement (VAS)

The VAS provides a social dimension to the earning of profits by a business. Additionally, it also indicates a more progressive atmosphere surrounding the business, putting the focus on all the partners rather than simply on shareholders. The measurement and disclosure of value-added per se should generate a new spirit of cooperation between the workers, investors, and governments and a new responsibility of the economic entities to all stakeholders. The new responsibility and atmosphere may be fairer, taking into account each individual contribution as a basis for the distribution. Added to this is the important fact that a user of accounts will see at a glance the allocation of resources distributed to the various stakeholders in the VAS, thus reflecting on the social aspect of the information. In contrast, the income statement primarily focuses on the 'bottom line' (i.e. on how much the entity makes). Figure 9.3 clarifies this.

Specific to Islamic financial institutions (IFIs), the Accounting and Auditing Organization for Islamic Financial Institutions (AAOIFI) suggests additional reports that IFIs should provide. From a CSR perspective,

Value-Added Statement		Income Statement	
Sources of value-added	RM'000		RM'000
Revenue	3000	Sales	3000
Less: Bought in items	1000	Less: Materials used	1000
	2000	Wages	500
		Interest	300
Distributions:		Depreciation	300
Employees (wages)	500	Profit before tax	900
Beneficiaries (*zakat*)	100	Less: Taxes	100
Government (taxes)	100	Profit after tax	800
Owners (dividends)	400	Less: Dividends	400
Charities (e.g. *waqf*)	500	**Profit retained**	**400**
Reinvest funds:			
Profit retained	400		
	2000		

FIGURE 9.3 The VAS and income statement compared

AAOIFI recommends IFIs to prepare the statement of sources and uses of zakat funds, Disclosure of earnings or expenditures prohibited by Islam and the statement of sources and uses of qard funds.

Statement of Sources and Uses of Zakat and Charity Funds

Islam greatly emphasises zakat, the third pillar of Islam, and charity. Given this, AAOIFI suggests that Islamic financial institutions should prepare such a statement if such institutions are authorised to collect zakat. Thus, the amount of zakat collected and how this has been disbursed to the eight categories of people (as stipulated by the Quran) is important to Muslims. Further, Islamic banks should also indicate whether the bank pays zakat on behalf of its unrestricted investment account holders.

In the case of companies other than Islamic banks that are not zakat collectors, such organisations must disclose the amount of zakat paid on behalf of Muslim shareholders if the companies have been so authorised (see Chapter 6 on zakat). Additional information disclosed should be on the calculation of zakat. The latter is important particularly for companies not paying zakat. This is to enable individual shareholders to determine their own zakat based on the company's disclosure of relevant information.

Statement on Earnings or Expenditures Prohibited by Islam

It is important for a company to disclose prohibited income and expenditure. Examples of prohibited income include interest obtained on deposits in conventional banks. Specific to Islamic banks would be the commissions from *Sharia*-noncompliant merchants of Islamic credit card businesses.

The manner in which prohibited income is disposed off should also be a subject for disclosure. More important, the company should indicate the specific steps it has taken to avoid such income in the future. The following examples clarify the disclosure on prohibited earnings.

Examples of Disclosure in the Annual Report of Prohibited Earnings of Two Islamic Banks

Bank I

All earnings that have been realized from sources or by means prohibited by *Sharia* rules and principles have been put aside in a separate account and disposed of to charitable causes.

Bank II

For any earnings discovered to be prohibited by *Sharia* (for example when involving the payment of interest), it is permissible for the Group and the Bank to accept such earnings. However, these earnings shall not be utilised and expended for any private purpose of the Group and the Bank. Instead, it must be channelled to a designated account to be consumed for public benefit referred to as *Maslahah Ammah*.

Islamic banks that do not have prohibited income should specifically indicate that fact as follows:

The main sources and investments of the Bank disclosed to us conform to the basis that had been approved by us in accordance with Sharia rules and principles.

Statement of Source and Application of Qard Funds

Qard funds are those financings extended to individuals where there is no return to the Islamic bank. The 'borrower' will only pay the principal amount. An Islamic bank may organise a fund for qard as a means of achieving social objectives. The amount of qard financing extended will, to a certain extent, indicate the fulfilment of the social responsibility of the organisation. While Islamic banks are in the business of extending financing and such loans are expected, companies other than Islamic banks may also extend such financing. For example, qard (loans) can be given to employees to help in the education of their children. This is part of social responsibility.

AAOIFI even suggests that proceeds of prohibited earnings of Islamic banks may also be included as funds available to the fund on a temporary basis until such proceeds are properly disposed off.

Report on Fulfilment of Other Social Responsibility Issues

While issues pertaining to interest and unfair trading practices are not being considered as social issues from a Western perspective, in Islam these matters are specifically addressed in the Sharia because of their potential to affect the well-being of the community. Thus, one would expect such matters to form part of CSR practices of a firm operating in an Islamic environment. Evidently, the scope of social responsibility accounting in Islam would be wider. Activities that may be categorised as having the possibility of impairing social and economic justice include meeting contractual obligations, hoarding, fraud, price manipulation, exploitation, and monopoly practices.

Contractual Obligations Keeping one's promises is considered desirable in any society, be it Islamic or otherwise. However, Islam intensifies the feelings of social obligations in an individual by specifically providing for the fulfilling of contractual obligations in the Quran.

> *Oh ye who believe! Fulfill (all) obligations [5:1].*

While it is inconceivable that any company would include information on their breaches of contract, a firm closely following the tenets of Islam should do so. If at all, this fact will ensure that the company will refrain from such practices.

Price Manipulation Other provisions in the Sharia that safeguard the wider interests of society include those concerning price manipulation, hoarding, and the giving of incorrect weights and measures. Islam forbids the hoarding of essential goods (*al-ihtikar*) as this may ultimately lead to price manipulation. Price manipulation may arise if there is *collusion* between companies. Competition is only effective and healthy if there are a large number of firms with none having the ability to influence price. Thus, Islam prohibits monopoly and oligopoly if such practices harm the interests of society. Additionally, Islam forbids every type of fraud and deception as explicated in the following verse.

> *O ye who believe! Stand out firmly for Allah, as witnesses to fair dealing and let not the hatred of others to you make you swerve to wrong and depart from justice [5:8].*

The preceding discussion suggests the need for transparency in disclosure practices. More specifically, the preceding emphasises the importance of reporting on the number of complaints the company receives in any financial period. Whilst this issue is not the focus of corporate reporting from a Western perspective, in Islam, reporting on such issues is pertinent. From the Western perspective, knowing the number of complaints levelled at a company simply points to a need for more efficient operations, and subsequently, this would tie in with the improvement of the bottom line. However, from Islam's perspective, the issue of injustice comes to the fore. Perhaps the following hadith reflecting on the concept of brotherhood in Islam sums up the conduct of a business in an Islamic society.

> *Do not envy one another; do not inflate prices one to another; do not hate one another, do not turn away from one another; and do not undercut one another, but be you O servants of Allah, brothers.*

Riba (Interest) One pertinent issue in Islam relates to interest (*riba*). Although the provisions for the disclosure of interest payments in external financial reports currently in force in many countries were not legislated with Islam in mind, they are, nevertheless, consistent with what a devout Muslim would advocate. However, while current practice is usually to simply show the amount of interest paid, under an Islamic system, companies would have to avoid such payments altogether (for instance, by borrowing from Islamic banks).

A Declaration?

While it is inconceivable that any business would report on the unfair trading practices just discussed, a form of deterrent is for companies to actually provide a statement specifically indicating that they do not have such practices. A true believer will refrain from making such a statement if the company indulges in unfair trading practices. Although the following example from an Islamic bank relates to prohibited earnings, a somewhat similar statement can also be included for other unfair trading practices.

> *The main sources of income of the Bank during the financial year ended March 31, 2018, that we have reviewed are in compliance with the* Sharia *rules and principles.*

For the specific case of unfair trading practices, the following statement would be appropriate.

> *There are no unfair trading practices leveled against the company for the financial year ending December 31, 2018.*

It is important for the preceding statement to be included in the annual report, as this will act as a deterrent for companies to undertake such practices.

CONCLUSION

CSR is about reporting more than just economic events. Thus, its objective is beyond reporting financial success. The reporting of CSR issues need not necessarily be expressed solely in monetary terms. Most important, organisations should realize that they do not operate in a vacuum. A corporation's relationship with society and the environment is critical. Given this, companies must realize that their accountability is to a wider group of stakeholders.

Perhaps, the director of Global Programs at GE, Krista Bauer, sums up best what exactly is meant by CSR. According to her, CSR is knowing about:

> *For every dollar that we spend, how many people do we impact? And for every activity that we engage in, how do we make it sustainable. It's got nothing to do with units out the door, with margin to the company, or with any sort of commercial angle or metric. And that's been entirely liberating because it has opened our eyes to a lot of things ... that GE doesn't make but that GE can enable.*

Specific on environmental issues, EL Artz, the chairman and CEO of Procter & Gamble, had this to say,

> *We simply can't protect the interest of the shareholders unless we do our part to protect the environment.*

Finally, Frank Popoff, the CEO of Dow Chemical, warns,

> *No matter how competitive you are and how globally you trade, if you are environmentally irresponsible, someone can and will – and should – padlock your door.*

Examples of CSR Reporting

Following are some examples of CSR reporting taken from the annual reports of some multinational companies, such as Starbucks and Bank of America.

Starbucks: 2016 Global Social Impact Performance Report We will focus in four areas where our commitment and scale can make the biggest impact:

- Making coffee the world's first sustainable product by doing our part to improve the lives of at least One Million people in coffee communities around the world
- Building and operating the world's largest green retail business

- Creating pathways to employment for 1 million people
- Strengthening communities by welcoming all and creating impact on issues that matter[1]

Bank of America, 2014 Corporate social responsibility plays a critical role in our business strategy of responsible growth and connects us to our core purpose of making people's financial lives better around the world.

At Bank of America, corporate social responsibility is an important way we live our purpose of helping make financial lives better. How we engage in the communities in which we operate is tied closely to the business we do with customers and clients in those communities. Corporate social responsibility begins with the lending and investing we do, helping the economy grow.

We established a Global Corporate Social Responsibility Committee that regularly reports to the Corporate Governance Committee of our board of directors.

The Chairman and Chief Executive Officer, BRIAN MOYNIHAN, had this to add:

> *What is our role in a global economy? And how do we deploy all of our assets and resources to be a positive force in society?*

In 2014, we strengthened our corporate social responsibility governance structure by launching a new Global Corporate Social Responsibility Committee, chaired by our global chief strategy and marketing officer and comprising senior leaders from across every business line and support group. The committee meets quarterly and is accountable to the chief executive officer.

We want to take a leadership role in helping remove barriers to investment in clean energy projects around the world. The capital we commit and our strong global client and institutional investor relationships can lead to considerable additional investments in a lower carbon future.

The Environment Specific to the environment, Bank of America reported the following:

To our stakeholders:

Bank of America has been a strong supporter of environmental sustainability for many years. Our leaders and employees recognize that businesses – and the communities and people they serve – rely on a clean and healthy physical environment to thrive and grow.

---

[1]2016 Global Social Impact Performance report, https://www.starbucks.com/responsibility/global-report.

Greenhouse gas emissions

We have established a goal to reduce our absolute GHG emissions by 15 percent from 2010 to 2015. The goal spans our global operations in more than 40 countries and builds on our previous GHG reduction of 18 percent from 2004 to 2009. If achieved, our new goal would represent an overall global reduction in aggregate GHG emissions of more than 30 percent from 2004.

VOCABULARY

accountability
adalah (justice)
current value balance sheet (CVBS)
economic performance indicators
economic sustainability
environmental indicators
equilibrium (balance)
Islamic worldview
khilafah (vicegerency)
responsibility
rubbubiyyah (perfect state)
shura (mutual consultation)
social performance indicators
statement of sources and uses of zakat funds
statement of sources and uses of qard funds
tawhid (unity)
tazkiyah (growth and purification)
ummah (community of believers)
value-added statement (VAS)

MULTIPLE-CHOICE QUESTIONS

1. ____________________refers to God's arrangement for directing things towards a perfect state.
   a. Adalah
   b. Tawhid
   c. Rubbubiyyah
   d. Shurad

2. The Quranic view of life divides man's functions into:
   I. Khilafah
   II. Hablumminannas
   III. Hablumminallah
   IV. Tawhid

   a. I, II, and III
   b. I and II
   c. II and III
   d. I, III, and IV
3. Why is a current value balance sheet important for an Islamic society?
   a. To indicate there is inflation
   b. To ensure that shareholders are not cheated
   c. To calculate zakat
   d. For the auditors, as auditors require current values to be reported
4. Which of the following is not included in the GRI Framework on Sustainability?
   a. Labor practices and decent work
   b. Human rights
   c. Product responsibility
   d. Corporate governance
5. The three basic categories of information in the GRI Framework on Sustainability are:
   a. economic, human rights, and ethics.
   b. economic, environmental and corporate governance.
   c. economic, environmental and product responsibility.
   d. economic, environmental and social.
6. There are various advantages in reporting CSR activities. Which of the following is not one of the advantages?
   a. Increased information for decision making
   b. More accurate product costing
   c. Maintaining organisation's legitimacy to operate
   d. Increased operating costs
7. Product responsibility in the GRI Framework on Sustainability consists of various issues. Which of the following is (are) not part of product responsibility?
   I. Customer health and community
   II. Bribery and corruption
   III. Advertising and respect for privacy
   IV. Competition and pricing

   a. I and II
   b. I and III
   c. I, II, and III
   d. I, III, and IV

8. Which of the following statements is (are) true?
   - I. Social performance indicators from an Islamic perspective should include congregational prayers.
   - II. It is acceptable for Islamic business enterprises to engage in interest-based transactions if the amount is not material.
   - III. In Islam, man is only accountable to God.
   - IV. The process of shura is fundamental to achieving the ideal Islamic society.

   a. I and II
   b. I and III
   c. I, and IV
   d. I, II, and IV
9. Which of the following is (are) not part of the proposed CSR model from Islam's perspective?
   - I. Statement of zakat and charity funds
   - II. Statement of qard funds
   - III. Profile of directors
   - IV. Amount of zakat paid by company

   a. I and II
   b. I and III
   c. III only
   d. All of the options are part of the proposed CSR framework.
10. Which of the following statements is (are) true?
   - I. From Islam's perspective, the GRI framework is adequate to reflect on the social responsibility of the organisation.
   - II. Zakat is emphasised in the Quran as a tool to address inequity.
   - III. Qard loans need not be paid back by the borrowers.
   - IV. Shura in CSR would refer to stakeholder engagement.

   a. I and III
   b. II and IV
   c. III and IV
   d. II, III, and IV

DISCUSSION QUESTIONS

1. What is corporate social responsibility?
2. What are sustainability issues?
3. What is the Global Reporting Initiative? What are the types of information suggested by the GRI to be disclosed by companies?
4. There are various guidelines on sustainability that companies can use to report on CSR. Discuss.

5. It has been suggested that CSR from an Islamic perspective has a wider focus. Discuss.
6. What are the advantages of a value-added statement?
7. Some Muslim scholars have suggested that the value-added statement may support socioeconomic justice of Islam to a greater extent than the income statement. Discuss.
8. The Global Reporting Initiative suggests three broad categories of CSR information that companies should disclose. Is this adequate for businesses operating in an Islamic economy? Discuss.
9. Islam emphasises the two concepts of accountability: Vertical as well as horizontal accountability. How would these accountabilities impact the CSR of a business?
10. Discuss the GRI Framework on Sustainability. What needs to be added to the framework for it to be useful to Islamic societies? Discuss.

Bibliography

CHAPTER 2: RECORDING TRANSACTIONS AND MARKET VALUES IN ISLAM

Accounting and Auditing Organization for Islamic Financial Institutions (1993). *Statement of Financial Accounting No. 1: Objectives of Financial Accounting for Islamic Banks and Financial Institutions*. Manamah: AAOIFI.

Accounting and Auditing Organization for Islamic Financial Institutions (1999a). *Accounting, Auditing and Governance Standards for Islamic Financial Institutions*. Manamah: AAOIFI.

Adnan Muhammad Akhyar. "An Investigation of Accounting Concepts and Practices in Islamic Banks: The Case of Bank Islam Malaysia Berhard and Bank Muamalat Indonesia," Doctor of Philosophy thesis, Department of Accounting and Finance, University of Wollongong 1996, http//ro.uow.edu.au/thesis/1015.

Gambling T., and Karim, R. A. (1991). *Business and Accounting Ethics in Islam*. London: Mansell.

Omar Abdullah Zaid (2004). Accounting Systems and Recording Procedures in the Early Islamic State P149, *Accounting Historians Journal* 31(2), December 149–170.

Thomson Reuters (2017) Fatina Jabir: Planning is first step to creating a brand, http://www.zawya.com/mena/en/multimedia/video/VID20131110105137/.

CHAPTER 3: ADJUSTING ISLAMIC ACCOUNTING RECORDS AT THE CLOSE OF THE ACCOUNTING PERIOD

AAOIFI Statement of Financial Accounting No.2 (SFA 2), Concepts of Financial Accounting for Islamic Banks and Financial Institutions. Manamah: AAOIFI.

Accounting and Auditing Organization for Islamic Financial Institutions (1993). "Statement of Financial Accounting No. 1: Objectives of Financial Accounting for Islamic Banks and Financial Institutions." Manamah: AAOIFI.

Holy Quran, Surat Al-Baqra verse No:282.

Malaysian Accounting Standards Board (2005). *Financial Reporting Standard I-1* (2004) presentation of financial statements of Islamic financial institutions, MASB financial reporting standard. Kuala Lumpur.

Malaysian Accounting Standards Board (2011). MFRS116, Clarification of Acceptable Methods of Depreciation and Amortisation (Amendments to MFRS 116 and MFRS 138), MASB financial reporting standard. Kuala Lumpur.

Malaysian Accounting Standards Board (2011). MFRS132, Financial instruments: Presentation, MASB financial reporting standard. Kuala Lumpur.

CHAPTER 4: ISLAMIC FINANCIAL STATEMENTS

Accounting and Auditing Organization for Islamic Financial Institutions (AAOIFI) (2015). "Financial Accounting Standard No.1 General Presentation and Disclosure in the Financial Statements of Islamic Banks and Financial Institutions, Appendix E, Examples of the Financial Statements and Disclosures Therein," AAOIFI, *Accounting, Auditing and Governance Standards.*

Accounting and Auditing Organization for Islamic Financial Institutions (AAOIFI) (2010). *Conceptual Framework for Financial Reporting by Islamic Financial Institutions*, http://aaoifi.com/

Bahrain Islamic Bank (2015). *Annual Report.* Bahrain Islamic Bank, Manama, Kingdom of Bahrain.

Baydoun, N., and Willet, R. (2000). "Islamic Corporate Reports." *Abacus*, 36(1), pp. 71–90.

Birchfield Mosque and Community Center (2009). *The Birchfield Mosque and Community Center Financial Statements for the Year Ended 31 March, 2009*, https://www.gov.uk/government/uploads/system/uploads/attachment_data/file/350997/arbmosquepb.pdf.

Birchfield Mosque and Community Center (2009). The Birchfield Mosque and Community Center Financial Statement for the Year 2009, https://www.gov.uk/government/uploads/system/uploads/attachment_data/file/350997/arbmosquepb.pdf.

The Dubai Financial Service Authority (DFSA) Rulebook: http://dfsa.complinet.com/

KPMG (Qatar) (2012). "AAOIFI Illustrative Consolidated Financial Statements for Islamic Banks," Annexed number 131.

Kuwait Finance House Malaysia Bernhard (Incorporated in Malaysia), http://www.kfh.com.my/

Malaysian FRS116. Property, Plant and Equipment [Compiled May 2010]. The Malaysian Accounting Standard Board.

Mosque Foundation (2013). *Annual Report*, http://mosquefoundation.org/images/annual-reports/pdf/2013_MF_Annual_Report.pdf.

Seif, E. I., and Tag, El-Din (October 2004). *Issues in Accounting Standards for Islamic Financial Institutions.* Leicester, UK: Markfield Institute of Higher Education, https://www.coursehero.com/file/12128272/Accounting/.

CHAPTER 5: ACCOUNTING FOR SUKUK

Amin, M. (2011). "Accounting for Sukuk under IFRS and AAOIFI Accounting Standards." In Sohail Jaffer (Ed.), *Global Growth, Opportunities and Challenges in the Sukuk Market*. London: Euromoney Books.
Ariff, M., Iqbal, M., and Mohamad, S. (2012). *The Islamic Debt Market for Sukuk Securities*. Cheltenham, UK: Edward Elgar Publishing.
Hassan, Z. (2014). *Islamic Banking and Finance: An Integrative Approach*. Oxford: Oxford University Press.

CHAPTER 6: ACCOUNTING FOR ZAKAT

Accounting and Auditing Organizations for Islamic Financial Institutions (AAOIFI), *Financial Accounting Standard (FAS) 9: Zakat*.
El-Badawi, M. H., and Al-Sultan, S. M. (1992). "Net Working Capital versus Net Owner's Equity: Approaches to Computing Zakatable Amount: A Conceptual Comparison and Application. *The American Journal of Islamic Social Sciences*, 9(1), 69–85.
Sulaiman, M. (2003). "The Influence of Zakat and Riba on Islamic Accounting." *The Indonesian Management and Accounting Review*, 2(2), 149–167.

CHAPTER 7: ISLAMIC COMMERCIAL CONTRACTS

http://www.Islamicbankers.me
Lahsasna, Ahcene (2011). *Shariah Aspects of Business and Finance*. Kuala Lumpur: International Centre for Education in Islamic Finance.
Shahul Hameed bin Mohamed Ibrahim (2009). *Accounting and Auditing for Islamic Financial Institutions*. Kuala Lumpur: International Centre for Education in Islamic Finance.
Wahbah Al Zuhayli (2003). *Al Fiqh Al-Islami wa Adillatuh (Islamic Jurisprudence and its proofs): Financial Transactions in Islamic Jurisprudence: Volume 1 (Translated by Mahmoud A. El-Gamal*, Damascus: Dar Al Fikr.

CHAPTER 8: APPLICATION OF ISLAMIC FINANCIAL CONTRACTS TO ACCOUNTING

http: Islamicbankers.me; downloaded on 21/12/2016
http://www.albawaba.com/news/mashreq-al-islami-launches-personal-finance-retail-customers; downloaded on 21/12/2016.

Shahul Hameed bin Mohamed Ibrahim (2009), *Accounting and Auditing for Islamic Financial Institutions*, Kuala Lumpur: International Centre for Education in Islamic Finance

CHAPTER 9: SOCIAL RESPONSIBILITY ACCOUNTING

Baydoun, N., and Willett, R. (2000). "Islamic Corporate Reports." *Abacus*, 36(1), 71–90.

Sulaiman, M. (2005). *Islamic Corporate Reporting: Between the Desirable and the Desired. Research Centre*. International Islamic University Malaysia Press.

Sustainability Reporting Guidelines, G3.1 (2011). The Global Reporting Initiative. https://www.globalreporting.org.

Index

Page references followed by f indicate an illustrated figure and t indicate an table.

Printed and bound by CPI Group (UK) Ltd, Croydon, CR0 4YY

06/01/2025

14620924-0001